RELATIONAL FOUNDATIONS

Experiencing Relevance in Life and Ministry

David Ferguson
in cooperation with
The Center for Biblical Leadership

Relationship Press

Relationship Press • P.O. Box 201808 • Austin, TX 78720-1808
Phone: 1-800-881-8008 • Fax: 1-512-795-0853

ISBN–1-893307-49-2

Table of Contents

Acknowledgements

As you begin this exploration of the relational foundations of our faith, a significant challenge will emerge: the challenge to view life and ministry "from above." You will be invited to move beyond man-centered perspectives on the Christian life, perspectives that are all too common, yet sadly misplaced. Instead, you will be encouraged to embrace a God-centered or "theocentric" perspective, a perspective that has the potential to bring restoration and relevance to your life and ministry. Does such an approach imply that people are unimportant? Absolutely not! Indeed, a theocentric perspective allows us to more fully see the critical importance of people as we continually consider this crucial question: "How is God's Spirit at work among His people to accomplish His purposes?"

It is this very question that leads me to give thanks for all of the saints that have shared in this journey with sensitivity and dedication. For the past decade, elders within our ministry such as Lewis Alexander, Gene Bender, Bruce Walker, and Jim Walter, along with our trustees Teresa Ferguson and Brian and Wetonnah McCoy, have collaborated on the implications, potential, and pitfalls of the relational theology presented in this resource. For these special saints, I give God great thanks. Furthermore, well over ten thousand ministry couples in the United States and abroad have participated in Galatians 6:6 ministry retreats and other training events, during which these principles have been shared and shaped. I would also like to express thanks to Pastors Roger and Julie Barrier in the United States and Alister and Christine Mort in the United Kingdom, along with the network of accredited trainers who deliver relevant relational training in various aspects of this message. I am filled with deep gratitude because I have not been on this journey alone.

My heart has been particularly touched by God's initiative and leading through the Great Commandment network of denominations and movements, a group of churches and ministries that our team has the privilege to serve. I have been filled with joy as I have watched His Spirit bring together such diverse people and perspectives within His body for the simple purpose of Great Commandment/Great Commission relevance, and I can only imagine that this spirit of unity and cooperation has brought great pleasure to God's heart as well.

Among the network's strategic partners, Larry Duncan and the Center for Biblical Leadership (CBL) at the Church of God of Prophecy have shared in the vision-casting, field-testing, and publication of this resource. John Duncan provided innumerable hours of editorial support, while the staff of the White Wing Publishing House, including Virginia Chatham, Lonzo Kirkland, Joann Nope, Diann Stewart, and Elizabeth Witt, lent their creative and editorial skills in order to polish this course and maximize the success of its presentation.

Supportive media resources have been developed through the creative work of Mike Frasier, with the support of our strategic partners like Christ for the Nations Institute and Campus Crusade for Christ's Life Builders. "Thanks" is too small a word for the seemingly endless hours these saints have contributed to the audio/video production work.

Finally, the one person who co-labored with me most energetically throughout the development of this resource was my daughter, Terri Snead. She knows and lives out this relational message, and shares in the wonder of its effectiveness through her ministry of teaching and counseling. Her creative writing and skill with words provide invaluable refinements to my sometimes wandering thoughts. Very importantly, she knows her father's heart and passion, his limitations and constraints. God could not have provided more abundantly than He did through Terri, a true gift from the Lord!

David

Preface

Imagine the irony of watching someone frantically trying to rearrange the deck chairs on the Titanic, even as the ocean liner begins to break apart and sink into the icy waters of the Atlantic. What an incredibly sobering image of good intentions marred by a focus on the wrong things. Unfortunately, one might have the same reaction to much of Christianity today. It is often marked by frantic attention to peripheral things, even as the church steadily sinks into irrelevance.

As we journey through *Relational Foundations*, we will be challenged to move beyond simply dealing with surface symptoms and outdated methods. While conflicts rage over worship styles, the visible church is sinking. While seeker-friendly environments and small group gatherings compete for our attention, the visible church is sinking. After successive emphases on church growth, political correctness, and postmodernism, the visible church is sinking. Even with billions of dollars spent on conferences, events, training, and promotion, the visible church is sinking. But let us remember, there once was a day when the church had more impact on our world than the media, entertainment industry, or sports heroes. There was a time when the church faced the same evils of relativism, materialism, immorality, corruption, and persecution that we face today, yet turned the world upside down for Jesus Christ.

What was it that the 1st century saints possessed that we seem to lack? They embraced the fresh and powerful foundations of their new faith, they possessed passion that was ignited by a Person – Jesus Christ, and (perhaps unlike the church of today) they had not "gotten over" the wonder that they had been called and privileged to relate to God's Son, God's Word and God's people through the person of the Holy Spirit, and to join Him in sharing the wonder with others.

We are blessed and humbled to journey with you as we seek to restore the passion and relevance of the 1st century Christians to the 21st century church. May God renew you and your ministry through these *Relational Foundations*.

Welcome to *Relational Foundations!*

Relational Foundations is a course of study designed to encourage you and your ministry team to reassess the foundations of your faith, and to equip you to restore relevance to your life and ministry.

This *Relational Foundations* workbook is intended to serve as the participants' guide for the course. It includes everything participants need to thoroughly experience the *Relational Foundations* resource.

This workbook includes the following features:

- **Key Relational Foundations Principles**—These are introduced as text boxes in each chapter. These foundational principles are then discussed in the text of the workbook.
- **Experiences With God's Word**—Each chapter includes an opportunity to truly experience God's Word together. At these times, participants will have the opportunity to become "doers of the Word" (James 1:22 KJV).
- **Experiences With God's People**—Each chapter includes an opportunity for you to allow the Lord to work through His people. As true fellowship is experienced, you will be empowered to reflect His character and to demonstrate His care and compassion for each other.
- **Experiences With God's Son**—Each chapter also includes an opportunity for participants to pause and reflect on God's Son. Through these times of quiet reflection and meditation, a deeper love for Christ will be born.
- **For Further Study**—Most chapters contain a section of additional study material related to the chapter content that can be explored by those who wish to deepen their understanding of the relational foundations of the faith.
- **Additional Resources**—Each chapter includes a list of resources that may prove helpful to participants as they continue their growth in these relational foundations.

Participants should note that the *Relational Foundations* course can be experienced . . .

- individually, as a self study.

- with a partner.
- with a class or small group.
- with your ministry team.

Relational Foundations sessions can also be formatted for use . . .

- as a weekly "stand-alone" course.
- as a curriculum for a weekend retreat.
- as a "continuing education" component of regular leadership meetings.

HOW TO GET THE MOST OUT OF THIS RESOURCE

In order to get the most benefit and blessing from this resource, we urge you to do the following:

1. **Set aside time each week to read the chapter and work through the Experiential Exercises.** This will prepare you for your interactions with a partner or small group and enrich your personal understanding of each chapter.

2. **If you are working through this resource with a friend or ministry partner, we urge you to make time each week to work through and discuss the exercises.** Make your meetings a priority in your schedule and come prepared to interact appropriately.

3. **If you are working through this resource with a small group, we urge you to make it a priority to attend each small group session.** Make your meetings a consistent part of your schedule and come prepared to interact appropriately. You may also want to make notes and then reflect on the responses of fellow group members from each meeting. We urge you to get to know each person in your group in a meaningful way, show interest in their lives, and demonstrate supportive care.

4. **The following "Participant Promise" page presents some ways in which you can make the most of your experience with this workbook.** We suggest that you read it over and carefully discuss it with your partner or group before making this commitment.

PARTICIPANT PROMISE

We invite each participant to commit to the following in order to enhance their personal and communal experience of this resource:

1. I will spend time between sessions completing the chapters with honesty and sincerity.

2. I will participate in learning sessions fully, openly, and honestly.

3. I will seek to give care as others may need it and receive care as I may need it.

4. I will be willing to receive feedback from those who know me in my group, team, or family so that I might experience the growth and change that God intends for me through this course.

Name   Date

Chapter 1

Experiencing Relevance in Life and Ministry

I remember the exact moment it happened. I was sitting in an airport with my wife, Teresa, when it unfolded right before my eyes. I, like many of you, was traumatized on September 11, 2001. Things happened on that day that we thought could never happen. There were things shaken that we thought could never be shaken. There was a shaking of our security, of our economy, and of our priorities. Yet I also remember that the Lord brought to my mind a passage from the Book of Hebrews that day. "Once more I will shake not only the earth but also the heavens . . . so that what cannot be shaken may remain" (Hebrews 12:26, 27).

God certainly did not cause this horrific event. He was grieved for every soul whose life was touched by the tragedy. But even now, as I reflect on that horrible day, this thought comes to mind: "Could the Spirit of God be shaking His church, just like we were shaken after September 11?" As the body of Christ continually fails to be relevant to the needy world around us, God may be shaking us in order to bring us back to the very foundations upon which the first-century church was built.

> **Could the Lord be shaking His church so that it might reclaim its relevance and restore its impact on the world for Christ?**

The Spirit of God seems to be shaking His individual followers as well, in order that they might obtain clarity about their life purpose and direction. Perhaps God is shaking those that follow Him in order to draw His people back into deep, loving relationships with Him and with those He loves.

This shaking of God's church and His children is being done with a purpose in mind: to restore relevance to our lives and ministries. What does it mean to be relevant? According to Webster, something is *relevant* when it has "significant and demonstrable bearing on the matter at hand." A relevant solution is clearly applicable and pertinent, significantly impacting the needs of the current situation. A solution that does not meet these needs is deemed "irrelevant" or "extraneous."

There is evidence of the irrelevance of our lives all around us. The busyness of life seems to have rearranged our priorities so that eternal things have become marginalized. Economic pursuits have driven us into "making a living," while we have lost the burden and skills to impart our lives. We fight to keep our marriages and families together. We struggle to live lives of moral purity and ethical behavior. We seem to be vulnerable to the same corruption and bondage that has taken our world captive. Even those of us who still call upon the Lord from a pure heart struggle to pass on the faith to our own children, and often ask within the quietness of our hearts, "Is this all there is to following Christ?"

We also see increasing evidence of the irrelevance of ministry. People in Western societies are simply *not* streaming to the church because the vast majority of the Western world does not perceive our message as relevant to the deep needs of their lives. Within this phenomenon lies a critical paradox: the unchurched of our culture often consider religion and spirituality very important to their lives. Yet, ironically, an overwhelming majority of non-Christians feel that the church is not sensitive to their real needs. In other words, what they hear and see in us is largely not applicable or pertinent to their situation. They find us irrelevant.

Is it possible that our culture no longer sees us as relevant to its needs because we have lost touch with the very heart of who we are? Could it be that the Holy Spirit is drawing us back to our true identity as followers of Christ? Fundamentally, the Gospel promise of new life is about a Person; it is about the One who lived and died and rose again on our behalf. It is for this reason that the foundations of our faith must be relational. Jesus lived and died so that we might have life eternal with Him. He has now equipped us to live out the wonder of this relationship as His light in a darkened world.

> **The Gospel promise of new life is about a Person; it is about the One who lived and died and rose again on our behalf. It is for this reason that the foundations of our faith must be relational.**

Is it possible that in the complexity of our lives and ministries, we have been led astray from our sincere and pure devotion to Christ? Is it possible that God would say of us, as Paul did of the Corinthians, "I am afraid that . . . your minds will be led astray from the simplicity and purity of devotion to Christ" (2 Corinthians 11:3 NASB)? Have we made the journey so complex and, as a result, so irrelevant that the Spirit of God is shaking things in order to bring us back to the core of our faith?

It is our hope that through our journey together in this course, the Lord will bring us back to some of the relational foundations of our faith because with such a restoration, relevance will return. With a fresh grounding in these relational foundations, we will have a significant and demonstrable impact on our world. We will experience a greater love for Christ than we ever dreamed, and that love will overflow into our lives and ministries, thus bringing to a needy world the One who is eternally relevant. Our personal lives will begin to take on a sense of divine calling and purpose. We will begin to sense God's answer to our souls' deep question, "Why am I here?" His response will go beyond simply explaining why He has put six billion of us on this planet. We will discover how our individual lives can have relevance and meaning. We will be able to answer the question, "What significant, even eternal impact is possible for me?" Is this not a question of your heart at the deepest level? If it is, our time together may produce the "shaking" from the Lord that will transform your life.

Join us now as we begin our journey toward restoring the relational foundations of the Christian life.

Road Sign #1

As you travel this road with us, you will find three "signs" along the way that will guide the restoration of relevance to life and ministry. Throughout this workbook, we have used three icons to represent three different types of experiential exercises, each of which corresponds to a type of encounter through which God works to transform lives and ministries. The first exercise you will complete focuses on the ways in which God desires to transform and shape our lives through encounters with His people. This type of exercise, labeled "An Experience With God's People," encourages you to share your responses with a partner or small group. This is a vital way in which God may restore relevance in your life and ministry. Only as we are vulnerable before God and others can relationships be real and relevant. Only when we lay down our "look good and sound spiritual" mentality can we hope to experience genuine relationships.

Vulnerability with God and His people will contribute to the Spirit's shaking of false pride and self-reliance, challenging us to live out a testimony of humility and interdependence. In our ministry, authenticity toward God and others will contribute to the restoration of the church as a safe place where people can be known, accepted, and loved.

The other two "road signs" will be introduced later in this chapter, and a more detailed discussion of the importance of these three types of experiences can be found in Chapter 2.

An Experience With God's People

"This is the confidence we have in approaching God: that if we ask anything according to his will, he hears us. And if we know that he hears us—whatever we ask—we know that we have what we asked of him" (1 John 5:14, 15).

The Book of Acts describes several important characteristics of the early church. These defining traits enabled that body of believers to impact their world in an astounding way. Read over the characteristics identified below, and explore the accompanying Scripture passages:

- They were devoted to teaching the Word of God (Acts 2:42).
- They were devoted to fellowship with other believers (v. 42).
- They were devoted to the breaking of bread together (v. 42).
- They were devoted to prayer (v. 42).
- They had a reputation for unity (v. 44).
- They were generous toward those in need (v. 44).
- Others took note that they had been with Jesus (4:13).
- They were willing to speak the Word of God with boldness (v. 31).
- They were of one heart and mind (v. 32).
- They gave witness of Christ with great power as abundant grace was upon them (v. 33).
- People hold them in high esteem (5:13).
- Through Spirit-prompted ministry, multitudes of men and women were constantly being added to the kingdom (v. 14).
- They rejoiced at being considered worthy to suffer shame in Jesus' name (v. 41).

As you read each Scripture, pause to listen for God's prompting. Ask Him to help you answer the following questions:

- Which of these characteristics are most true of my life?
- Which ones may need to be restored in my life?
- Which of these characteristics are most true of my ministry?
- Which ones may need to be restored in my ministry?

Be still before the Lord as you reflect on these questions, then complete the following sentences:

Concerning life relevance, I sense a need for _____. *This would add relevance to my life as*_____.

For example: *concerning life relevance, I sense a need for a greater experience of fellowship with other believers. This would add relevance to my life as deepened relationships with other believers challenged and encouraged me in my faith.*

Concerning ministry relevance, I sense a need for _____. *This would add relevance to our ministry as*_____.

For example: *concerning ministry relevance, I sense a need for more unity among God's people. This would add relevance to our ministry as we give a better testimony of unity and increase our effectiveness through greater cooperation.*

After you have had time with the Lord, share your responses with a partner or small group. Then pray for one another, asking the Lord to make these characteristics true of each individual and ministry.

Pray that your partner(s) would be open to God as He removes anything that can be "shaken," leaving only that which is eternal. Pray that each would be open to the Spirit's transforming work in their lives and ministries.

Claim the promise of 1 John 5:14, 15. Because these requests are "His will," we can be confident that He hears and that we will have what we ask of Him. Thank Him in advance for helping you to make these characteristics true of your life and ministry. Thank Him that your life can be changed, even today.

(For example: *Heavenly Father, I pray that our lives would be shaken. Please make us into a likeness of You, leaving only that which is eternal. I pray that You would add relevance to our lives and ministries. Make me more devoted to Your Word. Make my partner more devoted to prayer. Shake our ministry so that others will take note that we have been with Jesus. Thank You in advance for accomplishing these things. May Your Spirit continue His work in us this very hour. In Jesus' name, Amen.*)

LOVING THE REAL GOD: OUR FOUNDATION OF CHRISTOLOGY

The first relational foundation that is critically important for us as followers of Jesus is our Christology—our view of Jesus. The health of our relationship with Him is connected to how well we know Him, which is, in turn, dependent upon how we see Him. Do we see Him as He really is, or might we have a distorted picture of Him? As we take this journey toward the restoration of our relational foundations, it is important that we allow the Holy Spirit to challenge us with the question, "Do we see Jesus as He really is?"

My Personal Journey

One morning during my devotional time, God began to use a particular passage to speak to me about my view of Him. Isaiah 30:18 reminded me that "the Lord longs to be gracious to you; he rises to show you compassion." I had studied just enough Hebrew to know that the word *long* meant "a passionate excitement." Thus, the passage seemed to suggest that the Lord was passionate, even excited, about the opportunity to give me grace. That morning, God spoke to my heart: "David, you have not seen Me as a God of excited grace. You have too often seen Me as a God of reluctant grace. It is almost as if you think that I will give you grace one more time, but there is no way that I am happy about it. It is as if you believe that I am reluctant to be gracious."

The Father began to show me how my concept of a God of reluctant grace was reflected in my own life. His Spirit produced brokenness within me as I realized how often I had been slow to accept, forgive, and comfort those around me. Because I saw God as reluctant to give grace to me, I was often reluctant to give grace to others. I often waited until people around me "earned" or "deserved" my love. My distorted view of God was hindering the relevance of my life and ministry.

> **It is important to allow the Holy Spirit to challenge us with the question, "Do we see Jesus as He really is?"**

Thankfully, the Holy Spirit began to confirm that the real God is One who is excited to love me, who is passionate about forgiving me, accepting me, and lavishing grace upon me! I began to feel a greater, deeper love for Jesus than ever before. Loving Him was easier and more heartfelt because I now knew that He was excited about first loving me (1 John 4:19). This new view of God not only began to change my relationship with Him, it began to impact my relationships with other people (both in ministry and at home). When my God was reluctant to give grace, I, too, was reluctant to give grace—reluctant to accept my wife or forgive my children. But as I came to see Christ for who He really is and received more of His love for me, I was empowered to love others with some of that same excitement and passion.

In Chapter Two, we will explore our Christology in greater depth. We will examine the connection between our view of Christ and the Great Commandment: "Hear, O Israel! The Lord our God is one Lord; and you shall love the Lord your God . . ." (Mark 12:29 NASB). We will explore how our capacity for loving God and others is connected to our ability to see Christ as He really is.

Pause and Reflect

Pause now as we look forward to this exploration of our Christology. Offer the following prayer: *Lord Jesus, open the eyes of my heart to see You as You really are. Remove any distortion that might hinder me from truly knowing and loving You.*

The Forgotten Purpose of Truth: Our Foundation of Biblical Hermeneutics

The second relational foundation we will address deals with our approach to the Bible. God wants to reshape our view of His Word just as He longs to transform our view of His Son. We will ask ourselves, "Is it possible that we may not be doing everything we need to be doing with the Scriptures?" We will see that God's Word is necessary for sound doctrine (Titus 2:1) and critical for right living (2 Timothy 3:16, 17). But we will also see how God may want to shake our approach to His Word in order to bring us back to the relational purpose of Scripture. Our Biblical hermeneutics, or principles of interpretation, must contain an emphasis on our relationship with the Author of the Book. After all, the Bible is a God-breathed Book, and God has put inside of us the Holy Spirit, who longs to draw each of us into a deep, loving relationship with God as we encounter His Word.

My Personal Journey

For many years I had a conviction that the Bible would indeed give us right doctrine. I also knew that God's Word was to guide us in how we were to live and what rules we were to obey. But the Spirit of God began to show me that there was another purpose for which His Book was written.

I was reading a very familiar text one evening, and I pictured in my mind the scene from the Gospel of Luke. I imagined Christ seated with His disciples as they shared their last meal together. I read those words that are spoken at

> **Is it possible that we may not be doing everything we need to be doing with the Scriptures?**

every communion: "This is my body given for you. . . . This cup is the new covenant in my blood, which is poured out for you" (Luke 22:19, 20). I then read with fresh eyes and heart the words that described the next scene: "Also a dispute arose among them as to which of them was considered to be greatest" (v. 24). The Spirit of God touched my heart, and tears came to my eyes. I was startled by the emotions within me. Here was Christ being totally vulnerable concerning His impending death, and His "near ones," His dearest friends, were fighting over status and prestige. Tears flowed down my cheeks as I imagined the disappointment and sense of rejection that Jesus felt. His Spirit had met with me in the Word and moved my heart with compassion for the Savior. That evening, the Spirit of God revealed to me another purpose of His Book: the Bible was written to lead us into a deep, loving relationship with the Author of the Book, which then empowers us to love others as well.

In Chapter Three, we will explore these relational hermeneutics in greater detail. We will discover how Christ presents and reinforces this approach to Scripture within the Great Commandment: "On these two commandments depend the whole Law and the Prophets" (Matthew 22:40 NASB).

Road Sign #2

We invite you now to stop and give attention to a second "road sign" that will appear throughout this resource. This time, we welcome you into "An Experience With God's Son." We believe that as you come to know Christ in a deeper way and begin to see Him as He really is, the Spirit will deepen His transforming work in your heart and life. As you experience the real Jesus, you will be drawn further along the road of loving Him and will be additionally empowered to love others.

An Experience With God's Son

"But you are not to be like that" (Luke 22:26).

We live in a world filled with crises. It is no wonder that many Christians believe that the Lord will be coming soon to claim His own. The Bible shows us what our world will look like just before Christ returns. We might even describe these characteristics as symptoms of the irrelevance in our culture. In a world of irrelevance . . .

- people will be lovers of self, focusing on their own plans, needs, and desires.
- people will be lovers of money, giving priority to what they can acquire.
- people will be boastful and arrogant.
- people will be unloving, irreconcilable, and prone to gossip.
- people will be lovers of pleasure.
- there will be only a form of godliness.
- people will indulge the flesh.
- people will become self-willed.
- people will speak arrogant words.
- people will be enticed by fleshly lusts and sensuality, and will become entangled in the world's defilements.

(See 2 Timothy 3:1–5 and 2 Peter 2:10–18 for reference to these characteristics.)

Prayerfully and humbly look at this list again. Which of these characteristics might you struggle with? Which of these symptoms of irrelevance might be true for you?

I sometimes struggle with _____ .

(For example: *I sometimes struggle with selfishness when faced with the needs and demands of my family and friends.*)

(For example: *I sometimes struggle to give loving responses. My boss tells me that I can be harsh and critical when I interact with customers.*)

Let us return to the saddened heart of Jesus in the Gospel of Luke. Recall the words, "but you are not to be like that." The disciples' selfish response was too much like that of the world, and Jesus seems sorrowed by this likeness.

Now consider the truth of Hebrews 7:25. We have a Great High Priest who "always lives to make intercession for [us]" (NASB). In this passage, Christ is revealed as the One who intercedes for us at the right hand of the Father. But consider this: what is Christ praying? If He is interceding and praying for us, what would His prayers include? Surely He prays for the Spirit's work of conviction in us, and possibly that His people would boldly pursue those who do not know Him.

But consider this: as the interceding Christ looks upon the sin, compromise, and complacency of His people, His heart is burdened that we look too much like the world. He is saddened that we, like His disciples, respond like those who do not know Christ.

Recall now the personal struggle that you noted earlier. Pause to meditate on how Jesus is interceding for you. Envision the Savior bowed in prayer for you. He is burdened by the fact that His church is acting so much like the world. Then He looks up with saddened eyes and you hear Him whisper these words, "Let it not be so among you."

As you hear His words and reflect on His love, is your heart touched with humility, sadness, or regret?

As I reflect on my struggle and how it saddens Jesus, my heart is touched with . . .

Share your response with a partner, and pray for one another. Ask God to continue to bring fresh encounters with His Spirit that would change, restore, and empower you.

As you continue your journey through this course, God may want to shake the very foundations of your faith. We encourage you to be open to His presence and His Spirit. As He works in our lives, the Spirit will restore the heart of Christ in us so that we may give praise and glory to God.

SEEING PEOPLE AS GOD SEES PEOPLE: OUR FOUNDATION OF ANTHROPOLOGY

The third relational foundation we will examine concerns our perspective on people. We can only love people as God loves them if we see them as God sees them. We know that God sees people as sinners in need of a Savior, but we will also discover that God's heart is broken because those same people are desperately alone. In Chapter Four, we will explore this first human crisis of aloneness, and confirm that any hope of fulfilling Christ's Great Commandment to "love our neighbors" rests in seeing our neighbors as God sees them. In our study of man and human anthropology, we will be reminded that God has placed in every human a need to relate to his or her Creator. We all need a relationship with God. At the same time, we will also discover that God has designed each individual with a need for human relationships. It is no flaw in design; we need one another. In Chapter Five, these dual needs for relationships with God and others will be explored as we discuss the Creator's provision of relationships like marriage, family, and the church.

My Personal Journey

> **We can only love people as God loves them if we see them as God sees them.**

Many years ago in a couples' Bible study, I asked everyone present to share a little bit about their concept of God. I prefaced my question with a few statements about how there is often a connection between your early experiences with your earthly father and your concept of your heavenly Father. In her response that evening, my wife shared a memory that I had never heard her share before. As she was sitting next to me, telling about a five-year-old little girl who was anxious for her Daddy's attention, the Spirit of God broke my heart. Teresa told a story about how she felt desperate to spend time with her father one particular Saturday morning. She got out of bed, went outside, and took it upon herself to climb a steep ladder up to the roof of their house. She was so anxious to spend time with her father that she ignored the danger and fear she felt in order to join her father as he repaired the roof. During the years that we were married, I had seen her as someone who was anxious a great deal of the time, and I was often irritated by her anxiety. I had seen her as someone who was very self-reliant, always doing things herself, and I had been judgmental and critical. On that day, I began to see her as God sees her. He moved my heart with compassion for this little girl, this precious partner who was neglected and alone. My heart was also broken over how I had often communicated a message to Teresa that she should only need God. My misguided message was too often one that would encourage her to pray, memorize Scripture, and study God's Word, but never to need me.

In Chapters Four and Five, we will explore the painful consequences of experiencing aloneness and see that God desires for each of us to help remove aloneness from the lives of those around us. We will also consider the truth that God wants to love others through their relationships with us.

REDISCOVERING CHURCH: OUR FOUNDATION OF ECCLESIOLOGY

The fourth relational foundation concerns our view of the church. Just as God wants to change the way we see people, He also wants to help us rediscover the nature and calling of the church. As we fulfill Christ's call in the Great Commandment to "love our neighbors," we will want this love to move out from our nearest "neighbors" (like our spouse, children, family, and close friends) to extend to the entire household of faith.

As the church, we know that we are called into fellowship with one another as fellow travelers in the light (1 John 1:7). We also know that God exhorts us to not give up meeting together (Hebrews 10:25) so we may be encouraged as "the Day" approaches. But do we have a testimony of "no divisions" within the body of Christ (1 Corinthians 1:10)? And if there are divisions, do we live out God's remedy for such divisions: to have equal concern for one another (12:25)? In Chapter Six, we will explore the mystery of the "called-out ones" or *ecclesia,* and we will explore the wonderful truth that we have been made parts of one body (v. 24). Through our study together, we hope to restore some of God's vision for the body of Christ: when one member suffers, we all suffer. When someone is honored, we all rejoice (v. 26). Coming to better understand the relational nature of the church will bring both personal calling for life relevance and corporate calling for ministry relevance.

> **Just as God wants to shake the foundation of the way we see people, He also wants to help us rediscover the nature and calling of the church.**

My Personal Journey

I can still recall the shock and sadness in my heart as I opened the local newspaper and read a particularly painful headline: "Protecting Your

Kids From Abuse at Church." A series of sexual abuse scandals had rocked our city, and I grieved over the victims and their families. Among the many painful losses they had experienced, these precious people had lost the witness of His church. Now the newspaper was giving practical advice on how parents could better protect their children from abuse. It was unimaginable to me that parents needed to protect their children when involving them in church activities. After all, the church is to be a safe place for the children of God, a place of refuge from the world. It is also to be a safe place for those outside of Christ, a haven for those seeking answers and needing hope. My sadness and shock had barely begun to subside when, just a few days later, I experienced a similarly painful event.

While attending an inter-denominational gathering of church leaders, I observed that the regularly scheduled program had been set aside in order to address the concerns over the sexual abuse cases within our community. As we began to discuss this crisis, my heart was sorrowed at how quickly many of those in attendance seemed to turn against the "offending" churches. One minister noted that one of the sexual abuse incidents took place in a thriving mega-church. He surmised that God must have allowed these events to take place in order to bring humility to the church. Another pastor commented on the "liberal" doctrine of one of the churches involved. In his mind, "their liberal doctrine contributed to a lack of righteous standards."

My heart was grieved as I left the meeting that afternoon. Not only had many of God's children suffered because of the abusive acts of others, but now God's people were turning against one another. The place of refuge had become a place of conflict and accusation. The place of safety had been filled with turmoil and blame.

In Chapter Six, we will explore the blessing of living out Christ's vision for His church. We will prioritize our relationship with other believers and learn what it means to experience true fellowship with one another.

IMPARTING NOT ONLY THE GOSPEL, BUT OUR VERY LIVES: OUR FOUNDATION OF APOLOGETICS

The final foundation that may need to be shaken as we seek to regain relevance for life and ministry is the foundation of apologetics—our means of giving a defense for Christianity. We will explore the need for a relational witness. We will have to ask ourselves, "Have we become

> **Have we become so rational in our beliefs and so propositional in our evangelism that we have forgotten the Person of the Gospels?**

so rational in our beliefs and so propositional in our evangelism that we have forgotten the Person of the Gospels? Have we become so preoccupied with convincing people of the reliability of Scripture and the certainty of Christ's death and resurrection that we may have forgotten to love others? Have we forgotten to not only share the Gospel, but our very lives (1 Thessalonians 2:8)?" Our world needs the testimony of our lives as "living letters" (2 Corinthians 3:2, 3). As we experience His life and love, we are able to share with others.

My Personal Journey

My own journey toward a relationship with Christ provided an unforgettable reminder of this need for a relational presentation of the Gospel. Through two decades of sporadic church attendance, I had heard most of the rational arguments for becoming a follower of Jesus. On occasion, I had even listened as zealous believers fulfilled their evangelistic duty and presented the "Roman Road" to salvation (Romans 3:23; 6:23; 5:17; 10:9, 10). My reluctance to embrace a faith in Christ was not primarily because of rational issues of belief, or even because of behavioral issues in my life that needed repentance. Rather, I longed for the answer to a deeper question: "If all of the espoused propositions are true, and if my commitment brought the needed changes to my life—so what? What then? What is the rest of the story?" Was the Gospel only a matter of conformed belief and compliant behavior?

During my very rebellious teenage years, my grandfather's faith provided an example of how Christ can change a heart, not just readjust beliefs or eradicate certain behaviors. My grandfather's love and acceptance of me, in spite of my sinful behavior, planted seeds in my heart that God began to nourish.

During my senior year in college, the caring concern of a church custodian began to soften my heart toward faith in Christ. As this man showed interest in my life, the Lord used him to answer the question, "So what?" Just as certainly as that custodian shared the Gospel with me, he also imparted a "living Gospel." That blessed servant of the Lord shared his own life with me.

In Chapter Seven, we will explore more of this relational apologetic. We will learn what it looks like for a church to share the Gospel both with their words and with their love. We will discover how relevance returns to life when we know how to share both the plan of salvation and the provision of relationship.

THE GREAT RESTORATION

One chilly evening in 1517, a brilliant theologian made his way across the campus of a German monastery. He walked alone that evening, needing time to deliberate his course of action. With the certainty of enormous risk, Martin Luther carefully counted the cost of his dissent. For months, he had formulated a daring plan to oppose the church's practice of selling spiritual pardons. Luther knew that by defying the church he would lose his credibility and position within the monastery. He also knew that heretics were punished and sometimes executed. If he followed through on his decision, his life would be changed forever. On this night, Luther contemplated the significant changes that were needed in the life and ministry of the church, and carefully considered what he might do to effect such change.

Martin Luther's decision to challenge the church set the course for dramatic change in the lives of many that would follow. On the morning of October 31, 1517, Luther mounted the steps to the Castle Church of Wittenberg, Germany. He reached into his pocket and pulled out a document that contained the ideas and concerns he had agonized over for months. With the swift strike of hammer against nail, Luther posted his document on the door of the church for the entire world to see. With quiet resolve, Martin Luther turned toward home. The Reformation had begun.

Centuries ago, the Spirit of God moved among His church in what we now call the Great Reformation. There was a restoration of the essentials of grace and faith, along with a renewed emphasis on the centrality and reliability of Scripture. The church of today needs a similar restoration. We need a fresh emphasis

> **The Great Reformation brought significant and lasting changes within the church. The church of today needs a similar restoration.**

on relationships and an accurate view of Christ. We need to refocus on truly experiencing His Word. We need God to restore our compassion for the people around us and breathe new life into our presentation of the glorious Gospel of Jesus Christ.

The Great Reformation brought significant and lasting changes within the church as its leaders sought to restore the purity of man's relationship with God. It is our prayer that the Spirit of God would begin a new movement among His people that will be just as real, relevant, and lasting as that brought about by the Reformation of the 16th century. It is our hope that God will bring about significant change in the 21st century church—that we will experience a Great *Restoration* within the body of Christ.

> **This Great Restoration may be God's way of bringing us back to some simple truths: "Could you love Me with all of your heart? Could you love your neighbors as you love yourself? Now, go and make disciples and teach them everything I have commanded you."**

This Great Restoration may be God's way of bringing us back to some simple truths. God has given us 66 books of the Bible, but I wonder if He is clarifying our focus so that we regain the simplicity of the Gospel (2 Corinthians 11:3). I can imagine that God may want to bring about this Great Restoration by challenging us to ground our life and ministry on a few simple parts of His Word. All other Scripture will depend on how well we have laid this simple but powerful foundation. I can imagine that He might say, "Dear ones, could you love me with all of your heart, mind, soul, and strength? And then could you love your neighbors as you love yourself? Then go—go forth and make disciples of all nations, baptizing them in the name of the Father, Son, and Holy Spirit and teaching them to obey everything I have commanded you" (Matthew 22:37–39; 28:19, 20). Is it possible that we need a relational foundation that is centered upon Great Commandment love and a Great Commission passion?

Life relevance might then return as we rediscover the wonder and privilege of intimately relating to the Creator. Our motivation for following Jesus would shift as feelings of duty, obligation, and the pressure to perform are replaced by joy, a sense of privilege, and a sincere desire to please Him. Righteousness would be empowered by the dread of displeasing such a special and loving Savior. Life significance would be found, not in what we acquire, accomplish, or achieve, but in the blessing of co-laboring with Christ in loving others. As we joined Him in loving well, we would then "love" many into His kingdom.

Ministry relevance might then return as Christ's followers focused on recapturing an identity of love and pursuing a mission of multiplication. Sharing the Gospel would involve more than passing out tracts or taking spiritual surveys. Evangelism would be empowered by a love and concern for those outside of Christ, and prioritized within the context of relationship. Believers would not only be equipped to lead others to salvation in Christ, but to journey with others in a loving relationship that reveals Christ. As we demonstrated love to those outside the church, their hearts would be turned toward the One who is love.

Such a radical restoration of 1st century relevance will require new methodologies. It will necessitate both a relational message and relational approaches to ministry. As an illustration of this principle, Christ speaks in Matthew 9:17 of the fresh message of the Gospel and how it requires "new wineskins." The good news of Christ could not be contained in the "old wineskins" of Judaism. Similarly, we must explore not only the relational message found in the Great Commandment, but also the "new wineskins," or methods, which will be required to convey this message.

As we begin this journey, the Holy Spirit may begin a needed shaking of both our ministry message and our methods. Such a shaking may prompt a measure of anxiety and uncertainty as the familiar gives way to restoration. During such an uncertain journey, security in something or Someone is imperative. Our prayer will be that God, by His Spirit, will come alongside us to provide reassurance and peace. Our closing time of experiencing His Word together is intended to reveal Christ as the cornerstone of our life, faith, and ministry.

Ephesians 2:20 reveals that Jesus Christ is the Chief Cornerstone. He is the foundation of our hope and our redemption. As we make this Great Restoration journey, we must not forget the foundation upon which our faith is built. That foundation is our relationship with a Person— Jesus Christ. The apostle Paul also reminds us that, "No one can lay any foundation other than the one already laid, which is Jesus Christ" (1 Corinthians 3:11). Our relationship with Christ is the critical foundation upon which all believers build their faith. It is the underpinning and groundwork for all that we will experience in this course. As the Lord begins to shake certain areas of your life, we invite you to go back to the foundation of your relationship with Him.

Finally, Scripture encourages us to rest in Christ, our Cornerstone. "I lay a stone . . . a chosen and precious cornerstone, and the one who trusts in Him will never be put to shame" (1 Peter 2:6). The apostle gives us a description of Jesus Christ as a living stone who possesses invincible strength and everlasting presence. It is because of our relationship with the Cornerstone that we have protection and security. Therefore, as God continues to shake His church, we will have the security of knowing that Christ is always with us, and can rest in the certainty of His protection and provision.

Road Sign #3

Join us now for a final experience that will help launch our journey toward life and ministry relevance—"An Experience With God's Word." Rest securely in Jesus Christ, the Chief Cornerstone. Let us begin our exploration of *Relational Foundations* with an expression of gratitude for our relational foundation in Him.

An Experience With God's Word

"The Lord longs to be gracious to you; he rises to show you compassion" (Isaiah 30:18).

As we begin this journey toward relevance, let us take time to consider what Christ may be feeling or desiring for us.

What does Christ feel toward us even if we do not see Him clearly, for who He really is?

How does Christ respond even if we do not see His people (our spouse, children, friends, and family) as He sees them?

What is His heart toward us? From His place at the right hand of the Father, is He longing to prove us wrong? Does He hope to expose our error? Does He want to embarrass us before others?

May it never be!

Christ longs to show us grace! He longs to give us His unmerited favor!

But what if our consideration of the Great Restoration forces us to admit that we have not done everything we need to be doing with the Bible?

What if we have misunderstood the mystery of our connectedness to one another within the church?

How does He respond if we have misrepresented the Gospel by quibbling over minor, rational truths rather than imparting our lives?

What might be the Savior's response? Will it be one of judgment, criticism, or rebuke? Or could His response be one of lavish, extravagant grace?

Pause and consider the truth that Christ longs to show you grace. He is excited to show you favor. He earnestly desires to shower you with undeserved, unexpected blessings. Our prayer will be for this truth to overtake your heart as you experience each chapter of this resource.

Picture the Savior seated at the right hand of the Father. Use your imagination to paint the scene in the throne room of heaven. God the Father sits on His throne. God the Son sits to the right, the place of power and of honor.

The One who sits at the Father's right hand will be interceding for you as you make this Great Restoration journey (Hebrews 7:25). At any and every point along the way, as His Spirit begins a divine shaking to restore relevance to your life and ministry, Christ will show you grace. Picture it now: Christ rises from His seat in the throne room. Jesus invites you close and welcomes you to Himself. With excitement in His eyes and graciousness in His voice, the Savior speaks a blessing over you.

Meditate on the person of Christ, who, with outstretched arms and nail-pierced hands, welcomes you into His presence and is excited to bless you. As certainly as the prodigal son was welcomed with compassion and excitedly embraced by the Father (Luke 15), we have a Savior who longs to show us grace and rises to show us compassion (Isaiah 30:18).

Pray now with a partner or one of the members of your small group. Share with them what it does to your heart to encounter such a "cornerstone."

As I imagine Christ, and think about how He is excited to welcome and bless me, how He rises to show me compassion, my heart is filled with . . .

(For example: *"My heart is filled with gratitude and joy,"* or *"My heart is filled with humility and confidence,"* or *"My heart is filled with reassurance and security."*)

Additional Resources

David Ferguson, *The Great Commandment Principle* (Wheaton, IL: Tyndale House Publishers, Inc., 1998).

David Ferguson, *Relational Leadership* (Austin, TX: Relationship Press, 2004).

Alan Wolfe, *The Transformation of American Religion: How We Actually Live Our Faith* (New York: Free Press, 2003).

Chapter 2

Loving the Real God: Our Foundation of Christology

'Have I been so long with you, and yet you have not come to know Me" (John 14:9 NASB)?

Imagine the sadness that must have been in the Savior's heart as He uttered these words. Picture the scene in the upper room. Jesus' faithful followers surround Him. His closest friends encircle the room. Christ has already experienced the painful distraction of the disciples' argument about who was to be the greatest in the Kingdom. He has vulnerably shared how His body is about to be broken and His blood is about to be shed, only to be met with the dispute of His closest friends (Luke 22:17–26). Then, as a testimony of humble servanthood, Christ takes a basin of water and a towel and begins to wash the feet of each disciple. He washes the feet of Peter, James, John, and even Judas. He washes the feet of His betrayer, extending love and grace to him one final time. During the Passover meal, Christ turns to Judas and says, "What you are about to do, do quickly." Judas then departs to complete the terms of his agreement to betray Christ (John 13:26, 27).

As you revisit this familiar story, pause and reflect upon the heart of the Savior. What might Jesus have been feeling as He experienced the dread of crucifixion and the insensitivity of His disciples' response, and anticipated the imminent betrayal of one of His followers and the departure of His closest friends? What feelings might have been in Christ's heart in the upper room? Has your spirit connected with His Spirit on this level? Have you come to know Him in this way? Now imagine that this One who is "a man of sorrows, and familiar with suffering" (Isaiah 53:3) experiences additional pain as He utters His next words. Allow the Holy Spirit to gently lead you to respond to the heart of Jesus as you hear Him say, "Have I been so long with you, and yet you have not come to know Me?"

Pause and Reflect

Jesus, my heart is moved with _____ as I encounter Your sorrow in a fresh way.

Now that you have taken the time to pause and reflect upon the heart of Jesus, allowing His Spirit to engage your heart with His, consider this: we, at times, are very much like the disciples—we may not know Christ as He really is. We must be open to the possibility that each of us, at times, may be hindered in our view of Christ. As we journey together, we hope that you will be open to seeing Christ more clearly and loving Him more intimately. We pray that your heart might be open to the possibility of knowing Him in ways that are new and fresh.

My Personal Journey

While putting the finishing touches on promotional plans for one of my recent books, I was challenged with a fresh perspective on Christ's declaration of the Great Commandment: "You shall love the Lord your God with all your heart, and with all your soul, and with all your mind. . . . You shall love your neighbor as yourself" (Matthew 22:37, 39 NASB). I began to ponder, "Why am I so often hindered from loving God with all my heart, mind, soul, and strength?"

My own self-interest and misplaced priorities often caused me to struggle to love the Lord as I desired. But at other times, my love for God was hindered by something deeper: a distorted concept of who He really is. The Spirit impressed upon me the truth that my only hope of fulfilling the first part of the Great Commandment more consistently was to see God more clearly. If I was going to love the real God, I needed to truly **know** the real God.

God sometimes uses the simplest things in life to teach us great lessons. He gave me liberating insight into who He really is through my first grandson, Zachary. During Zachary's first several weeks of life, I was amused by Teresa's childish excitement over being with him. When she would hear him waking up from one of his many naps, a smile of joy would light up her face. Her exuberance communicated the message, "He's awake! He's awake, and I am looking forward to playing with him!"

One morning, after witnessing Teresa's response to Zachary, the Lord surprised me through a devotional reflection on Psalm 139:3: "You . . . are intimately

> **If we are going to love the real God, we need to truly know the real God.**

acquainted with all my ways" (NASB). As I pondered this passage, the Spirit reminded me that the Psalmist was referring to the special, caring involvement of the Lord in each of our lives. The Lord knows us intimately, and He delights in caring for us. The Holy Spirit seemed to say to me, "David, when you wake up in the morning, My heart is filled with excitement over you. Just as Teresa's heart is filled with excitement over Zachary, I rejoice over you! My heart is filled with the same realization in the morning: 'He's awake! He's awake, and I am looking forward to sharing the day with him!'"

I was deeply touched by this realization, and the thought of a God who was "intimately acquainted with all my ways" blessed my heart. This refreshing view of God seemed so different from my previous concept of Him. Through much of my life and ministry, God seemed to say, "He's awake, and I am going to watch him closely." At other times, I believed that God's response was, "Oh no, he's awake. There's no telling what kind of mischief he will get into today." Occasionally, it was difficult to believe that God even noticed I had woken up at all. The Lord began to sadden my heart as I realized that for many years I had missed knowing the real God and missed His love for me. He began to reveal how my concept of God had hindered my intimate walk with Him and, just as importantly, my love for Him.

Along with these fresh insights into the true nature of God, the words of the Great Commandment came flooding back to me: "Love the Lord your God with all your heart and with all your soul and with all your mind and with all your strength" (Mark 12:30). God impressed me with this thought: loving God as the Great Commandment exhorts is only possible when it is the **real** God that I am seeking to love. Loving someone who is excited to see me every morning is easy. Loving someone who regrets that I am awake is not. Loving the God who is intimately involved in all my ways comes easily. Trying to love a god who is just waiting for me to mess up is difficult.

Take the next few moments and consider this concept of God, which may be new to you. As you reflect on your own view of God's heart, how do you respond to His caring involvement?

An Experience With God's Word

"You . . . are intimately acquainted with all my ways" (Psalm 139:3 NASB).

"He will take great delight in you, he will quiet you with his love, he will rejoice over you with singing" (Zephaniah 3:17).

Imagine the expression that was on the face of Jesus as you woke up this morning. In your mind's eye, picture His kind, gentle eyes and warm, tender smile. Imagine that as you awoke, God looked down and smiled at you, His precious child. With joy in His heart, He announced, "I am looking forward to sharing the day with you!" The real God, who knows you intimately, could not wait to care for you today. The Creator of the universe, who knows every hair upon your head and sees every tear that you cry, cannot wait to show you how much He loves you. The holy God of heaven knows your darkest secrets and deepest failures; yet because of His relationship with you, He longs to show you grace (Isaiah 30:18).

What does it do to your heart to consider a God who is acquainted with all your ways and longs to be caringly involved in your life? How does your heart respond to the amazing truth that God takes great delight in and rejoices over you?

As I reflect upon the real God, who cannot wait to care for me, I feel _____.

As I consider the real God, who rejoices over me and looks forward to spending the day with me, my heart is filled with _____.

Pause now and say a prayer that communicates your gratitude, humility, and wonder toward the God who knows you and rejoices over you. Pray with a partner or member of your small group.

Heavenly Father, I feel _____ *as I reflect upon your heart toward me. Thank you for being the kind of God who* _____.

CHRIST: THE CORNERSTONE

As we journey toward relevance in our lives and ministries, we must begin with an assessment of our view of and relationship with Christ—the cornerstone of our faith. Scripture reminds us that "No one can lay any foundation other than the one already laid, which is Jesus Christ" (1 Corinthians 3:11), and that the "stone which the builders rejected has become the chief cornerstone" of our faith (1 Peter 2:7 NKJV). Therefore, we begin our study of *Relational Foundations* with Christology (the study of Christ). He is the Alpha and Omega, the Beginning and the End, the Cornerstone of our foundations.

Throughout this chapter, we will be challenged to assess our view of God, taking a careful look at how we see Him and how we interpret His character and response toward us. As we examine our view of Him, we will make reference to Jesus Christ and God the Father

> **Our view of God impacts every aspect of our Christian faith. Every part of our spiritual journey is either hindered or empowered by our view of Him.**

interchangeably. After all, Christ said, "Anyone who has seen me has seen the Father" and "I and the Father are one" (John 14:9; 10:30). Finally, it is important to note that this discussion of Christology precedes the other elements of *Relational Foundations* because our view of God impacts every aspect of our Christian faith. Every part of our spiritual journey is either hindered or empowered by our view of Him.

Our View of God Will Hinder or Empower Our Love for Him.

Trying to sustain an intimate walk with anyone other than the real God will leave us frustrated and empty. We will find that it is easy to love the God who is excited to care for us, but it will be difficult for any view of God that differs from that to inspire love. We will discover that our worship can be hindered if we are trying to relate to anyone other than the real God. Our prayer life may involve more duty and obligation than intimate fellowship and love. If we cannot see the real God, our relationship with Him will have little impact on our lives and our experience of love for Him will be incomplete at best.

Our View of God Will Hinder or Empower Our Ability to Experience His Word.

If we cannot see the real God, we will be hindered in meeting with Him at the point of His

Word. Every sermon or Bible lesson is filtered through our concept of God, and any distorted view of Him chokes out the impact of the Word upon our heart. For instance, if you view God as One who is constantly disappointed with you, Scripture may seem to bring only God's criticism. Such a distorted view of God will push you away from a relationship with Him. Similarly, if God seems impersonal or distant, the most glorious spiritual truths may have little impact because you might assume that such truths are only meant for the "important" people within the body of Christ.

It is difficult to look forward to a devotional time with a god who is judging or condemning. We may be reluctant to read the words of a god who only inspects or criticizes. By contrast, as we come to see the real God, the God who is excited to love us, we will approach His Word with expectation and hope. Hearing, reading, and studying Scripture will become a joyous pleasure not to be missed. We will return to this discussion in Chapter Three in order to further our understanding and experience of this relational approach to God's Word.

Our View of God Will Hinder or Empower Our Love of Other People.

If we cannot see the real God who is love, our ability to demonstrate love will be hindered (1 John 4:8). We will discover that if our god is harsh and condemning, we may display these same characteristics in our relationships with others. If our god is inspecting and critical, we may easily find fault with others. If our god is distant and remote, we may have a tendency to keep our emotional distance from those around us, or to cling to people as if they are our only hope. But seeing the God who is excited to love us will empower in us an excited love for other people. We will examine our relationships with people more closely in Chapters Four, Five, and Six.

Our View of God Will Hinder or Empower Our Heart for Evangelism.

If we cannot see the real God, our message to an unbelieving world may be characterized by irrelevance and little effect. We may struggle with being "a living epistle" of His life and love, focusing more on sharing the Gospel than actually "imparting" it to others through the example of our life (see 1 Thessalonians 2:7, 8). If we cannot see the real God, we may also struggle to look beyond the sins of others to see their needs. Effective, relevant evangelism will find the followers of Jesus telling stories of the real God's love at work in their lives and hearts. There will be an experience of God's Great Commandment love that empowers a Great Commission lifestyle. We will discuss additional principles of relational evangelism in Chapter Seven.

My Personal Journey

As the Lord began to renew and reshape my view of Him, the Holy Spirit allowed me to see how my previous concept of God had negatively affected many aspects of my life. Having come to Christ after many years of rebellion, I embraced my newfound faith with intensity and enthusiasm. Even as a young adult, I found myself immersed in Bible studies, Scripture memory programs, service at our local church, and ministry in the community. But my hindered view of Christ began to impact each of these areas of my Christian life:

My Love for the Lord

As my walk with the Lord continued, it became increasingly difficult to sustain the initial excitement that followed giving my life to Christ. I knew that I loved the Lord, but my daily experience of love for Him seemed to diminish.

My Longing for the Word

I made commitment after commitment to have daily devotionals with the Lord, but I felt only defeat as I followed the encouragements I was given to "Look for sins to avoid and commands to obey." The list of things to do as a follower of Christ and the list of things to avoid seemed to sap my love for His Word.

My Love for Others

Since I tended to view God as inspecting and disappointed, I often took on that same role with the people in my life. Because of my own concept of God, I was careful to point out the sin in the lives of others, believing that it was my job to help them become more like Christ. As a result, my wife had a husband who frequently saw her faults instead of her needs. My children had a father who noticed their misbehaviors but too often ignored their heart. My fellow church members had a friend who gave more advice and spiritual pep talks than care and concern for the struggles of their lives.

My Ability to Effectively Share the Gospel

Finally, because of my hindered concept of God, my efforts to share the Gospel with those outside the church were characterized by subtle and not-so-subtle messages of condemnation. Because my god was mostly concerned with sin, there were times when I focused only upon sin and the need for repentance, with the result that the "good news" failed to sound very good. While others did come to know Christ as I shared my faith, they often came to see God in much the same way that I had presented Him to them. Their view of God often became just as distorted as my own.

Thankfully, as God began to reshape and restore my view of Him, all of these things began to change. My view of people became drastically different. My ability to see the needs and heartfelt concerns of those around me increased, and as I experienced more of God's love for me, I was able to demonstrate more of His love to others.

Join me now in looking at your own concept of God and considering how it might be impacting your relationships with Him and with other people. Allow the Lord to reveal any areas of needed restoration so that He might enrich the relevance of your life and ministry.

ASSESSING OUR VIEW OF GOD

When Christ gave us the Great Commandment in Mark 12:29–31, He actually referenced the Old Testament *Shema*, the Hebrew call to worship. The *Shema* begins with a declaration about the God of the Hebrew people: "Hear, O Israel! The Lord is our God, the Lord is One! You shall love the Lord your God . . ." (Deuteronomy 6:4, 5 NASB). During Old Testament times, when pagan and idolatrous cultures were the norm and nations frequently worshipped gods of their own making, the first declaration of the Hebrew nation was about the one true God. The Hebrew call to worship clearly defined the One who is worthy of their adoration and loving obedience. We must also notice that before there was a call to love Him, there was a clear declaration of who He is. In much the same way, before we can truly come to love the Lord our God, we must come to see God as He truly is. In essence, this chapter is our own call to worship. We will spend the next few moments giving clearer definition to the real God so that, by seeing Him more clearly, we will gain greater freedom to truly love Him.

> **Many of us have never even considered our view of God. We have believed certain things about Him and have never questioned them or been challenged with an alternative.**

Many of us may have never even considered our view of God. We have believed certain things about Him and have never questioned them or been challenged with an alternative. But for the next few moments, we would like for you to consider how your view of

God might differ from who He really is. You may discover that when different people read the same Bible verses, their perceptions and characterizations of God can be quite different.

Read the following verse of Scripture several times. Imagine that Christ is standing before you in the upper room. Listen as He speaks these words. Listen to the inflection of His voice. Where is the emphasis? What tone of voice accompanies these words? What are the subtle implications behind the words you hear?

"If you love Me, you will keep My commandments" (John 14:15 NASB).

John 14:15 can be an effective assessment tool as we seek to discover our own view of Christ. Now that you have read the verse several times, contemplating the tone of voice and words of emphasis, consider the following possibilities. Can you identify with one of these concepts of God? Does the voice that you heard reflect one of these characterizations of God?

Is Your God an Inspecting God?
"**If** you love Me, you will keep My commandments" (John 14:15 NASB).

Some of us view God as an inspecting god. As you read the verse above, you may have imagined a tone of expectation and demand. An inspecting god might raise his eyebrows as he utters the words, "If you love me you will keep my commandments." The words might carry a questioning tone, conveying the sense that there is a test to be passed or a measurement to be taken. "If you love me, then you'll do what I say! I'll wait and see just how much you really love me." You may have even imagined your inspecting god shaking his finger at you as he speaks these words. His stern tone and gestures warn of his constant inspection.

If we have an inspecting god, it seems as though he is constantly recording what we do on a heavenly tally sheet. Every time we sin or fail to measure up, he frowns and records it. He may also keep track of things we have done well, but he inspects our every move and relates to us only on the basis of the number of positive and negative tally marks we have accumulated.

If our god is an inspecting god, we may become defensive and consider innocent comments or events to be personal attacks. If we believe that our god is constantly seeking to find fault with us, it is easy to assume that others are doing the same, and thus we may react defensively to anyone who attempts to share their disappointments, or even their needs.

My Personal Journey

I can still recall one of my reactions to Teresa during our early years of marriage. We were driving down the freeway together when she casually pointed out a purple car in the lane next to us. Since her favorite color is purple, her eye was simply drawn to this vehicle. All Teresa said was, "Look, isn't that a pretty car?"

My next thoughts came quickly and gave evidence of how defensive I was about any comments that could be interpreted as critical: "She doesn't like the car we have. She doesn't think we'll ever have a nice car!" My view of God as an inspecting god left me self-protective and somewhat cynical. Since my god was constantly inspecting me, I interpreted Teresa's casual comment as an "inspection" as well.

If we have an inspecting god, our lives may be filled with an underlying anxiety about the number of tally marks we have been given, and we may be prone to inspecting other people. If our god is closely and suspiciously monitoring our behavior, we may be inclined to do the same to those around us. Our spiritual life may be robbed of gratitude and joy. It is hard to get excited about times of prayer, solitude, or meditation with the Lord if they include a "daily inspection." It is hard to experience consistent joy under the scrutiny of an inspecting god.

Is Your God a Disappointed God?

"If you **love Me**, you will keep My commandments" (John 14:15 NASB).

Some of us may view God as disappointed in us. As you read the verse above, you may have heard a voice that seemed full of dissatisfaction: "If you **love me**, you will keep my commandments." This kind of god might look down at you with arms crossed, shaking his head as he says, "If you really loved me, then you would be able to keep my commandments. In fact, I have known all along that you did not **really** love me, and what you just did proves it!"

If we have a disappointed god, we may live out our Christian faith with a sense that we will never measure up. Our god looks down at us but seldom likes what he sees. He notices our attempts at living a righteous life, but ultimately shakes his head in displeasure. He shrugs his shoulders as he watches us as if he has given up, certain that we will never "make it." For this kind of god, no amount of right behavior will ever be good enough.

If our god is disappointed in us, it will be difficult to experience contentment and peace in our spiritual journey. If we believe that we will never measure up, our personal worth will always be in question, and we may strive to perform for God and others in order to feel worthy of their love. If we have a god who is disappointed, we may be inclined to use our own disappointment as a form of coercion. Statements like, "You **will** be at tonight's service, won't you?" or "I sure hope I can count on you to help in the nursery" may permeate our ministry efforts to motivate others. Likewise, an attitude of "nothing is ever good enough" may pervade our homes and family relationships. If our god is a disappointed god, we may become hard to please, find ourselves driven by perfectionism, or seek to control the things and people around us.

Is Your God a Distant God?

"If (you) love Me, (you) will keep My commandments" (John 14:15 NASB).

Hard to trust

Fear

& someone besides me

Some of us may see God as a distant god. As you read the verse above, the voice you heard may have seemed cold or disinterested. A distant god would speak the verse with half-hearted enthusiasm or great indifference. This kind of god might seem preoccupied with other things. You might picture him looking up absentmindedly and saying, "Oh, if you love me, then you will probably keep my commandments. Thanks for stopping by."

If we see God as a distant god, then we may believe that He is really only listening to the "important people" or taking care of the "important things." We may wonder, "Out of all of the millions of people on this planet, why would God even notice me?" Our hearts may approach this kind of god with reluctance. A distant god seems to listen with only one ear when we pray, and, therefore, we may not truly believe that our needs and concerns are of interest to him.

My Personal Journey

For many years, I struggled with a god who inspected and was often disappointed. My wife, Teresa, came to see that she had viewed God as distant. She noted one day that "It was hard for me to imagine that God even noticed when I woke up in the morning. I was never convinced that He truly knew me or what was important to me. I saw God as someone who only had time for the 'big stuff' of this world, and I certainly wasn't included. This distant god was hard to get to know or to trust, and seemed disinterested in knowing me."

If our god is distant and uninvolved, we may relate to others with similar emotional detachment. We may politely interact with family, friends, and ministry companions, but there may be little intimacy and true fellowship. Because trust is difficult for those of us who have a distant god, we may resist getting to know others and allowing them to know us. We may live self-reliantly, believing that, ultimately, we are on our own. If our god is emotionally distant and uninvolved, our love for him may be characterized by a sense of duty or obligation, and we will find it challenging to love others in a relevant, meaningful way.

Pause and Reflect

Look back over the three characterizations described above. Can you see yourself in any of these descriptions? Can you identify with any of the illustrations? We know that each person's view of God is uniquely their own, and that your view of God may not be described perfectly above, but consider for a moment how you at times might be hindered in seeing God as He really is.

Take time to consider your own view of God. When you are **not** experiencing Him as "excited to love you," how do you see Him? Is your god sometimes inspecting, disappointed, or distant (or defined by some other characteristic that makes it difficult to love him)?

At times, I am hindered from experiencing God as He really is—excited to be lovingly involved with me. Instead, I see Him as _____.

(For example: *disappointed in me, distant from me, inspecting me, angry with me, uninterested in me, constantly testing me, or another description of your choice.*)

FACTORS THAT CONTRIBUTE TO HINDERED VIEWS OF GOD

As you have begun to reflect upon your personal view of God, you may have considered some of the same questions that I asked as the Lord began to reshape my view of Him: "How did I come to see God in this way? How did my view of Him become hindered and distorted?"

After many years of trying to help others with their concept of God, as well as pursuing a better understanding of my own, the Holy Spirit brought insight into three factors that often contribute to hindered views of God: family relationships, religious experiences, and painful life events.

Family Relationships

Both formal research and intuitive thought leads us to the conclusion that family relationships can have a significant impact on our concept of God, particularly during our early, formative years. Positive or painful interactions with caregivers shape our experiences of trust, intimacy, and affection. It is through the lens of these early interactions with family members that we come to view other relationships, including our relationship with God.

There were many aspects of my childhood that shaped my life and concept of God in positive ways, but I have also come to recognize that my view of God as an inspecting god partially grew out of early interactions with my father. As a Marine drill sergeant, my father was a strict disciplinarian, and he carried many of his military traditions into our home. Inspections of closets, clothes, and shoes were commonplace. He even held frequent bed inspections, during which a quarter was flipped onto the bed to see how tightly the bed was made. If the quarter did not bounce high enough, the covers were thrown to the floor and the bed was to be remade. My father had the best of motives—he wanted his son to become diligent, dependable, and disciplined—but his methods were sometimes painful. My relationship with an inspecting father became connected to my view of an inspecting God. In later years, however, it was a blessing to experience the deepening of an adult friendship with my dad that was actually used by the Lord to help me see God as He really is.

Pause and Reflect

Could aspects of your family relationships have, at times, hindered you from experiencing God as He really is?

At times, I may have been hindered by . . .

Religious Experiences

A second source of my hindered view of God were some of my religious experiences. I became a follower of Jesus at the age of 21, just as the Holy Spirit was ushering in the "Jesus Movement" of the 1960's and 70's. God allowed me to pass on to others the wonder of His work in my life with great zeal and passion. Over the next few years, He multiplied His blessings in my life and ministry, but I was also frustrated by the challenges of rigid church structures, religiosity, and the pressure to conform. In the midst of these clashes between revival and the status quo, a much more subtle attack was underway.

It was during this time of spiritual renewal that a very popular devotional guide found its way into my hands. With hundreds of thousands of copies sold, this daily devotional became a foundational part of our campus ministry. But looking back, I grieve over the long-term impact of this devotional on my life and the lives of those around me. As we read this devotional day after day, our concept of Christ became tragically distorted. Each devotional reading contained a lengthy Scripture passage followed by three penetrating questions:

1. What sin is to be avoided?
2. What commands are to be obeyed?
3. What now needs to change in your life?

The impact of this devotional was subtle, but severe. I was trained to read the Bible only in order to identify sins, commands, and things that were wrong with my life.

As I look back upon those years, there is no doubt that I needed more of Christ's sanctifying work in my life. But ever so slowly, the wonder of being saved by Christ was replaced by the dread of these daily encounters. The childlike excitement of experiencing the One who wrote the Scripture was being hindered by this approach, which suggested a god who was inspecting and displeased.

Pause and Reflect

Could some of your religious traditions or experiences have, at times, hindered you from seeing Christ as He really is?

At times, I may have been hindered by . . .

Painful Life Events

As we walk through life in a world of tribulation, we inevitably encounter painful events, critical losses, and life-altering traumas (John 16:33). Such events often leave us wondering, "Where was God when . . .?" If such questions are not sufficiently processed, our hearts are left with unresolved pain and uncertainty. When we are uncertain of God's care or His presence, we are left vulnerable to misconceptions of who He really is.

I have come to realize that my distorted view of God was impacted by certain painful life events. Ironically, one of these events occurred during our family's celebration of the Christmas season. I recognize now that I was going through a time of spiritual stagnation, but life with Teresa and our three children seemed to be going quite well. Our ministry as a couple had even been receiving considerable accolades. But just when I thought that God's exceeding abundance was right around the corner, the bottom fell out.

Our family had just celebrated the purchase of our first, new house. We were able to choose a neighborhood, a lot, and a view that were ideal. We had deliberated over the building plans and carefully chosen the decorations and finishing touches for our home. We even arranged to lease the house for a few months before the actual purchase so that we could celebrate Christmas there. We were grateful for what appeared to be God's blessings. But as we settled into our new home, the financial challenges of our church soon commanded our attention.

I served on the staff of a large church in our city. The church was growing, but was financially overextended in a relocation and construction project. All of the church leaders were shocked when the purchasers of our old facility defaulted on their payment and the loan institution holding the church note went bankrupt. In a matter of a few weeks, 14 ministers lost their jobs. I was among them. My unemployment meant that the purchase of our new home was impossible. We were forced to move out after only a few weeks of residence.

We piled our belongings in the back of a pickup truck, took down the Christmas decorations, and loaded up the presents that had been placed under the tree. Our last trip to the house brought the most tears. In one of the saddest and most telling scenes, my young son, Eric, unplugged the Christmas tree, and we loaded the still-decorated tree onto the truck. Eric and I rode in back with the tree, in order to avoid losing all of the decorations. I remember riding in silence most of the way, not really knowing what to say to my son or my family.

More than any other family member, this life event hit me hard and personally. I struggled with feeling like a failure. I even labeled myself as "inadequate" because I, as the husband, father, provider, and leader, had not passed "inspection."

My self-doubts and disappointment turned to questions about God. Had He not seen this coming? Why did He not stop us from designing, building, and moving into this new house? Why did He allow us to experience this loss and embarrassment? Could God not have provided for His church? Did He not notice how faithful our family had been? How could He treat us like this? All of these questions stole the blessing of my Christmas that year. Although my family adjusted amazingly well, I still struggled and questioned the heart of God.

As God's plan played itself out, my rational questions that had no answers gave way to a healthier, more relational focus. I still have few answers as to why God allowed these events to occur as they did, but I did encounter the real Jesus in a very special way. My self-doubts and despair gave way to renewed joy and gratitude as I meditated on God's Word. During the last week of December, when Teresa and I typically spend time on goal-setting for the New Year, God led me to the Book of Isaiah. As I meditated on the children of Israel's wilderness journey, I was struck by God's heart toward His people. My heart was gripped by His Spirit as my eyes fixated on His Word: "In all their affliction He was afflicted" (Isaiah 63:9 NASB).

The real God was afflicted, touched, sorrowed, and saddened by His children's pain. My eyes filled with tears—not tears of sadness, but tears of wonder and gratitude for the real Jesus, who noticed and cared. In the midst of my pain, Jesus became Someone who was compassionate, comforting, and understanding. From that moment, everything about that painful time became new. As I will share in later chapters, God brought much good from this difficult circumstance. But none of His subsequent blessings could compare to that moment of encounter with the afflicted heart of a saddened Jesus!

Pause and Reflect

Could certain painful life events have, at times, hindered you from experiencing Christ as He really is?

At times, I may have been hindered by . . .

We hope that you have taken this opportunity to assess your own view of God and reflect on how you might have been hindered in seeing Christ as He really is. It is our prayer that you will continue this journey of knowing Him and experiencing His heart on a daily basis.

An Experience With God's People

"Be kind and compassionate to one another" (Ephesians 4:32).

Consider how you might respond to these questions: How might you be hindered from seeing the real God? How might your hindered view of God have impacted your life and ministry?

I am sometimes hindered in seeing Christ as One who is excited to love me. Instead, I sometimes see Him as . . .

(For example: *I am sometimes hindered in seeing Christ as One who is excited to love me. Instead, I sometimes see Him as distant and detached.*)

I think that this hindered view of Him has impacted my life and ministry in the following ways . . .

(For example: *I think that this hindered view of Him has impacted my life and ministry in the following ways: I tend to forget that God is concerned about the details of my life, that He loves me enough to care about the "little things." I also have a tendency to be somewhat detached or distant from other people, especially when I am feeling stressed or overwhelmed.*)

Share your responses with your partner or small group. As you hear the responses of others, you will want to communicate your care and concern. Avoid giving advice or spiritual pep talks to one another during this time. Instead, focus upon living out Ephesians 4:32 as you respond with comfort and compassion. Give a response that is kind and tenderhearted. Your response might begin with caring words such as . . .

I am saddened that . . .
I am sorry that you . . .
I regret that . . .
I feel compassion for you because . . .

55

(For example: *I am saddened that you have a distant view of God at times. I was especially saddened when you talked about feeling detached and separated from your kids,* or *I felt compassion for you as I heard you say that you sometimes view God as disappointed and displeased. My heart hurt for you when I heard you say that you only wished you could please Him.*)

After each person has shared their responses to the questions above and received comfort from their partner(s), take a few moments to pray for one another. Ask God to make the prayer of Philippians 3:10 come alive in each person's heart, so that each of you "might know Christ" in a deep, personal way. Pray that God would reveal His true identity and heart to each person present. Your prayer might sound like the following:

Heavenly Father, I ask that Your Holy Spirit might reveal the true identity of Jesus to my brother/sister in Christ. May he/she come to know the real God—the One who is excited to love him/her. Please remove any mistaken view of who You are, in order that he/she might know You and the love of Your heart. It is in Jesus' name I pray, Amen.

KNOWING THE REAL CHRIST

"If you love Me, **you will** keep My commandments" (John 14:15 NASB).

Now that we have assessed our view of God, let us go back to our Scripture passage in John 14:15. We have seen that our God is not an inspecting, disappointed, or distant god. If each of these views is inaccurate, then how would the real Christ speak the words of this verse? To find our answer, we must go back to the context of the passage. The fourteenth chapter of the Gospel of John took place in the upper room, where Jesus began to comfort and prepare the disciples for His upcoming death and departure. It was a sacred time of tender care from the Savior toward His followers.

Christ began to reassure His followers with several promises: "Trust in God, trust also in me. In my Father's house are many rooms. . . . I am going there to prepare a place for you" (John 14:1, 2). Next, Jesus gave the promise of His return: "I will come back and take you to be with me that you also may be where I am. You know the way to the place where I am going" (v. 3). The Savior went on to make a promise about all that they would do as a result of their faith in Him. "I tell you the truth, anyone who has faith in me will do what I have been doing. He will do even greater things than these, because I am going to the Father" (v. 12). Finally, notice the verse immediately preceding our Scripture of interest: "If you ask Me anything in My name, I will do it (v. 14 NASB). This, too, is a verse of promise. Now, pause and reread John 14:15 as it was intended—as a **promise** for every believer. "If you love me, **you will** keep my commandments!"

It was within the context of this list of promises that Jesus made the declaration of John 14:15. This verse is a promise that was meant to bring reassurance, blessing, and security to our hearts. Indeed, Christ might have smiled and proclaimed the certainty of this connection: "If you love me you will keep my commandments. If you and I have a love relationship with one another, you will keep the commandments. It will happen. I promise." When you woke up this morning, Jesus was not checking to see if you were keeping His commandments in order to prove your love. Rather, He was longing for you to love Him, knowing that as you do, you **will** keep His commandments! This is the same promise that Paul relates to the church at Galatia when he reminds them, "So I say, live by the Spirit, and you will not gratify the desires of the sinful nature" (Galatians 5:16). The real Christ is not inspecting, disappointed, or distant. He is excited to love us, and longs for us to share in His love!

The real Christ is attentive and caring, sensitive and compassionate. He does not have a tally sheet in heaven, and is not too preoccupied to care about each of us individually. He is not detached or distant, disappointed or displeased. In fact, Christ, the Savior of the world, wants a relationship with us! The real Christ wants to be

> **The real Christ is not inspecting, disappointed, or distant. He is excited to love us, and longs for us to share in His love!**

close, intimate friends with you and me. He is excited when we wake up in the morning, and cannot wait to talk with us and relate to us. He is delighted to know us and be with us. The real Christ generously and graciously gave up His life because He could not bear the thought of eternity without you. He is pleased with you because He sees you with the eyes of a Master Creator, One who admires His handiwork and values each of His treasures because they are unique and wonderful. Of course, the real God is also holy, without spot or blemish, and His plan is that, out of our deep love for Him, we would live out His commands. For this reason, He has sent His Spirit to empower us with His holy life and abundant love. This is the character of the real Christ, the One to whom we have the privilege and honor to relate.

Pause and Reflect

What does it do to your heart to consider that the real Jesus desires a love relationship with you?

As I come to see Christ as One who longs for me to share in His love, my heart is touched with _____.

(For example: *As I come to see Christ as One who longs for me to share in His love, my heart is touched with gratitude, humility, and deepened love.*)

Can you imagine the joy that is possible as we are able to experience the love of the real Christ? Our life can overflow with gratitude and love. Our worship will be meaningful and fulfilling as we celebrate the special relationship with our trusted Friend. Our prayers will be more than an obligatory routine; they will be filled with expressions of thanksgiving, faithfulness, and vulnerable need as the Spirit prompts and empowers us. The life we live will become more and more "His life" as we walk worthy of our high calling in Christ, fulfilling the challenge to be holy as He is holy (Ephesians 4:1; 1 Peter 1:16). As we experience the love of the real Christ, our ability to love others will increase through the empowerment of the Spirit. Our ministry will be characterized by grateful service instead of compulsion or dutiful obligation. Finally, as we come to experience the love of the real Christ, our lives and ministries will reflect the heart of God. We will begin to look more like Him, and as our "appearance" changes, we will bring Him the glory of which He alone is worthy (2 Corinthians 3:18).

Reshaping Our View of God

Many of you may be asking a critical question at this point in our journey together: "I have come to realize that my view of God may need some reshaping; I cannot always see the real God clearly. But how do I go about removing the hindrances to seeing Him clearly? What can I do to reshape my view of Him?"

Scripture again gives us insight into the loving and abundant provision of God as the psalmist declares, "In your light we see light" (Psalm 36:9). Our view of Him is reshaped as we look beyond our human experience and life events toward the light that only He can give. It is God's light that reveals who He really is, and while God certainly reveals Himself in creation and circumstances, much of His "light" comes through relationships. God reveals His true identity through the testimony of His Son, through the revelation of His Word, and through the love of His people. You may recognize these three elements of transformation as the "road signs" we encountered in Chapter 1, but we might also describe them as "three sources of light."

The Light of God's Son

Jesus boldly proclaimed that He is "the light of the world" (John 8:12), so as we encounter the real Jesus and experience His love, we experience one source of His transforming light. And when we have seen the real Jesus, we have seen the real God (14:9).

The Light of God's Word

When we walk in the light of God's Word, we experience a second source of His transforming power. Psalm 119:105 makes it known that His Word is a lamp to our feet and a light for our path. As we experience God's Book and are drawn into a deepened relationship with Him, we see Him for who He really is. Our concept of God is reshaped as the Holy Spirit leads us into a deepened love relationship with the God of Scripture. We come to find that His Word is "living and active," bringing transformation as we encounter Him at the point of His Word (Hebrews 4:12).

The Light of God's People

A third source of light is God's love as it is demonstrated through His people. Christ reminded us that we are "the light of the world" (Matthew 5:14); and as we love one another, His love is perfected in us. Through our demonstrations of love to one another, we are able to see the real God more clearly (1 John 4:12).

In John 12:35, Jesus exhorts us to "Walk while you have the light, before darkness overtakes you." Our journey together in this study is one that is undertaken in the light of God's Son, God's Word, and God's people. We trust the Holy Spirit to illumine the Word, to empower fellowship among God's people, and to restore relevance to our lives and ministries as we walk together in His light.

Join us now for the final experiential exercise of this chapter. Take the next few moments and prayerfully ask God to reveal His true identity through this experience with His Son.

An Experience With God's Son

"But while he was still a long way off, his father saw him and was filled with compassion for him; he ran to his son, threw his arms around him and kissed him" (Luke 15:20).

The well-known story of the prodigal son gives us a picture of the real God. The most gripping scene in this biblical account finds the father waiting for his wayward son. He scans the horizon day after day, straining his eyes and hoping to catch a glimpse of his son—the son who demanded an early inheritance, ran away from home, and squandered every cent his father had so graciously given him.

Before you read the familiar story of the prodigal son and his father, please take a moment to reflect on your own life. Do you have anything in common with the prodigal?

Has there ever been a time when you have made **selfish** demands? It could be as subtle as preoccupation with your own plans, agenda, and goals, or as overt as manipulating others or pursuing iron-fisted control. Have you made demands of the Lord, hoping for Him to meet your needs in your time and your way instead of His?

When faced with difficulties and challenges, the prodigal son tried to take care of things himself. Has your own **self-reliance** ever led you to foolishly conclude that you could "take care of it"? Have you ever minimized your need for God or other people because of a mistaken conclusion that you are better off on your own?

The wayward son also discounted his own worth to his father. Have you ever questioned your worth to your heavenly Father, thus allowing **self-condemnation** to rob you of joy and passion for the Lord? Have you mistakenly concluded that you are not worth the loving care of the Father?

Finally, have you, like the prodigal, fallen victim to a lifestyle of poor choices and pain-filled consequences? Have you been in places that you should not have been? Have you been demanding toward those you love rather than giving honor to them? Have you squandered precious things? Have you made life choices that you regret?

Even now, as you read the story of the prodigal and his father, allow the Lord to sensitize your heart to the real God. Spend some time meditating on this passage of Scripture. Ponder not only the story itself, but also the ways in which the heart of the Lord is revealed through the story.

Picture in your heart this man who has selfishly taken from his father and wasted all he was given. He finds himself feeding pigs, and eventually comes to question his own value and worth. Then he decides to go home. Picture him walking along dusty, winding roads. Finally, he turns the last corner toward home and catches a glimpse of the livestock in the distance. For a moment, imagine that this prodigal is not just any prodigal. **The prodigal is you.** You are returning home; you see your former residence in the distance.

Now allow the Holy Spirit to lead you in experiencing the testimony of God's grace. Experience afresh the power of God's love for each of us, which is revealed in Luke 15:20, when the father sees the prodigal: "But while he was still a long way off, his father saw him and was filled with compassion for him; he ran to his son, threw his arms around him and kissed him."

Imagine that Christ is waiting for you to return home. When He sees you in the distance, He is moved with compassion in spite of your selfishness, pride, condemnation, and sin, and He **runs** toward you. He leaps quickly, anxiously off the front porch because he cannot wait to see you. He embraces you, kisses you, and whispers in your ear. He does not offer lectures or criticism. There is no rebuke or scorn. His voice is filled with compassion as He embraces you. There's a ring, a robe, and the announcement of a party. The real God welcomes you with outstretched arms, ready to embrace you and excited to love you!

Let God now fill your heart with gratitude for the grace that you have received. Ask Him to bring you back often to a time of fresh reflection upon the grace of the embracing Christ. Pray that He would fill you with wonder and gratitude for His care that would compel you to love those around you.

Spend the next few moments praying with your partner or small group. You might offer a prayer of gratitude and then one of calling. Your prayers might sound like the following:

A prayer of gratitude—*"Fill my heart, Holy Spirit, with the wonder of an embracing, celebrating Christ; may my joy and gratitude for being so loved empower my love of others."*

A prayer of calling—*"I sense your calling, heavenly Father, to love others around me with this same caring initiative. Make my heart especially sensitive to passing on your love to my* _____ (for example: *husband, wife, child, friend, family member,* or *co-worker).*

For Further Study

EXPERIENCING CHRIST: THE KEY TO SIGNIFICANT LIFE CHANGES

Jesus was often misunderstood and misrepresented during His time on Earth, just as He is today. But the New Testament reveals that many people experienced significant positive changes in their lives when they encountered the real Jesus.

We pray that the following Scripture passages might be used by the Lord to renew hope and excitement in specific areas of your life. Approach each passage prayerfully, asking the Spirit to encourage and impact your heart. Notice the dramatic life changes that occurred as these 1st century followers encountered the Savior.

From Self-Preoccupation to Glorifying Praise (See Luke 17:11–19.)

The Samaritan leper referenced in this text experienced a significant transformation: rather than single-mindedly focusing on his own life (including his miraculous healing and his hope for restoration to his family and community), he returned to relate to Jesus—the One who had given those blessings. "He threw himself at Jesus' feet and thanked Him" (v. 16), and as a result, Christ affirmed him as one who brought praise to God (v. 18). There may be no greater life or ministry objective than this: to bring praise and honor to God!

Read a related passage in John 17:1–3, then pause to listen as His Spirit floods your heart with reminders of your own manifold blessings. Allow the Spirit to lead you into a prayer of thanksgiving and praise to the One who gives these blessings.

From Denial to Bold Witness (See Matthew 26:69–75 and Acts 2:14–41.)

Peter's transformation from one who fearfully denied Christ to one who courageously witnessed at Pentecost gives evidence of his encounters with the real Jesus. We witness Peter's brokenness and tears of contrition when he looked into the eyes of Jesus immediately following the denial (Luke 22:61). We see how Christ took special notice of Peter after the Resurrection (Mark 16:7), and how He restored and commissioned him at the Sea of Tiberias (John 21:15–22).

These encounters with the real Jesus helped prepare Peter to receive the divine empowerment of the Spirit that enabled him to boldly witness to the resurrected Christ on the day of Pentecost: "Peter stood up with the Eleven, raised his voice and addressed the crowd . . . and about three thousand were added to their number that day" (Acts 2:14–41).

Pause now and ask the Lord to bring additional boldness to your own life. Pray that He would reveal His special care for you, perhaps even in the midst of your own denial or abandonment of Him. Ask Him to show you how He takes special notice of you. Pray that His Spirit would bring any needed restoration to your life and ministry, empowering you with the same transforming power that Peter received.

From Skepticism to Service (See John 3:1–21; 19:38–42.)

Nicodemus probably would not have been voted "most likely to believe" based on his encounter with Jesus (John 3:1–21). This Pharisee may have felt fearful, unsure of himself, concerned about his future, embarrassed, or insecure as he waited until dark to approach the Savior (v. 2). Within the safety of darkness, Nicodemus posed the question, "How can a man be born again?" and in so doing, revealed the uncertainties and misunderstandings of his heart. Christ patiently addressed the leader's questions, revealing His desire to bring change to this man's heart and life: "You should not be surprised at my saying, 'You must be born again.' The wind blows wherever it pleases. You hear its sound, but you cannot tell where it comes from or where it is going. So it is with everyone born of the Spirit" (vv. 7, 8).

Something about this encounter with Christ piqued the curiosity of this religious leader. We do not hear about his immediate conversion following that evening discussion, but we do read of Nicodemus after Christ's death. We cannot be sure how often Nicodemus listened to the Master as He spoke to the crowds. We do not know how often he may have witnessed the miracles of Christ or sensed the Messiah's compassion. We do know, however, that these encounters must have occurred because Nicodemus' life was transformed. Perhaps he heard Christ cry out at Calvary: "Father, forgive them, for they do not know what they are doing" (Luke 23:34). Nicodemus might have overheard Jesus' promise to the thief on the cross: "Today you will be with me in paradise" (v. 43). Or maybe he heard Christ's declaration of faith upon His death: "Father, into your hands I commit my spirit" (v. 46).

We can be certain that something was changed inside of Nicodemus because the same man who was afraid to go to Jesus during the light of day boldly approached Pilate, asking for permission to bury Jesus' body. Along with Joseph of Arimathea, Nicodemus took the body away, brought a mixture of myrrh and aloes, wrapped the body and the spices in strips of linen, and laid Jesus in the tomb (John 19:38–42). The one who had approached Christ in secrecy and uncertainty was now apparently willing to be identified with Him.

Pause now and consider any uncertainties or questions in your own heart. Have you, like Nicodemus, been afraid to boldly identify yourself with Christ? Have you been fearful, embarrassed, reluctant, skeptical, or insecure? Ask the Holy Spirit to empower you with the same power that transformed the life of Nicodemus. Ask Him to make the changes inside of you that prompted the bold steps of this religious leader. May the Spirit lead you to serve the Savior in courageous ways!

From Knowing Scripture to Experiencing Scripture
(See Luke 24:13–35.)
The disciples who walked along the Emmaus Road were certainly familiar with Scripture; they knew the Word of God. We know that these disciples rationally embraced the truths of the Messiah because they made their way to Golgotha during the Passover. They were among the crowd who saw Christ's torture and crucifixion. Yet Scripture tells us that "they were kept from recognizing him" (Luke 24:16).

It is important to notice that Christ did not leave them in this state of "knowing Scripture," but missing Him. The Gospel recalls that, "Beginning with Moses and all the Prophets, he explained to them what was said in all the Scriptures concerning himself" (v. 27). As Christ seized the initiative to reveal Himself, transformation took place in the lives of these disciples: "Were not our hearts burning within us while he talked with us on the road and opened the Scriptures to us" (v. 32)?

How long has it been since your heart "burned within" as the Spirit revealed the Son through His Word? Perhaps it has been too long. Pause now and ask the Lord to meet you in His Word, bringing revelation and life. Ask Him to join you often and open the Scriptures to you, making them come alive by His Spirit. (Further discussion and emphasis will be placed upon this topic in Chapter Three.)

For additional study (personally or in a small group), consider the following Scripture passages, which speak of the revealed Christ and the lives He transformed:

- John 11:17–36 (Christ's compassionate response to Mary, Lazarus' sister, makes an impact upon the unbelieving Jews.)
- Luke 10:38–42 (Mary sits at the feet of Jesus, giving priority to listening to Him.)
- John 4:4–42 (The woman at the well brings others to Christ.)
- Luke 19:1–10 (A tax collector's priorities are transformed.)

Additional Resources

Judson Cornwall, *Let Us Worship* (So. Plainfield, NJ: Bridge Publications, 1983).

Rob Currie, *Hungry for More of God* (Chattanooga, TN: AMG Publishers, 2003).

Ron Owens, *Return to Worship: A God-Centered Approach* (Nashville, TN: Broadman and Holman Publishers, 1999).

Alan D. Wright, *Lover of My Soul: Delighting in God's Passionate Love* (Sisters, OR: Multnomah Publishers, 1998).

Chapter 3

The Forgotten Purpose of Truth: Our Foundation of Biblical Hermeneutics

My Christian walk began at the age of 21. The Lord worked through the janitor of a local church, along with the lifestyle example of a few others, to introduce me to a personal relationship with God. I was blessed to begin my journey with Christ as a young adult. But almost two decades later, while serving in local church ministry myself, I began to realize that I had traveled only a short distance in my journey toward an intimate relationship with the Lord. Thankfully, He began to change all of that.

While preparing a message from the seventeenth chapter of Luke, an encounter with the Lord redefined my perspective on life and ministry. In a few short moments of meditating over this passage, my perspective on preaching, teaching, Bible study, and the Christian life itself was forever changed.

It was a Tuesday. I was in my study, feeling grateful for a few hours of uninterrupted time to get ahead on the next week's message. After my typical reading and reflection on the text, I began scribbling a few tentative thoughts for a teaching outline.

"Obey the Bible" was my first handwritten entry on an otherwise blank notepad. I interpreted Christ's interaction with the ten lepers as a reminder for us to obey God's commands. I noted that as the lepers approached Christ with the words, "Master, have pity on us," He responded with a command they were to obey: "Go, show yourselves to the priests" (Luke 17:13, 14). Old Testament law spoke of cleansing from leprosy and required these men to show themselves to the priest in order to be declared ceremonially clean (Leviticus 14:2). Just as Christ commanded the lepers to obey the Levitical law, there was little uncertainty in my mind that this passage was our reminder to obey biblical laws.

Next, I scribbled the words, "Exercise Faith" on my notepad. By reading and interpreting the text, I knew that the lepers were called upon to exercise faith as they traveled back to Jerusalem. Their healing was not immediate; Scripture tells us, "*As* they went, they were cleansed" (Luke 17:14). I gleaned from this the truth that God also wants us, as His children, to exercise faith in His Word. After all, God declared that "without faith it is impossible to please God" (Hebrews 11:6), and that "faith comes from hearing the message, and the message is heard through the word of Christ" (Romans 10:17).

As I continued to reflect upon the Savior's interaction with the one leper who returned to express his gratitude, the emotion of the passage began to impact my heart. After the leper threw himself at Jesus' feet and thanked him, Christ asked a series of remarkable questions. My eyes were fixated on the red letters of my Bible: "Were not all ten cleansed? Where are the other nine? Was no one found to return and give praise to God except this foreigner" (Luke 17:17, 18)?

For the first time, the Lord's reaction seemed important to me. Did He not know whether the other lepers were cleansed? Was Christ really questioning the whereabouts of those nine? Certainly not—He is the omniscient One. Then why did He ask such questions? The Spirit began to move in my heart as sadness overwhelmed me. Jesus was not asking these questions because He did not know the answers. This was a brokenhearted Savior expressing disappointment because of the apparent lack of gratitude of the nine. This was Christ revealing His hurt. This was Jesus expressing His pain.

Tears began to fill my eyes. Sadness moved over my heart. Why was I crying? Where was this sadness coming from? After a few moments of reflection, I realized that I was actually hurting for Jesus. I was living out a measure of what the apostle Paul spoke of in Philippians: "the fellowship of sharing in His sufferings" (Philippians 3:10).

The contrast was remarkable: I had engaged in careful exegesis of this passage of Scripture many times and preached several effective sermons on the text before. But on this day, it was as if God said, "David, you know a lot about my Son's teaching. You know a lot about my Son's preaching. But would it be all right if I helped you get to know Him in a deeper way? I would like to help you know Him and His sufferings, in order to deepen your love for Him and for others."

On that day, my relationship with Christ grew more intimate; my love for Him was deepened and enriched. Mercifully, God opened my heart to a new way of approaching His Word.

Since that day, I have come to believe that the Spirit of God wants to draw each of us into this same sensitivity for the Christ of the Bible. He wants to soften your heart with this same tenderness for Jesus and then revolutionize how you read, study, and teach His Word. He wants to make the pages of Scripture come alive and lead you on a journey toward a loving, deeply intimate relationship with God.

Tragically, most Christians would say they desire this close relationship with the Lord. Some would even say they are pursuing it. But this kind of deep, intimate relationship eludes many of us. We come to salvation, begin our relationship with the Lord, and learn to walk in His Spirit, but never travel very far down the road toward intimacy and closeness with

> **He wants to make the pages of Scripture come alive and lead you on a journey toward a loving, deeply intimate relationship with God.**

Him. We may diligently study the Bible, pray faithfully, and even convey His truths to others, yet neglect to continue this journey toward intimacy. How can this be?

THE FORGOTTEN PURPOSE OF TRUTH

We all begin our relationship with God by declaring ourselves to be separated from God and in need of a Savior. From that moment, we begin our walk with Christ. Thankfully, God also provides several avenues through which we can continue our growth and pursuit of Christlikeness. We have the opportunity to approach God through prayer. We have the provision of fellowship with the body of Christ—His church. We can relate to God through corporate worship. Additionally, God has given us His Word so that we might come to know Him and His desires for our life and ministry.

It is to this provision of Scripture that we want to give our focus. Could it be that, in our efforts to grow and mature in Christ, we are not doing everything we are supposed to be doing with the Bible? Could it be that, even in our best attempts at discerning God's truth and working to apply it, we have not done all that we need to do with Scripture? Could we have missed a critical purpose of God's truth?

For more than a decade in church ministry, I fully embraced and defended the reliability and importance of 2 Timothy 3:16, 17: "All Scripture is God-breathed (Greek: *Theopneustos—Theos*—"God"; *pneustos*—"breathed") and is useful. . . . " I had understood Scripture's usefulness for teaching doctrine (Greek: *didaskalia*—"context of teaching") and rebuking or correction (Greek: *elegmos*—"reproving wrong" and *epanorthosis*— "restoring proper condition"). But on that particular day when God moved me with compassion for the sufferings of Jesus, He seemed to take me beyond these two purposes. I came to see that while Scripture is most certainly useful for determining what we are to believe and how we are to live, God desires something more as we encounter His Word. There is a "forgotten purpose" of truth that His Spirit made real for me that day. It is this forgotten purpose that can serve His longing to restore relevance to the 21st century church.

> **It is this forgotten purpose that can serve His longing to restore relevance to the 21st century church.**

Many of us clearly see the **rational purpose** of God's truth. We know that Scripture tells us what we should believe and that God's Word is our determiner for what is true, immovable, unchangeable, and eternal. For example, Acts 4:12 tells us, "There is no other name under heaven given to men by which we must be saved." This boundary of right doctrine lets us know that to claim there is any way to salvation other than Jesus is error, or sin. Consider this diagram as a way of representing the rational purpose of God's truth. Right doctrine serves as a boundary for our journey in life. Straying past that boundary leads us into sin.

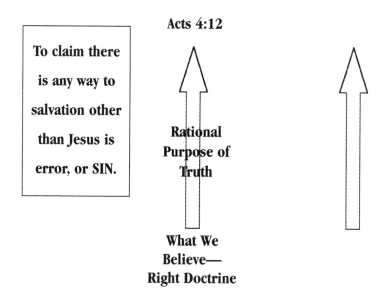

To claim there is any way to salvation other than Jesus is error, or SIN.

Acts 4:12

Rational Purpose of Truth

What We Believe— Right Doctrine

Most of us are also acquainted with the **behavioral purpose** of God's truth. We look to God's Word to tell us how to live our lives. We know that the Bible gives us commands and principles for how to live a life that is pleasing to God and in harmony with one another. Ephesians 4:29 speaks of not letting any unwholesome talk come out of your mouth (reproof), but only what is helpful for building others up (correction). Therefore, to revile, judge, or gossip with our words is to fall outside of the boundary of right living; these are sin. The diagram below shows us that the behavioral purpose of truth forms another boundary for our lives, in that it gives us guidance for how we should live. To stray past this boundary also leads us into sin.

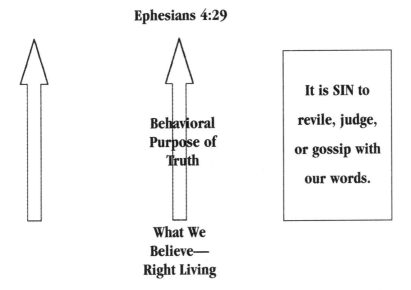

Ephesians 4:29

Behavioral Purpose of Truth

What We Believe— Right Living

It is SIN to revile, judge, or gossip with our words.

While these two purposes of truth are critical for life and ministry, they are not sufficient in themselves. Consider the third diagram below as a way to summarize our representation of God's truth. God's Word gives us boundaries for our life and ministry. The Bible defines the limits of sound doctrine and clearly sets the boundaries for what we are to believe. God's Word also gives us boundaries for how we are to live our life and outlines how we should behave. Yet we must see that these are boundaries given by God in order to direct our journey toward a relationship with Him and with those He loves. In fact, we might consider these boundaries for doctrine and behavior as the "curbs" alongside our road to intimacy with God.

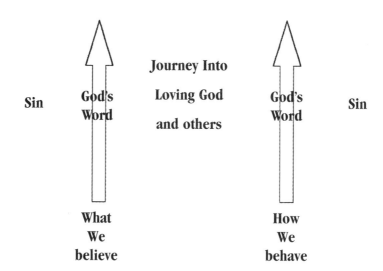

Sin — God's Word — **Journey Into Loving God and others** — God's Word — Sin

What We believe — How We behave

Many of us, though, get sidetracked on this journey toward a deep, intimate relationship with God. We carefully look to Scripture in order to tell us what to believe and how we should behave, but we end up simply veering toward one curb or the other, and miss the opportunity to more deeply know the God of the Bible. As a result, our lives may suffer from a lack of significance and diminished, eternal impact for the cause of Christ. Our ministries may be void of relevance and demonstrable impact because week by week we leave church knowing what to believe and how to behave, but we never take the journey into a deeper relationship with the God of the Bible. Tragically, many of us have been unable to consistently experience the **relational purpose of truth**. As we will elaborate in the section to follow, the relational purpose of truth is this: God's Word was written so that we might have a loving, intimate relationship with the One who wrote it, as well as with those He loves.

> **Week by week, we leave church knowing what to believe and how to behave, but we never take the journey into a deeper relationship with the God of the Bible.**

Matt 22:40

CONFIRMATIONS OF THE RELATIONAL PURPOSE OF TRUTH

The Lord used my experience of suffering with Jesus over the ungratefulness of the nine lepers to challenge the way I interpreted Scripture. My general guidelines for interpreting Scripture had been to ask questions like, "What does the passage say? What does it mean? What does it mean to me?" My experience with Christ in Luke 17 seemed to argue that Scripture was most certainly given to us in order to provide us with right doctrine and instruction for right behavior, but there was more. Could it be that it was also given in order to lead us into loving relationships with God and other people? As I looked carefully through Scripture, I discovered countless confirmations of this relational purpose of truth.

Confirmation From the Old Testament

When challenged to identify the key truth of the Old Testament, many scholars would cite Micah 6:8: "What does the Lord require of you? To act justly and to love mercy and to walk humbly with your God." In these few words, we find concise instructions for relating to both God and other people. This verse summarizes all of Old Testament Scripture with **relational** commands—walk humbly with the Lord, and treat others with justice and compassion.

I was amazed to discover that the Old Testament law also confirms God's relational purpose of truth. We may have to look a little deeper, but even within the old covenant, we can see a God who wants to draw His people into a loving relationship with Him and one another.

We all know that church curricula and teachers of the Word regularly emphasize the importance of the Ten Commandments. From preschool classes to adult Bible Studies, we frequently revisit these instructions that are so central to the Old Testament. Effective teachers explain the context in which the commandments were given, challenge us to pursue the behavioral lifestyle that the commandments exhort, and speak of the truthful insights that the commandments provide into God's character and holiness. But when we study the Ten Commandments and do not experience the heart of the compassionate Father who gave us those commandments, we cannot fully see the God who is love. We miss the relational purpose behind the Ten Commandments when we see only the "thou shalt not's" without recognizing the heart of love that lies behind them. A relational focus would lead us to ask the question, "Why did God give us these commandments?" Was it to raise a standard of moral behavior? Yes. Was it to give testimony of a righteous God? Of course. But Deuteronomy 10:13 also speaks of these commandments being given "for your own good." What good does God have in mind for us? Evidently, our loving Father gave us these commandments because He did not want to see His children hurt themselves or one another. In order to see the relational purpose behind this passage, we must ask ourselves: "What does it prompt within me when I consider that His 'Thou shalt not's' are given for my good, so that I will not be harmed nor cause harm to others?"

Pause and Reflect

Sit quietly before the Lord, and consider how He has given you certain commandments for your good. He has articulated specific "thou shalt not's" that will keep you from harm. He loves you and does not want to see you hurt. What does it do to your heart to consider His care?

As I consider the Lord's care for my good, my heart is touched with _____.

Express your feelings with God. Tell the Lord about your gratefulness, humility, love, or joy. Offer your heartfelt prayers to Him.

As we approach any passage of Scripture, we must not only look at the rational meaning of the text and extract behavioral applications from the text. We must always ask ourselves: What is revealed in the text about the character, person, and heart of God? We must then allow His Spirit to lead us into a heartfelt response. This relational perspective will be critical to developing a more intimate relationship with the One who is Truth.

Confirmation From the 1st Century Church

Confirmation of the relational purpose of truth is also found in early church history. No one who reads the New Testament can miss the amazing impact and immediate relevance of the 1st century church. The Book of Acts clearly chronicles how the Holy Spirit enabled these believers to change their world for Christ. What could they have been doing differently? What did they know that the 21st century church may be missing?

> **That's what a hurting world needs to see: A model of God's Word in action, a body of believers experiencing God's Book and loving God and one another. That is relevance.**

We can say with certainty that part of the early church's success was due to its emphasis on the application of truth. They taught that the truths of

God's Word were to be experienced in our attitudes and actions. The apostle John admonished, "Dear children, let us not love with words or tongue but with actions and in truth" (1 John 3:18). Truth was to be both believed and lived out. The members of the early church learned to demonstrate this identity of love as they became passionately committed to loving Jesus and one another. They lived out Christ's prediction from the upper room: "By this all men will know that you are my disciples, if you love one another" (John 13:35). Paul continued to affirm this relational purpose of God's Word when he wrote to Timothy, "The goal of our instruction is love" (1 Timothy 1:5 NASB). Finally, Peter affirmed the scattered saints of the 1st century because they had purified themselves by obeying the truth (they believed and behaved rightly) and developed a sincere love of the brethren, but then encouraged them to do more: "Love one another deeply, from the heart" (1 Peter 1:22).

The 21st century church must likewise take a firm stand for the truth. We must proclaim that Scripture is the authoritative, absolute truth of God. But we must go further. We can have Bible-believing, Bible-teaching churches that are still irrelevant to the needs of people. If we misapply God's Word by appealing only to the rational mind, hearers of the Word may leave unaffected or even "turned off" by the truths we hold so dear. When we experience scriptural truth in our relationships with God and others, we put God's love into action. That is what a hurting world needs to see—a model of God's Word in action, a body of believers experiencing God's Book and loving God and one another. That is relevance.

An Experience With God's Son

"I want to know Christ and the power of his resurrection and the fellowship of sharing in his sufferings" (Philippians 3:10).

Let us revisit the story of the ten lepers (Luke 17:11–19). Consider the scene: as Jesus and His disciples approach a village on their way to Jerusalem, a ragged band of men begins to call out to them. They shout their request from afar. You cannot see their faces because they have grown accustomed to hiding in shame. Days or even years of rejection have made them cower behind their cloaks. On this day, however, the rumors of a teacher who can bring healing to the sick have made the men unusually bold. Out of desperation, they call out, "Jesus, Master, have pity on us!"

Scripture tells us that when Jesus saw the men, He gave an immediate response. The Savior took one look at the torn flesh and diseased bodies. He saw the rejection and condemnation they had suffered, the sadness of their hearts as they were forced to leave family members and friends. And as soon as the Savior saw these men, He was driven to action. He was moved with compassion, and guaranteed their healing with the words, "Go, show yourselves to the priests."

Scripture records that as the men walked toward the temple, they were cleansed. Can you picture the faces of the men as they approach the city? Perhaps one man looks down and watches as the flesh is restored to his arms. Another stops and stares with amazement at the face of his friend as he sees him whole and healthy for the very first time. Their steps quicken as they remember a wife at home alone, a child whom they have never seen, or a friend who is dearly missed. They hurry toward the temple, knowing that the priest's blessing is the only thing that stands in the way of restoring these relationships that they have missed so much.

Pause now and consider the next scene of the story. Jesus has moved further down the road toward Jerusalem. The ten lepers have been sent ahead to show themselves to the priest. But as Jesus and the disciples make the turn in the road toward the city, they find that one of the lepers has doubled back. He runs to Jesus and throws himself at the Savior's feet. Tears of joy stream down his face. He is out of breath, yet his words are very clear: "Thank You! Thank You! Praise You!"

The words of appreciation and praise still hang in the air, but words have now been replaced with quiet tears. The man still kneels before Jesus, just weeping. If we look carefully, we might notice that Jesus is peculiarly still. His face is saddened. His expression is grieved. Christ kneels in front of the man, grasping his shoulders. We hear pain in the Savior's voice as He asks, "Were not all ten cleansed? Where are the other nine?"

Pause now and reflect on Christ's questions for the leper. What do they seem to suggest is in the heart of Jesus?

Jesus seems to be experiencing _____.

What does it do to your heart to reflect on the pain that Christ experienced?

As I consider how Jesus was saddened and disappointed, my heart is moved with

_____.

Pause and pray a prayer of care and concern for Christ. Tell Him how it makes you feel to know of His hurt.

Lord Jesus, my heart is _____ *as I consider* _____.

As you finish your prayer, share your feelings for Jesus with a partner or small group.

As you were able to hurt with Jesus and feel a sense of sadness for Him, you were beginning to fellowship with Christ and share in His sufferings. You were living out Philippians 3:10. Now, as you have come to feel compassion for Jesus and as your heart has been sorrowed for Him, has that not deepened your love for Him? Have you not been drawn closer to the Lord because of your relational encounter with Him in His Word?

Confirmation From Christ: Re-hanging the Mirror of God's Word

James 1:23, 24 tells us, "Anyone who listens to the word but does not do what it says is like a man who looks at his face in a mirror and, after looking at himself, goes away and immediately forgets what he looks like. But the man who looks intently into the perfect law that gives freedom, and continues to do this, not forgetting what he has heard, but doing it—he will be blessed in what he does."

Therefore, we can imagine that God's Word is like a mirror that hangs on a wall in our home. We can look into this mirror and see how closely we resemble Jesus. We can gaze into the glass and see a reflection of God's glory as the Spirit works to transform us into the likeness of Christ (2 Corinthians 3:18).

Just as the mirrors in our home hang from nails, God's "mirror" (the Bible) must hang upon something as well. In dramatic fashion, while answering a question concerning which commandment was greatest, Christ revealed that God's Word actually "hangs upon" two commandments: "Love the Lord your God with all your heart and with all your soul and with all your mind. . . . Love your neighbor as yourself. All the Law and the Prophets hang on these two commandments" (Matthew 22:37–40). Christ said that all of Scripture "hangs," "depends," or "must be considered in relation to" the way we love God and one another. Every book of the Bible, every command and scriptural principle, hangs on the "nails" of loving God and loving one another.

The New Testament reveals that God intends for us to look into the mirror of His Word and allow the Spirit to transform us into His image, thus bringing glory to God. Christ's answer to the Pharisee in the Gospel of Matthew expands that vision. Jesus' response reveals that it is not enough to simply know God's truth and study His commands, but that all of Scripture must be lived out in the context of loving relationships with God and one another.

Imagine what might happen if you removed the nail that holds a mirror on the wall of your home. That mirror would fall and shatter into pieces as it hit the floor. If you picked up one of the pieces that fell to the ground, would you still have a mirror? Yes. But could you see everything as clearly as before? No. Without the nail supporting the mirror, your view would be distorted. Without the nail, you would not be able to see the image as a whole.

The Pharisees seem to have had a mirror that had fallen to the ground. They seem to have only been able to see certain pieces of God's truth. They were masters at picking up one piece of God's mirror and, with an incomplete and distorted view, looking for others who were not living up to that piece. Their knowledge of Scripture consistently contrasted with the testimony of their lives, provoking anger and rebuke from the Lord. Jesus revealed the

> **It is not enough to simply know God's truth and study His commands; all of Scripture must be lived out in the context of loving relationships with God and one another.**

disparity between the Pharisees' knowledge and their relationship when He said, "You diligently study the Scriptures because you think that by them you possess eternal life. These are the Scriptures that testify about me, yet you refuse to come to me to have life" (John 5:39, 40). These religious leaders were the most learned biblical scholars of their day, and had spent years in the pursuit of knowledge of the Scriptures, but they missed the chance to experience a deepened love relationship with the One who is Truth and those He loves.

On one occasion, Scripture tells us that Jesus and His disciples were passing through the grain fields, and the disciples began to pick some heads of grain. The Pharisees asked the Lord, "Look, why are they doing what is unlawful on the Sabbath" (Mark 2:24)? The religious leaders were looking for someone who was not living out the command to "keep the Sabbath holy" (see Exodus 20:8–10). Did God command that we observe the Sabbath and give honor to the Lord? Yes. Were the Pharisees correct in their study and knowledge of this truth? Yes. They understood the rational purpose of truth and embraced the behavioral purpose of truth, but they missed the overarching relational purpose of truth. They neglected to see that the command to "keep the Sabbath" must be interpreted in the context of loving God and loving others.

Jesus responded to the Pharisees by recounting the story of King David and his men. Christ reminded the Pharisees that when David and his men entered the house of God, they ate the consecrated bread because they were hungry (Matthew 12:3–8). Jesus "re-hung" the Sabbath requirements back on the nail of Great Commandment love as He said, "The Sabbath was made for man, not man for the Sabbath. So the Son of Man is Lord even of the Sabbath" (Mark 2:27).

The New Testament contains many other instances of Christ confirming the relational purpose of truth. In Jesus' prayer for His disciples, He asks the Father to "Sanctify them by the truth;

your word is truth" (John 17:17). This prayer of Jesus reveals that God's Word consecrates us and sets us apart for a particular purpose. But what is that purpose? The last verse of Christ's lengthy prayer gives insight: "that the love you have for me may be in them" (v. 26). We are set apart in order to experience and express Christlike love.

Another confirmation of the relational purpose of truth is found in Christ's words in John 8:32 to the Jews who had come to believe in Him: "You will know the truth, and the truth will set you free." If God's truth is supposed to set us free, what is it that we are supposed to do in our freedom? Galatians 5:13 provides this insight: "You my brothers, were called to be free. But do not use your freedom to indulge the sinful nature, rather, serve one another in love."

Finally, Christ confirmed the relational purpose of truth as He interacted with other people. His responses to Zacchaeus, the woman at the well, and the man born blind all bear witness to a Savior who did not just live out the "letter of the Law," but who re-hung that law upon the nail of loving God and loving others. But there is perhaps no greater example of Christ's commitment to a relational purpose of truth than His interaction with the woman caught in adultery.

Jesus offered forgiveness and a new start to this woman, even as the religious leaders prepared to stone her. The Pharisees held up the truth of the Law: "Teacher, this woman was caught in the act of adultery. In the Law Moses commanded us to stone such women. Now what do you say?" (John 8:4). The Pharisees, armed with this "piece" of Scripture, were ready to pass judgment and carry out the swift execution the Law demanded. Did Christ know the truth of Scripture? Yes. Did He embrace and agree with it? Certainly. But Jesus did something different with that truth.

> **We may be arming saints with a small piece of God's truth and sending them out into the community to look for people who are violating it.**

He compassionately said to the woman, "Neither do I condemn you," but He added, "Go now and leave your life of sin" (v. 11). Christ showed His love for this woman who had been scarred by sin as He knelt beside her on the ground. Jesus demonstrated His lavish grace, offering protection and security. Then, and only then, did He address her behavior. Only after Christ had demonstrated His love for the woman did He address her sinful acts. Only after He had shown compassion and mercy did He speak of her failure. We cannot help but conclude that this woman was moved with gratefulness and loving obedience.

The church of the 21st century must heed the example of Christ. We must not only dedicate ourselves to scriptural knowledge and purity of lifestyle; we must learn to hang all of Scripture on the Great Commandment—loving God and one another. We must do more than memorize Bible verses; we must live them out with God and other people. We must do more than arm ourselves with biblical knowledge and pass that knowledge onto others; we must model it and live it out in loving relationships. When we equip people with the knowledge of truth, but fail to show them the relational purpose of truth, we may promote a Pharisaical perspective. Week by week, we may be arming saints with a small piece of God's truth and sending them out into the community to look for people who are violating it.

Has the church of the 21st century lost the nail that should be holding the mirror of God's Word? Have we lost sight of the two commandments that all other aspects of God's Word hang upon? Could this explain why there is so much knowledge of God's Word, yet so few people who are actually living it out? Could this explain why so many Christians know the truth, yet too frequently find themselves in the same moral and ethical failures as those without a relationship with Christ? Could this have any relation to the alarming fact that Christian marriages fail as frequently as any others? Could this be the reason that William Hendricks, author of *Exit Interviews: Revealing Stories of Why People Are Leaving the Church,* listed the number-one reason that people leave the church as follows:

> People no longer evaluate Christianity on the basis of whether it is true, but how it is true in their own lives. The question today is not whether God exists, but what difference does God make. People are not merely searching for truth—they are searching for how truth can be applied to their lives.

The church of the 21st century must re-examine what we are doing with Scripture. We must reclaim the forgotten purpose of truth because when we only emphasize fragments of God's truth, we lose relevance and impact in a hurting world. In order to be effective in our efforts to reach the world for Christ, we have to move beyond giving intellectual assent to the Bible, debating over rational beliefs, or assessing standards of behavior, and begin to experience the Word with God and one another.

PAINFUL RESULTS OF MISSING THE RELATIONAL PURPOSE OF TRUTH

Christians in every church and leaders of every denomination, movement, and para-church ministry must take steps to return to the foundation of loving God and loving others as we teach, preach, and study God's Word. If we continue to miss this relational purpose of truth, our churches and ministries will continue in their irrelevance and decline. Our personal lives will lack the vibrant relevance and passion that fulfills Christ's promise of exceeding abundance (John 10:10 KJV). We will become vulnerable to each of these painful results of missing the relational purpose of truth:

If the Relational Purpose of Truth Is Not Prioritized, Hearers of the Word May Become Proud.

- The Pharisees only knew what Scripture said. They did not fully know the One who wrote it (5:39, 40). Their pursuit of knowledge without relationship produced pride and arrogance (Matthew 12:1–14).

- First Corinthians 8:1–3 contrasts knowledge with love: "Knowledge puffs up, but love builds up. The man who thinks he knows something does not yet know as he ought to know. But the man who loves God is known by God."

- James 4:6 warns us about God's perspective on those who are proud, arrogant, or "puffed up." "God opposes the proud but gives grace to the humble."

My Personal Journey

After becoming a Christian as a young adult, I quickly began to develop friendships with other men who were interested in spiritual things. We sincerely wanted to know more of God's Word and were committed to our faith. During one particular Bible study, our group decided to begin a rigorous course of Scripture memory. We challenged one another to memorize large portions of the Bible, and even set up a system for holding each other accountable. As we would gather together for lunch or a cup of coffee, one of my friends would begin to recite his assigned text (the entire tenth chapter of the Gospel of John, for example), and then look to another person to recite the following chapter. These memory challenges grew increasingly difficult, but we reveled in the challenge because we were taking our spiritual growth seriously. I was motivated in this effort because spiritual growth seemed certain if I could only "hide the word of God in my heart."

As the months passed, several members of our accountability group dropped out. We began our second year with a dozen young men who were "serious about their spiritual walk," but after a few weeks, our number had dwindled down to only three. The three of us would sit at the local coffee shop and share our latest insight from the original languages of Scripture, or recite the chapter or book that we had recently committed to memory. It was during this time that my heart grew increasingly proud. I looked around with an arrogant smile at the few of us who remained, and had pity on the others who "could not measure up." The three of us found perverse pleasure in verses like Matthew 22:14: "For many are called, but few are chosen" (NASB). After all, we were among the "chosen"! Another of our favorite verses was Matthew 7:13: "Broad is the road that leads to destruction." The way we saw it, those who had opted out of our group were on that road, while we, of course, were on the narrow road that leads to life!

In my pursuit of knowledge, I had missed the Person of the Bible. In my quest for spiritual maturity, the importance of a relationship with my brothers in Christ had gone unnoticed. Looking back, God's heart must have been broken by my pride and grieved by my arrogance.

If the Relational Purpose of Truth Is Not Prioritized, Hearers of the Word May Feel Condemned.

- Matthew 12:7—"If you had known what these words mean, 'I desire mercy, not sacrifice,' you would not have condemned the innocent." If we are not careful, we may adopt the "right" beliefs and look for opportunities to debate about those beliefs. Or we may claim the "right" truths of Scripture and, like the Pharisees, condemn people who are not living out those truths.

- Luke 6:37—"Do not judge, and you will not be judged. Do not condemn, and you will not be condemned."

- John 8:10—"Jesus straightened up and asked her, 'Woman, where are they? Has no one condemned you? . . . Neither do I condemn you.'"

My Personal Journey

My own family members could testify to the importance of prioritizing the relational purpose of truth. Their testimony comes from years of my overly zealous commitment to right beliefs and right behaviors. You see, before becoming a Christian, I was very good at being lost in my sin. My lifestyle was sinful and corrupt, and I lived in a state of enthusiastic and blatant rebellion. When Christ came into my life, I put that same fanatical energy and eagerness into my newfound faith. The pendulum swung, and my family experienced the painful results of my misdirected intensity.

As I grew in my knowledge of God's Word and in the "maturity" of my Christian faith, living a life that was characterized by purity, obedience, and Christlikeness became paramount. In this particular season of my life, God's truth in 1 Thessalonians 5:22, "Avoid every kind of evil," was foremost in my mind and heart. Unfortunately, like the Pharisees, I took that one piece of God's Word and started looking for evil in my home.

Predictably, "evil" was discovered. I found that my own daughter was listening to "evil" music. She had several albums by the Beatles, with songs like "Can't Buy Me Love" and "Yellow Submarine." They just had to be evil. Next, I discovered that even my wife was listening to "evil music." Teresa's albums were clearly displayed near the record player. I had not heard the songs on those albums before and was definitely unaware that the albums contained no lyrics, only instrumental music. But surely that music was evil; the name "Mantovani" just sounded evil.

Upon making these discoveries, I decided that it was up to me to help my family obey the command of 1 Thessalonians 5:22; they were clearly **not** avoiding every kind of evil. So I broke those records. When my wife and children were out of the house one day, I smashed that "evil" music and threw the pieces in the garbage can. As I sat down to wait for my family, it seemed only fitting to prepare a brief sermon for them about the necessity of avoiding even the appearance of evil as a Christian.

I am not proud to admit any of this. My heart cringes at the memory of my wife and daughter's faces as I told them what I had done. They left the room quietly, not angered by my actions but obviously condemned. What my wife thought was beautiful, instrumental music had been labeled "evil" by her husband. What my daughter thought was fun, contemporary music, her dad had called "evil." They both respectfully complied with my wishes, but I remember leaving the room that day puzzled by their lack of joy. My plan was to rid our home of "evil," but they seemed to only feel my judgment.

If the Relational Purpose of Truth Is Not Prioritized, Irrelevance Will Increase.

- Irrelevance increases when we learn more biblical truth, but never take the journey into a deeper relationship with God. Our loving relationship with the One who wrote the Book empowers us to live out the truths of the Book. Are we living out a genuine image of Christ, or do we have only a form of godliness (2 Timothy 3:5)?

- Is there a sense of irrelevance about our lives and ministries? Have we been emphasizing trivial matters while missing the "weightier provisions of the law" (see example in Matthew 23:23–33)? Irrelevancy increases when we leave church week after week knowing more and having been exhorted to obey more, but not having experienced deepened love for God and others.

Irrelevance in Our Personal Lives

Many years ago, I took my first of several trips to the Holy Land. My wife and I were blessed to walk the streets of Jerusalem, stroll along the Sea of Galilee, and even pray in the Garden of Gethsemane. We have countless memories of the Lord strengthening our love for Him as we actually saw the places where He lived and died.

There is one memory, though, that is distinct from all the rest. Our tour group stayed at a contemporary, multi-story hotel in the city of Jerusalem, with all of the modern conveniences. The hotel itself was beautiful, but what I remember most are the unique features that we discovered on the Saturday of our visit. You see, if you walked into the restroom of this modern hotel in downtown Jerusalem on a Saturday, you would find toilet paper that had already been torn for you and paper towels that had already been taken out of the dispenser. You would find that all of the buttons in the elevators had been pushed for you. In fact, if you were staying on one of the top floors of this hotel and wanted to go down to the lobby, you would have to stop at every floor on the way down. Likewise, if you were in the lobby and wanted to go to your room, you would have to wait as the elevator stopped at every floor on the way up.

I discovered that these unique features of the hotel were reflections of a cultural effort to live out the Old Testament command to keep the Sabbath holy (Exodus 20:8–10). The toilet paper was torn so that you did not have to "work" on the Sabbath. The elevator buttons were already pushed because to push an elevator button would be to "work" on the Sabbath.

I could not get over how silly these traditions seemed. *How could they be so concerned about trivial things like toilet paper and elevator buttons?* I wondered. Yet as I returned from my trip to the Holy Land, the Spirit of God spoke to my heart: "David, how often have you put enormous emphasis on trivial things? How often have you focused upon those things that do not really matter?" The Lord humbled my heart concerning the irrelevance of much of my own preaching, teaching, and exhortation.

Irrelevance in Ministry

Pastor Newman was more animated and intense than usual during Sunday's message. His text was 1 Thessalonians 4:3: "It is God's will . . . that you should avoid sexual immorality." The pastor knew that his topic was extremely relevant to his congregation at this time. He had recently learned that the son-in-law of Frank Johnson, one of his faithful members, had been caught in an extramarital affair.

Pastor Newman preached his sermon with conviction. He pointed out that fornication is one of the most heinous sins because it is a sin against one's own body. He gave powerful illustrations about the consequences of sexual sin, being careful to point out the certain availability of God's forgiveness, but also emphasizing the dreadful wages of disobeying God.

The congregation left that Sunday morning in a somber mood. They thanked their pastor for the powerful sermon. "Thank you, Pastor. That was just what the people needed to hear." Even Frank Johnson left the church with a tear-stained face and appreciative heart.

The message from Pastor Newman was crystal clear that Sunday morning. The Word of God was declared with authority and conviction: sexual immorality is sin, and sin brings consequences. There was no doubt where the pastor stood on the issue. That is why everyone in the community was stunned when, less than three months later, Pastor Newman was arrested for soliciting a prostitute on the other side of town.

The names have been changed, but the basic story is true. Incidents like this occur with disheartening frequency across our land as those who speak the truth fail to live the truth.

This is not to suggest that we must walk in sinless perfection to qualify as Christian leaders. But in order to avoid the trap that waylaid Pastor Newman and so many others, we must allow God's Word to take root in us until what we proclaim and how we live are one and the same. We must

> **We must allow God's Word to take root in us until what we proclaim and how we live are one and the same.**

maintain a deep, loving relationship with the God who gave us verses like 1 Thessalonians 4:3 if we are to have any hope of living them out. Otherwise, we may be left with a "form of godliness," but we will have denied the power of God (2 Timothy 3:5). Relevance in ministry will only be maintained as God's leaders learn how to love Him intimately and allow His Spirit to constrain their lives.

If the Relational Purpose of Truth Is Not Prioritized, We May Develop and Promote Distorted Views of God and the Gospel.

- We may come to believe that God is hiding in the grain fields like the Pharisees, seeking to catch us doing something wrong. This may lead to irrelevance in our personal lives as we seek to catch others doing something wrong. It may also lead to an irrelevant ministry focus where leaders see their primary role as "pointing out the wrong" in the lives of others. As a result, our relationships with others will likely be damaged by emotional distance, condemnation, or revenge. We may also come to view God as distant, condemning, or even vengeful.

- We may develop a distorted view of the Gospel: "If I just **knew** enough, then God would be pleased." The Holy Spirit was not only active in the writing of Scripture; He is also active in leading us into its truth. "We have not received the spirit of the world but the Spirit who is from God, that we may understand what God has freely given us. This is what we speak, not in words taught us by human wisdom but in words taught by the Spirit, expressing spiritual truths in spiritual words" (1 Corinthians 2:12, 13).

- We may develop a distorted view of the Christian faith: "If I just **did** enough, then God would be pleased." The wonder of the Gospel is that provision has been made through Christ that we might relate intimately and eternally to our Creator, and that from this relationship we might grow in our knowledge of Him and be empowered to do His will. "But when the kindness and love of God our Savior appeared, he saved us, not because of righteous things we had done, but because of his mercy" (Titus 3:4, 5).

My Personal Journey

For too many years, I focused upon the commands of Scripture, always highlighting the behavioral expectations of the Bible. During many of those years, I was also consumed by the pursuit of biblical knowledge, wanting to know more, memorize more, and make a careful study of Scripture. This biblical knowledge was certainly important for my spiritual growth, and the behavioral principles I found in the Word were critical for righteous living, but they were not sufficient. I developed a distorted view of God. Without the relational focus of God's Word and a clear view of His heart, I came to see God as One who was only concerned about how well I was behaving and how often I messed up. I viewed God as an inspecting God who was just waiting to see which of His commands I would fail to live out next.

This view of God impacted my relationships with others. As a parent, I viewed my job as "shaping up" my kids. Too often, my parenting involved phrases like, "Make that bed!" "Take out that trash!" and "You're listening to that?" As a minister, I thought that I was supposed to present the Bible to the congregation and see their hearts convicted. I thought my job was to teach the Word and convict the souls. Graciously, the Lord began to change my views of both His character and His Word.

A feeling of surprise and regret came over my heart during one of my devotional times with the Lord. The Spirit of God spoke to me through the words of the Gospel of John: "And He, when He comes, will convict the world concerning sin" (John 16:8 NASB). The Spirit began to work in me to change my view of an inspecting God, and at the same time reestablished the fact that it is His role to bring conviction, not mine! Not only did my view of God change, my inspection of others diminished as well.

He is no longer an inspecting God for me, but One who longs to show me compassion. It is now the Holy Spirit's job to convict, not mine. I have come to realize that His Word was written so that I can grow in my love for Him and those He loves. Thanks be to God, for restoring the relational purpose of His truth.

An Experience With God's People

"And let us consider how we may spur one another on toward love and good deeds"
(Hebrews 10:24).

Take a moment now to reflect on your own journey with God's Word. Consider your own tendencies
to focus upon the rational purpose or behavioral purpose of His truth. Reflect on your own habits of
emphasizing trivial matters or misrepresenting the character of God. Pause now and consider your
responses to each of these statements below. Allow the Holy Spirit to impress you with any needed
changes. Prayerfully consider which of these statements may be true for you:

*I have sometimes overemphasized the importance of "believing God's truth" or "agreeing
with God's truth" by . . .*

*I have sometimes overemphasized the importance of "behaving rightly" or "doing the
right things" by . . .*

I have sometimes misrepresented the character of God by . . .

*I have sometimes misrepresented the Gospel as being about something other than loving
God and loving others by . . .*

As you complete your responses, take a few moments to discuss your responses with your partner
or small group as directed by your leader. Encourage one another to pursue deeper relationships
with God and one another. Spur one another on toward vulnerability and genuine change.

Finally, offer a heartfelt prayer to God. Allow your partner or small group to overhear your prayer to the Lord. Ask Him to bring change to your heart and life as you approach His Word. Your prayer might sound like:

"God, change me so that I can more often experience loving relationships with You and others as I truly experience Scripture. Let me come to a deeper love for You as I encounter Your Word. Help me deepen my love for others as I read and study the Scriptures."

WHAT WILL IT LOOK LIKE TO TAKE THIS RELATIONAL JOURNEY INTO SCRIPTURE?

"For the word of God is living and active" (Hebrews 4:12).

This scripture tells us that the Word of God is living and active, but what is the evidence that God's Word is truly "living" in my life? What does it look like for the Spirit of God to take the Word of God and empower our experience of it?

What Will It Look Like in Our Personal Lives?

Taking this journey into a deepened, loving relationship with God is an experience because any relationship must be experienced. It involves more than knowledge and dutiful compliance. Our journey in loving the Lord will change our lives in relevant, meaningful ways. Here are some of the benefits of taking this journey toward a more intimate relationship with the God of the Bible:

- You will live life with an expectancy of actually encountering Him—the One who wrote the Book!

- You will experience freedom like never before. Your Christian life will move beyond duties and obligations, from "got to's" to "get to's." You will be constrained by the love of Christ (2 Corinthians 5:14 KJV).

- You will be empowered to actually live out what you believe. You will find that this power comes not from a doctrinal treatise or a code of conduct, but from a Person.

- You will express humility instead of pride. Your heart will not be able to get over the wonder of how the Creator of the Universe meets you in His Word.

- You will demonstrate vulnerability instead of judgment. You will be excited to share what God's Word is doing in you rather than only pointing out the failures of others.

What Will It Look Like in the Church?

Many church leaders seem to assume that their personal spiritual growth will occur as a by-product of ministering to others. As ministers, we study God's Word in order to preach it and teach it. But we may rarely slow down long enough to contemplate what God wants to do in our own lives, apart from what He does through us for others.

Many ministers and lay leaders are beginning to change the way they approach God's Word. Instead of spending time in Scripture primarily as a means of preparing to preach sermons, teach classes, or lead small groups, they study in order to know and to love God more intimately. This approach seems consistent with Paul's testimony: "I consider everything a loss compared to the surpassing greatness of knowing Christ Jesus my Lord" (Philippians 3:8). These leaders seek to know and love God first for who He is and what He wants to do **in** their lives, and, second, for what He wants to do **through** their lives.

Paul wrote, "Let the word of Christ dwell in you richly as you teach and admonish one another with all wisdom" (Colossians 3:16). Do you notice a paradox in this verse? The ministry of effective Bible teaching begins by allowing something to happen" in us." Teachers must allow the Holy Spirit to work the Word into the soil of their own hearts before fruitful teaching and admonishment can take place. As we set out to study, outline, and interpret the Word, we must also allow the Word to penetrate soul and spirit, to judge the thoughts and attitudes of the heart.

Pastors and teachers must give their attention to the ministry of the Word and to prayer, as did the first-century apostles (Acts 6:4). *Attention*, as used here, implies purposeful intent that includes time and focus. Churches may need to redefine leadership job descriptions and workloads to accommodate the priority of spending time in the Word. We must place greater focus on "the equipping of the saints for the work of service" (Ephesians 4:12 NASB), allowing many tasks now performed by ministry leaders to be assumed by trained laity. In order to effectively minister the Word, we must "serve" others with God's truth. The following experiential exercise will demonstrate how this might be accomplished.

> **Teachers must allow the Holy Spirit to work the Word into the soil of their own hearts before fruitful teaching and admonishment can take place.**

An Experience With God's Word

"Therefore, there is now no condemnation for those who are in Christ Jesus" (Romans 8:1).

The following sample lesson might be experienced as an adult Bible Study or worship service:

The session begins with worship and singing. Choruses and hymns describe God's justice and mercy. Each song reminds the congregation of the righteousness of God as well as His loving-kindness.

The leader might then begin the message with the bang of a gavel. A "bailiff" could shout the words, "Hear ye, Hear ye. All rise! The court is now in session!"

As the leader begins to explain the courtroom analogy, the congregation would hear the important elements of this passage in Romans:

- This passage does not say that we will never be accused. We may experience the harsh treatment of other people, but as far as God is concerned, any accusations will be thrown out, and any indictments quashed.

- The text does not imply that there is nothing about our lives that deserves condemnation. On the contrary, we must see our sin, own it, mourn over it, and confess it to God.

- The text also does not imply that there will never be affliction or struggle for those who believe. But we have One with whom we can seek refuge in the midst of trials and tribulations.

- The good news of this passage is that Christ is our advocate. Because we are one with Christ, we are free from God's judgment and secure in our position with Him. Because of Christ, God does not only refrain from condemning us, but is well pleased with us (Matthew 17:5).

The leader might draw the congregation's attention to this related passage: "Who will bring any charge against those whom God has chosen? It is God who justifies. Who is he that condemns?

Christ Jesus, who died—more than that, who was raised to life—is at the right hand of God and is also interceding for us" (Romans 8:33, 34).

During the closing comments of the message, the leader might challenge the congregation to answer these questions within their own minds and hearts:

- Do you come here today as one who feels accused? Have you experienced the rejection or criticism of others? Do you feel that others are often judging or evaluating you?
- Do you come here today feeling that you deserve to be condemned? Is there an area of sin in your life that has gone unconfessed or that repeatedly causes you to struggle?
- Do you come here today as one who is burdened by the struggles of this world? Are you weary because of the stress of this life? Are you tired of problems or discouraged by affliction?

To each of us who experience such feelings of accusation and criticism, the apostle Paul poses the question, "Who will bring any charge against you" (Romans 8:33)? Paul goes on to answer this question with a declaration of truth. He explains that there is only One person with the right and power to accuse, criticize, or condemn: "It is God who justifies" (v. 33). Knowing that we might resist such a liberating truth, Paul asks again, "Who is he that condemns" (v. 34)? Again, we read that there is only One who has the right to condemn us: Jesus Christ, the One who died and was raised from the dead. He has the right and power to judge, but notice what He is doing for those who believe: He is interceding for us (v. 34)! This is why the apostle can say, "There is now no condemnation" for us (v. 1). The only One who can condemn you is praying for you!

Finally, the pastor or teacher guides the congregation through the following meditation, allowing the Holy Spirit to lead those present into an actual experience of Romans 8:33, 34. As church members experience these verses, they will encounter Jesus along the way.

Close your eyes, and form a mental picture of a courtroom. Imagine that you have just entered through the ominous, wooden doors and found your seat at the front of the room. The atmosphere is cold and frightening. You feel the intimidation of your surroundings. All the seats in the room are filled with people who have criticized and accused you in the past. There are individuals who have judged you inferior to others, passing out evaluation and critique. There are those who have rejected you or demanded that you perform according to their lofty standards. You look around and see the faces of people who have spoken against you, been harsh and cruel, abandoned and neglected you. But who can condemn? Only Jesus Christ, the Righteous One.

Suddenly, the doors at the back of the courtroom open and Jesus enters the room. You see His flowing robes, sandaled feet, and bearded face. His presence commands respect and exudes an authority unparalleled among earthly judges. His gait is dignified as He walks purposefully down the center aisle.

Rather than taking His place behind the judge's bench, Christ surprises everyone in the courtroom by turning abruptly and stopping to stand by your side. Picture Christ standing beside you as your eyes scan the faces of everyone else in the room. You look at the ones who have condemned you. You lock eyes with the people who have offered criticism and rejection. You see the faces of those who have abandoned you.

Then Christ slowly eases His arm around your shoulder and gently leads you to join Him in a kneeling posture on the ground. Each eye in the courtroom has traced Christ's every move since He stepped through the door. You are quite certain that the crowd's collective eyes are also boring straight into your soul.

At this crucial moment, you sense a sudden respite and notice that Jesus has begun praying. You listen more closely and realize that He is praying for you! Your mind and heart are transfixed, not by the faces of the people in the room, not by their opinions or their behavior, but by the words of the Lord. He is praying earnestly, and He's praying for **you***! The Lord Jesus Christ—the One who lived as man, died as man, and was resurrected into glory, now stoops beside you and intercedes on your behalf. The only True Judge, the sole Person in the courtroom without sin, the only One who can claim the right to bring a charge against you, now prays earnestly to His Father for you.*

Keep this image in your mind and heart. Christ is kneeling beside you. His arm is cradling your shoulders, and you hear Him pause in prayer. Jesus turns His head toward yours and whispers, "Where are your accusers?" Suddenly, you glance up and realize that the courtroom is completely empty. Every one of those faces filled with condemnation has disappeared from the room. Each person who brought a charge against you has vanished. Everyone who had responded with neglect or abandonment is gone. As Jesus rises and draws you into His arms in a tearful embrace, He proclaims, "Neither do I. Neither do I accuse you." The only One who can condemn you prays for you! The only One who is equipped to judge, does not. The Holy One of the Universe cares for you!

Pause and allow the Holy Spirit to fill your heart with wonder and gratefulness for this kind of Savior.

After the meditation, the leader encourages participants to pray with one or two others in the room: "Thank God for His incomparable love that empowers Christ to pray for us rather than condemn us. Praise Him because there is no condemnation for those who are in Christ Jesus!"

Pray that kind of prayer now with your partner or small group. Having focused upon the courtroom scene above, spend a few moments thanking God for His lavish mercy and His grace.

Heavenly Father, we ask that You would relieve our hearts of any burden of shame or condemnation. We ask this because of the truth that is proclaimed in Your Word: that the One who is righteous, the One who can judge, now intercedes for us. Thank You, Father, for the miraculous love of Your perfect Son who, in His great mercy and compassion, stoops to join us on bended knee and liberates us from the bondage of sin. Holy Spirit, make the joy and wonder of this truth impact our hearts and lives. In Jesus' name we pray, Amen.

For Further Study

Relational Significance in Scriptural Interpretation

"On these two commandments hang all the law and the prophets" (Matthew 22:40 KJV).

We must not miss the significance of Christ's words in this text. Not only do these two commandments constitute the nail on which the rest of the instructions of Scripture hang, they also provide a framework for the interpretation of God's Word. Christ's words reveal how relevance returns when Scripture comes alive through relationships.

We must approach Scripture with eyes and hearts to see both objective meaning and relational significance.

Christ seems to argue for a relational hermeneutic (principle of Scriptural interpretation) in His declaration about the greatest of commandments (Matthew 22:40). His words suggest this principle of interpreting Scripture: we must both explore the objective meaning of Scripture and encounter the relational significance of it.

We might illustrate this approach to Scripture by exploring the limited number of New Testament passages that contain the Greek word *kremannumi* ("depends" or "hangs"):

- Matthew 18:6—"But if anyone causes one of these little ones who believe in Me to sin, it would be better for him to have a large millstone *hung* around his neck."

Imagine the scene described in this text. You see a man with a millstone hung around his neck. The stone's weight makes it difficult for the man to walk, and you see him stumbling toward the edge of a boat. You are quite certain that if this man falls into the ocean, the weight of the stone will cause his death. With this scene in your mind's eye, you cannot focus only on the millstone's objective meaning, for to do so would be to miss the relational significance. Consider the absurdity of reacting to the situation described above by simply asking objective questions about the millstone: "How much does that millstone weigh? How old might it be? Where might that millstone come from?" Limiting our response to such questions would be to miss the critical significance of what we were observing. The significant issue is that the millstone is hanging around a person's neck! To miss where the millstone is hanging is to miss its relevance entirely. Christ's declaration in the Gospel of Matthew reveals that we face a similar challenge as we interpret Scripture. We often observe its objective meaning but miss its relational significance: God's Word "hangs" upon loving Him and loving others.

- Acts 28:3, 4—"Paul gathered a pile of brushwood and, as he put it on the fire, a viper, driven out by the heat, fastened itself on his hand. When the islanders saw the snake *hanging* from his hand. . . ."

In this passage, it is certainly important to notice that a poisonous serpent came out of the fire, but to focus on its length, color, or type would be trivial in relation to the significance of the scene. The significance is found in the facts that the serpent was hanging on Paul's hand, and that Paul did not die from the poison. We may gain understanding of the meaning of a text by asking objective questions, but we must go further. We must examine the relational significance of the passage by asking ourselves, "How might this encourage my love of God or empower my love for others?"

- Galatians 3:13—"Christ redeemed us from the curse of the law by becoming a curse for us, for it is written: 'Cursed is everyone who is *hung* on a tree.'"

This text reminds us of the precious gift of redemption. Surely it is important to look toward Golgotha and see Jesus of Nazareth, but focusing only upon such objective issues as the age, weight, and physical condition of the man hanging on the tree would be preposterous, since the significance of the event is found in the fact that the Son of God was hung on a tree. (See also Acts 5:30, 10:39.)

Christ seems to argue in Matthew 22:40 that we have not finished the hermeneutic process until we have fully explored both the objective meaning and relational significance of Scripture.

Hope for Restoring Relevance

The Gospels portray Old Testament Scripture "coming alive" as it is fulfilled in the person of Jesus Christ. Christ's first recorded sermon in Luke 4:16–21 was a routine reading of the Isaiah text: "The Spirit of the Lord is on Me . . ." until He closed the book, sat down, and began to speak to the temple leaders. He said to them, "Today this Scripture is fulfilled in your hearing." Christ brought added relevance to the Scripture, the same Scripture that has continued to change lives for centuries.

In John 5:39, Christ seemed to affirm the Pharisees' search of the Scriptures but rebuked them because they had missed the significance of the Person they read about: "You diligently study the Scriptures because you think that by them you possess eternal life. These are the Scriptures that testify about me, yet you refuse to come to me to have life." Relevance is found in a person!

In Acts 2:12–21, notice the relevance of the Gospel message as Peter responds to the crowd's question at Pentecost: "What does this mean?" Peter confirmed the Holy Spirit's presence with these words: "This is what was spoken by the prophet Joel." The significance was not in the sound of rushing wind or the commotion of fire, but in the fulfillment of Jesus' promise that He would not leave them as orphans. His Spirit had come. We see, once again, that relevance is in relationship!

THE PARABLE OF THE SOWER

The parable of the sower (Mark 4:2–9) contains a critical message for the followers of Jesus. Christ warned us: "Don't you understand this parable? How then will you understand any parable?" (v. 13). In some significant way, this parable is fundamental to life and faith.

As we explore the parable of the sower, we may be shocked to learn the primary lesson that Jesus was trying to teach. Through the parable of a growing seed, Christ communicated that, while hearing truth and receiving truth are essential, they are not sufficient. Truth must also be experienced.

Truth must be heard.

It is not the wisdom of men that impacts lives, nor is it clever sayings, compelling statistical research, or lessons from history. Rather, it is God's Word that is "living and active" and "sharper than any double-edged sword" (Hebrews 4:12). In the parable of the sower, Christ's disciples and the multitudes heard the truth concerning the sower, the seed, and the soil. Jesus concluded this portion of His sermon with these words: "He who has ears to hear, let him hear" (Mark 4:9). Truth must be heard.

Truth must be received.

The disciples (and a few others) wanted to know more about this important parable. They not only heard the Word but received it and sought to embrace its significance and relevance. When they came to the Master and asked Him the meaning of the parable, Jesus gave this interpretation:

- The sower is the Son of God.
- The seed is the Word of God.
- The soil is the hearts of men.
- Satan steals some of the seed.
- Some seed is received but dies when afflictions and tribulations arise.
- Some seed is received but is choked out by caring for other things.
- Some seed is sown on good soil, where the heart hears the Word, accepts the Word, and bears fruit from the Word (vv. 10–20).

The multitudes heard the Word. The disciples went one step further—they understood the Word. But they had yet to experience it. When we hear God's Word and even understand its meaning, but do not truly experience it, we are vulnerable to what Paul cautioned the church of Corinth about—truth simply becomes knowledge that puffs up rather than love that builds up (1 Corinthians 8:1). Just like the disciples, we often hear the Word, and even receive it, but stop short of the life-changing, liberating power of experiencing it.

Truth must be experienced.

"That day when evening came, he said to his disciples, 'Let us go over to the other side'" (Mark 4:35).

With this declaration, Jesus began to challenge the disciples to experience the parable of the sower. The sower (Jesus) has just sown the seed (the Word of God): "Let us go over to the other side." Jesus had sown this seed upon the disciples' hearts. How did they respond? As predicted in the parable, the seed was attacked:

- Satan came to destroy the Word: "A furious squall came up. . . . He got up, rebuked the wind, and said to the waves, 'Quiet! Be still!' Then the wind died down and it was completely calm" (vv. 37, 39). The word *rebuke* in this text was used by Jesus in other passages to refer to the evil one (see also Jude 9).

- Tribulation came to destroy the Word: "And the waves broke over the boat, so that it was nearly swamped" (v. 37). In a world of tribulation, the stresses of life can come from many sources: family, friends, children, jobs, health, church, and ministry. If our hearts are not guarded, the Word can wither within us.

- Caring for other things choked out the Word: "Teacher, don't You care if we drown" (v. 38)? The cares of this life can focus our hearts on popularity, material possessions, or other people's success. If our hearts are not guarded, these cares will choke out the Word.

As the wind died down and the sea became perfectly calm, the Lord announced the disciples' failure concerning the parable of the sower: "Do you still have no faith" (v. 40)? The sowing of the seed, "let us go over to the other side" had brought forth no fruit. The disciples were not able to persevere through Satan's attack, tribulations, and self-interests.

What could the disciples have done differently with the Word? How could the Word have produced "much fruit"? They could have kept rowing the boat, confident that since the King of kings and Lord of lords had said, "Let us go over to the other side," they were going to get to the other side. Consider also what the Master was hoping for. What response would have pleased the heart of Jesus? The disciples had the opportunity to experience the Word of God. They had the chance to live out the promise of Jesus. Had they done so, the 12 men would have come to know Him better and grown closer to their Master. They would have discovered a deepened sense of love for the One who protects, guides, promises, and delivers. Having heard, received, and lived out His Word, they would have come to relate to Jesus in a more intimate way. That day, the disciples encountered the critical importance of hearing, receiving, **and** experiencing truth.

Consider and discuss the following:

- In Mark 4, the multitudes heard the parable and the disciples received it, but when they all left, no one had experienced the Word. Does this ever happen to you as you attend church or Bible studies? You may hear and receive the Word but leave without having ever experienced it. How could this dilemma be corrected? How could your church or Bible study group provide and encourage opportunities to truly experience the Word?

_____

_____

_____

Consider these verses:

Proverbs 15:1—"A gentle answer turns away wrath."
Romans 15:7—"Accept one another, then, just as Christ accepted you."
James 5:16—"Confess your sins to each other."
Ephesians 4:32—"Forgiving each other, just as in Christ God forgave you."

How might experiencing these verses relate to expressing Great Commandment love?

_____

_____

How might failing to experience these verses contribute to the irrelevance of our lives and ministries?

_____

* Pray a prayer declaring your openness to God and His work as He leads you into experiencing more of His Word.

Father, lead us beyond mere knowledge of truth to a genuine experience of it. Replace knowledge with love that builds up as Your truth is lived out.

Additional Resources

Walter C. Kaiser and Moises Silva, *An Introduction to Biblical Hermeneutics* (Grand Rapids, MI: Zondervan Publishing House, 1994).

Chapter 4

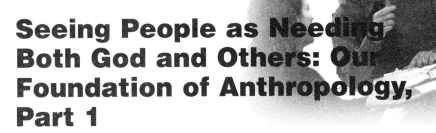

Seeing People as Needing Both God and Others: Our Foundation of Anthropology, Part 1

Almost two decades ago, as I was sitting in the Bodleian Library of Oxford University, God challenged the very foundations upon which my ministry had been built. Having arranged ahead of time for an ancient, Old Testament manuscript to be made available for research, I carefully studied the biblical perspective on human nature. On this particular day, God drew my attention to the first declaration of His displeasure, and His Spirit began to bring revolutionary, relational insights through the powerful simplicity of this passage.

Displeasure in Paradise

In Genesis 2:18, God uttered for the very first time this sobering phrase: "It is not good." He declared that something was missing in the Garden. Up to this point, everything in creation had been pronounced "good." Eden was a perfect paradise.

> **When God shows up and declares something to be "not good," we must sit up and take notice because we have a serious problem.**

Now if you or I were to declare that something was "not good," it might not make much of an impact. But when God declares something to be "not good," we must sit up and take notice because we have a serious problem. So what could have been "not good" about the Garden of Eden?

At this time, Adam lived in a perfect world. There was no crime, no traffic, no pollution, no disease, and no war. It was a totally problem-free environment. Most notably, the Fall had not yet occurred, so Adam was sinless, innocent in heart and mind. There was only good within the Garden.

Adam also possessed everything he could possibly need or want. The Garden and everything in it (with the exception of one unique tree) was his to use and enjoy. Adam had it all. He never suffered from a low bank balance, an empty pantry, or an investment loss. Adam was living a dream existence. He was in a perfect world, and almost everything in it was available for his use, enjoyment, and stewardship. What could have possibly been "not good"?

We also know that Adam had an exalted position. He had an excellent job with no competition for advancement. He was CEO over the "fish of the sea and the birds of the air, over the livestock, over all the earth, and over all the creatures that move along the ground" (Genesis 1:26). He had no problems with job security, jealousy from co-workers, or pressure to perform. Career-wise, he was at the top of the ladder. At this point, he was the only person on the ladder, but at least he was at the top! So where was the crisis? What could have been missing?

Adam even enjoyed an intimate relationship with God. Above all the earthly benefits and blessings in the Garden, Adam walked and talked in perfect, uninterrupted fellowship with his Creator because sin had not yet come between them. Can you imagine the thrill of communing with God face-to-face? You and I might talk about our daily "quiet time" with God, but Adam was blessed to be with God every day. Yet something was still "not good." What could have possibly been wrong in such an ideal setting?

There was just one thing missing, but apparently this one thing troubled God's heart. In Genesis 2:18, God declared what was not good—Adam was alone. Adam needed a human relationship. A sovereign God, free to create Adam any way He desired, chose to fashion him in such a way that Adam needed to relate intimately not only with his Creator, but also with others.

Adam was designed as a relational being. God had created Adam not only with physical and spiritual needs, but also with relational needs, which Adam could not meet on his own. These needs could only be met through meaningful relationships with both God and other human beings.

In Genesis 2:18, God also declared that He would solve Adam's dilemma, and He did so by creating another human, someone with whom Adam could be intimate. God said, "I will make a helper suitable for him."

God ministered to Adam's aloneness by giving him a human partner, Eve, thus establishing the core human relationship of marriage. God would later ordain family relationships (Genesis 4:1; Psalm 127:3) and fellowship within the body of Christ (Matthew 16:18;

1 Corinthians 12:25) as other avenues by which He ministers to the aloneness of the human heart.

> **God ministered to Adam's aloneness by giving him a human partner, Eve.**

Evidence of Our Need for Others

Several years ago, I met a woman named Sandy, who was a patient in a psychiatric hospital. She had been admitted to the hospital after attempting suicide. During several visits with her, I learned this woman's tragic story.

A year earlier, Sandy's husband had been killed in a head-on collision with a drunk driver, leaving her with three children under the age of six. Sandy was understandably devastated by the loss. But over a period of months she determinedly worked through her denial, her anger at God, and her bitterness toward the drunk driver. She finally began dealing with the enormity of her grief. When depressed or angry, Sandy was able to admit her feelings and deal with them. She came through the first nine months of her pain very well, all the while dealing with the ebb and flow of life-altering grief.

Finally, Sandy found the courage to get involved in the singles ministry of her church. Her church family had ministered to her often after the tragic accident, and well-intentioned people within the church continued to ask occasionally how she was doing. In the past, she had often answered, "I'm just numb" or "I'm getting by." But after processing much of her pain, she began to answer the question differently. Sandy would very honestly respond to church members' inquiries with, "I just feel very lonely."

But the responses she often received were less than comforting:
"You should not feel lonely. After all, God is with you."
"Lonely? That's not good. Maybe the pastor could get together with you this week."
"As Christians, we don't need to feel lonely. Just the other day I was feeling a bit sad, and I just thought to myself. . . ."

Self-doubt quickly set in for Sandy. "I still feel lonely," she admitted to herself. "Why doesn't God take away my loneliness? There must be something wrong with me."
Within three months, these feelings of condemnation, coupled with the pain of her devastating loss, prompted Sandy to try to take her own life. In the wake of her husband's death, Sandy had needed both the comfort of our heavenly Father and loving care demonstrated through

His people. Tragically, her glaring need and deep pain had been met by something less than compassionate care from those around her, and we almost lost her as a result.

What a difference it would have made in Sandy's life if those within her church had grasped the significance of her need for Christ in them. Imagine the impact that might have been made if Sandy could have heard these comforting words: "Sandy, I cannot even imagine the depth of pain you have experienced, but I want you to know that God has saddened my heart for you on several occasions. I am so sorry for your loneliness, and I just want you to know that I care."

God's Design, Our Acceptance

Two very significant implications for life and ministry derive from the truth that God created us to need both Him and each other. First, none of us can rightfully say, "All I need is God." To do so is to reject other people as a channel of God's loving provision. Adam lived in a perfect, sin-free world, and had a deeply personal knowledge of God. If anyone had grounds to think that an intimate relationship with the Creator was all he needed, Adam sure did. "It's You and me, God," he could have said. "You created the world, and I take care of it. Our relationship could not be any better. Together we can handle anything, right?"

> **None of us can rightfully say, "All I need is God."**

But God disagreed. "Adam, our relationship is primary," He might have said, "and I will be your most intimate friend. But I also desire to bless you through human relationships, persons with whom you will experience the joy of giving and receiving to meet relational needs. For you and many of your descendants, a spouse and other family member will meet your relational needs. For those who do not marry, I will provide close friendships. And one day, I will establish my church, where loving relationships will abound."

Meeting some of our relational needs through others was God's original plan in the Garden of Eden, and it remains His plan today. Claiming that we only need God discounts His purpose for human relationships.

Some people point to Philippians 4:13: "I can do everything through him who gives me strength." They contend that if God was all Paul needed, He is all we need. They equate a holy sense of self-reliance with spiritual maturity. "As long as I walk in constant fellowship with God, as long as I love God completely and exercise enough faith, I do not need anyone else."

But that is not what Paul conveyed to the Philippians. The apostle's expectations and faith were clearly and rightly focused upon Christ, but he follows with verse 14: "Yet it was good of you to share in my troubles." His message is clear: "I can do everything through Christ, and He has chosen to involve you!" Paul, the spiritual giant of the early church, recognized and accepted the fact that God often lovingly worked through others to meet his material, relational, and emotional needs.

The second implication is closely related to the first. Just as we cannot claim, "All *I* need is God," we must not convey the message, "*You* only need God."

To do so is to communicate a message of condemnation: "You should be able to take care of yourself without needing other people. If you still have needs, you do not have enough of Christ. If you were more consistent in your quiet time, if you had more faith, if you loved God with more of your heart, soul, and mind, you would not be needy." As important and necessary as faith and quiet times and loving God are, God has chosen to involve people in meeting the needs of other people.

> **Just as we cannot claim, "All I need is God," we must not convey the message, "You only need God."**

The "you only need God" message is crippling ministry after ministry today. This message is irrelevant to the real needs of people because it represents only half of the Great Commandment. We may have the "love God" part right, but love for God is incomplete without love for our neighbors. Dismissing our need for one another is the equivalent of saying to a starving beggar, "Go, I wish you well; keep warm and well fed" (James 2:16). To the single adult, it may sound like this: "You should not be lonely because Jesus is a friend that sticks closer than a brother." We might communicate to a faithful ministry worker: "Your need to be appreciated is nothing more than pride. God sees your labors, and His reward should be enough." Or we might say to people who have been abused or abandoned, "You just need to forgive and forget and move on with your life."

By God's design, we need Him and other people. Therefore, our complete message to a hurting world must be, "I need you, and it is all right for you to need me. And we both need an intimate, loving relationship with our Lord."

My Personal Journey

I can still clearly recall God's work in my heart concerning my need for other people. After an early morning breakfast with my discipleship group, staff meetings, counseling appointments, and a typically busy day on our church staff, my energy was gone. I was exhausted. As I prepared for the evening's sermon and looked ahead to another late-night committee meeting, there was a knock at my door. It felt like just one more interruption in an already hectic day.

> **Our complete message to a hurting world must be, I need you and it is OK for you to need me. And we both need an intimate, loving relationship with our Lord!**

"Brother David, have you heard anything more about my residency application?" Gabriel, my Nigerian friend, stood in the doorway, inquiring about the status of his citizenship. My wife and I had rejoiced in seeing Gabriel and his wife come to follow Jesus, and hoped to help in their quest for residency in the United States. This interruption, however, produced a strange response in me.

I stared at my Bible laying on the desk, opened to the passage in which Jesus asks His disciples, "Can you come and pray with me?" God broke my self-reliance. As a believer for more than ten years, and now in pastoral ministry, I had no memory of ever vulnerably asking for prayer. My prideful self-sufficiency was broken that evening as I heard myself say to Gabe, "I have not had the opportunity to check this week. Gabe, this may sound strange to you, but I am not sure I have what it takes to make it through the rest of the evening. Would you come pray for me?" It seemed like years of pain from my self-reliance were washed away through my tears. With a humble heart, I cried as Gabriel stood over me and prayed for me.

That was the night that my restoration began. God moved my heart with this reflection: if Christ in His humanity needed others, then it was all right for me to need people as well.

Pause and Reflect

"Forget none of His benefits" (Psalm 103:2 NASB).

Reflect on an occasion when God met a need in your life through another person. Consider a time when God blessed you by involving a family member, friend, or acquaintance in your life. It might have been a time of tragedy or loss, discouragement or disappointment, weariness or loneliness.

I recall a time when God met a need in my life, and He involved another person by . . .

Share your reflections with a partner or small group as directed by your facilitator. Pause to sense the Lord's pleasure as you actually experience His Word by "forgetting none of His benefits."

The Savior's Need

Come with me now into the New Testament for a more intimate picture of Christ's need for other people. Let us follow our Lord and the 11 into the Garden of Gethsemane. Picture yourself walking among the trees with the disciples, following the Master you love. His steps are agonizingly slow and deliberate as the weight of His impending death descends on Him. His breath comes in short, labored gasps. The mounting stress bows His back and forces from Him a low moan, then another, as if the heavy, wooden cross were already on His shoulder. Meanwhile, you notice that the disciples are puzzled at His behavior, perhaps thinking Him suddenly ill.

Reaching your destination, the Master turns to you. His countenance is clouded with gloom. Perspiration streams from His brow and drips from His hair and beard. In a quavering voice, He says, "I must . . . I must go . . . just a little farther." He looks past you to Peter, James, and

John, His closest and dearest friends on Earth. Imagine His imploring words: "Come with Me, My friends. I need you now. I really need you."

I wonder what some people might have said to Jesus if they had been with Him that evening. He was agonizing under the weight of "becoming our sin" and the impending crucifixion. The Savior was overwhelmed with sorrow and vulnerably shared His need with His friends. I am concerned that He might hear some of us today respond with, "Why do You need us, Jesus? Do You not know that You have the Father?"

Did Jesus have the Father? Of course He did. He and His Father were one! But at that moment, this Man of sorrows asked His closest friends on earth to be there for Him, to support Him, to pray with Him. Apparently, in His humanity, the Son needed others, just as you and I do. If the divine Son of God needed both the Father and human relationships, how much more do we, and the people around us, need both the Father and one another?

An Experience With God's Son

"I count all things to be loss in view of the surpassing value of knowing Christ Jesus my Lord" (Philippians 3:8 NASB).

Let us return to the Garden scene. Allow the Holy Spirit to move your heart with compassion for this One acquainted with sorrow and grief. As your heart is touched by His need, you will grow more sensitive to the needs of others.

Leaving the others behind, Jesus and the inner circle of three continue trudging up the darkened garden hillside. You follow them. The Master's body convulses from the mounting grief. His low moans turn into strained cries of deep pain. Jesus can hardly get His next words out. His voice is strained with emotion. "My soul is overwhelmed with sorrow to the point of death. Stay here and keep watch with me" (Matthew 26:38).

He leaves you behind and staggers farther up the knoll, bracing Himself on tree stumps and boulders. Loud cries of travail roll from Him. There He writhes and sobs and prays.

The Son of God faces the darkest hour in the history of creation. The One who knew no sin will soon become sin for His disciples—for you and me. He has vulnerably sought the prayerful support of Peter, James, and John. These men love the Master dearly. They have left their careers to follow Him. They have walked with Him, sat at His feet, and leaned on His breast. But now they seem oblivious to the Master's need.

Jesus returns to the place where you are watching the heartrending drama. He looks down at His dearest friends, who are asleep. Tears, soil, and blood streak His face and stain His cloak. He moves past you and wakes the men. Let yourself sense the pain-filled loneliness and grief of the Savior's heart as He asks, "Could you men not keep watch with me for one hour?" (v. 40). See the disappointment in His eyes as He returns to His place of agonizing prayer.

Amazingly, the scene plays out again and again. Three times, the Master shares His pain and need with His closest friends; and three times, they let Him down.

Can you care for Him in His sorrow? Can you hurt with Him? Can you feel compassion for the pain He felt when, at His time of greatest need, He was left alone? Ask the Spirit to prompt empathy for Christ within you as you reflect on His expressed need for other people and the disciples' failure to meet that need. Allow the Spirit to confirm and reinforce the validity of needing both God and others.

Meditate on Christ's words: "Could you not pray with me for just one hour?"

What does it do to your heart to meditate on the saddened Savior? How does it make you feel to hear the words, "Could you not pray with me?"

Lord Jesus, my heart is touched with _____ as Your Spirit leads me to encounter You in Your Word.

Share your responses with your partner or small group as directed by your facilitator. Allow the Holy Spirit to sensitize your heart to the needs of the Savior and the needs of others around you. Close in prayer for one another.

THE GREAT COMMANDMENT REINFORCES OUR NEED FOR OTHERS.

Come with me now to another scene in the life of Jesus—the day when Jesus gave the Great Commandment. The Pharisees and Sadducees are gathered around Jesus and His disciples. A lawyer has just posed the question, "Which is the most important commandment in the law of Moses" (Matthew 22:36 NLT)?

I can imagine the disciples' expectations as they hear the question. Peter elbows John and says, "Hey, this is important. The Master is about to tell us the greatest commandment." I can see John waving the other disciples into a huddle. "All right, fellows, listen up," he begins. "We are about to get our marching orders. We are about to hear the commandment that must become our top preaching, teaching, and ministry priority." They all turn to their Master and listen intently as Jesus replies, "You must love the Lord your God with all your heart, all your soul, and all your mind. This is the first and greatest commandment" (vv. 37, 38 NLT).

Imagine what might have happened if Jesus had stopped there. I can see Peter turning back to the other disciples and saying something like, "That is it! Our job is to preach a full and complete sellout to God. We are to love Him and Him alone. So let us go out and tell the world, 'You only need God.'"

Of course, Jesus did **not** stop after the command to love God. He went on to say, "A second is equally important: 'Love your neighbor as yourself.' All the other commandments and all the demands of the prophets are based on these two commandments" (vv. 39, 40 NLT).

Imagine Peter turning to the other disciples now. "Did you hear that? The greatest commandment is actually two commandments in one. We are to love God with everything we have, and we are to love our neighbor as we love ourselves. So we have to teach, preach, and live a message that demonstrates the importance of loving intimacy with God and others."

> **The greatest commandment is actually two commandments in one. We are to love God with everything we have, and we are to love our neighbor as we love ourselves.**

It is true that a relationship with God is to be primary in each of our lives. We are to trust Christ as Savior, yield to His Spirit, and obey His words. But we must also recognize that, in Jesus' eyes, our relationships with our neighbors (literally our "near ones") are just as significant as our relationship with God.

It is clear throughout Scripture that God, for reasons known only to Him, has opted to fill our longings for oneness through love relationships with both Himself and other human beings. The God of all comfort chooses, at times, to share His love and comfort with us through others, and with others through us (2 Corinthians 2:1–4). But how do we go about living out this Great Commandment on a daily basis? What does it look like to genuinely love both God and others?

How to Live Out the Great Commandment

Great Commandment love is relevant in human lives because it seeks to meet both spiritual needs and relational needs, thus removing the aloneness that God calls "not good." But what do we need in our relationships with one another? How do we identify valid relational needs? In short, by identifying passages of Scripture that tell us how God has demonstrated His love toward us, and that tell us how we are to love others in return. Throughout His Word, we find God demonstrating His love for human creation, and as we look deeper, we will also recognize relational needs that He desires to meet, at least in part, through us.

Identifying Biblical Relational Needs

In 2 Corinthians 1:3, 4, God is described as "the God of all comfort, who comforts us in all our troubles." This passage establishes that human beings have a need for comfort in times of trouble because God would not comfort us unless we needed it. But He does not stop there. We are to "comfort those in any trouble with the comfort we ourselves have received from God" (v. 4). Notice the pattern. The passage establishes our need for comfort in troubled times, declares that God is the ultimate source of the comfort we need, and calls us to lovingly share His comfort with those who need it.

Another example is found in Romans 15:7: "Accept one another, then, just as Christ accepted you." This passage establishes our need for acceptance, declares that God is the ultimate source of the acceptance we need, and calls us to meet the need for acceptance in others.

In Romans 15:5, Paul describes "the God who gives . . . encouragement," and in 1 Thessalonians 5:11 adds, "Therefore encourage one another." These verses establish our need for encouragement, reveal God as the source of encouragement, and command us to lovingly share encouragement with others.

These passages show us that a biblical, relational need is one that God has met in our lives and admonishes us to meet in the lives of others through the expression of Great Commandment love. Scripture urges believers to be "good stewards of the manifold grace of God" (1 Peter 4:10 NASB). One aspect of His multi-faceted grace is His comfort; another is His acceptance; and another is His encouragement. He has "graced" us by meeting these needs and calls us to express

> **Removing the aloneness that God calls "not good" requires meeting valid relational needs from the resources God freely supplies.**

His grace to others. As we live in loving intimacy with the One True God, freely receiving His abundant, manifold grace, we are to freely give to others (Matthew 10:8). This is what it takes to remove the aloneness that God calls "not good." It requires meeting valid, relational needs from the resources God freely supplies.

This view of needs is affirmed by the words of the apostle Paul, who assured the Philippian church of God's provision—"God will meet all your needs according to his glorious riches in Christ Jesus" (Philippians 4:19)—and gave testimony of the ways in which God had used them to supply his needs: "It was good of you to share in my troubles. . . . You sent me aid again and again when I was in need" (vv. 14, 16). God is Jehovah Jireh, our provider. He has promised to meet needs, and He sometimes chooses to do so through our families, friends, and church communities as we love Him and allow Him to share His life through us.

Ten Biblical Relational Needs

Dozens of passages in Scripture establish valid, relational needs from God's perspective, and call us to join Him in the ministry of meeting those needs. Consider the "one another's" of the New Testament: accept one another, encourage one another, be affectionate to one another, and bear one another's burdens. Each reveals an area of human, relational need where Great Commandment love may be applied in practical, caring ways.

In the following section, we will explore ten relational needs that appear to be among the most significant in Scripture. This list of ten needs is by no means exhaustive, but it will provide an excellent starting point for meeting the needs of others out of an abundance of God's love for us. When we become sensitive to the needs of others and give sacrificially to meet these needs, our lives and ministries will become increasingly relevant.

Below you will find a brief explanation of each of these ten needs, reflections on the ways in which Christ met each need in the lives of others, and practical examples that demonstrate ways in which churches and Christian leaders might meet each need as they live out a call to relational ministry. As you read these ten needs, make a quick personal and ministry assessment. How well are you doing at meeting these needs personally and corporately? (You may also wish to refer to the Relational Needs Questionnaire in the Appendix in order to make a more detailed assessment.)

1. **Acceptance**—The need for acceptance is met by receiving another person willingly and unconditionally, especially when the other person's behavior is imperfect or even offensive. It requires being willing to love others regardless of offenses and ways in which they are different from you (Romans 15:7).

Jesus met our ultimate need for acceptance in that "while we were still sinners," He died for us (Romans 5:8). He looked beyond our faults and met our needs. During His earthly ministry, Jesus accepted people regardless of background, race, or condition: the Samaritan woman (John 4:4–26), the thief on the cross (Luke 23:39–43), the Gentile centurion (Luke 7:1–10), and the woman caught in adultery (John 8:1–11). He helped people overcome failures, loved all people unconditionally, and forgave freely, even from the Cross: "Father, forgive them, for they do not know what they are doing" (Luke 23:34).

During any given week, you will find care teams from Hope in the City Church providing hot meals and blankets at a local homeless shelter. They lead support groups for recovering addicts in the community center and provide career counseling and tutoring at a women's shelter. The care teams are committed to reaching out with Christ's unconditional love to others, even if they seem different or have failed morally. Each member of the care team embraces and seeks to embody the mandate of Romans 15:7: "Accept one another, then, just as Christ accepted you."

> **2. Affection**—The need for affection is met by expressing care and closeness through physical touch and by verbally saying "I love you" (Romans 16:16; Mark 10:16).

Jesus frequently ministered to others through physical touch. He used touch to accompany several of His miraculous healings (Matthew 8:3, 15; 9:29; Mark 7:33–35), His consolation of the disciples (Matthew 17:7), and His ministry to children (Mark 10:16;, Matthew 19:13).

During months containing five Sundays, the Marrietta Church has dedicated the evening service on the fifth Sunday to intergenerational ministry. Families gather together in small groups. Those members without families present are "adopted" for the evening.

During one particular evening session, the families focused their sharing around this sentence: "I feel your love when. . . ." Four-year-old Aaron moved to sit next to his dad, and we heard him say, "Daddy, I feel your love when you come into my room and wrestle with me. I really like it when you give me back rubs at night, too. Thanks, Daddy!" As Aaron and his dad gave one another a hug, the Spirit touched Aaron's father with the imperative of loving his son well by meeting his need for affection.

3. **Appreciation**—The need for appreciation is met through expressing thanks, praise, or commendation. This involves specifically and intentionally recognizing someone's accomplishments or efforts (Colossians 3:15).

During His earthly ministry, Jesus frequently voiced appreciation to individuals, including the Canaanite woman (Matthew 15:28), a centurion (Luke 7:9), and John the Baptist (v. 28). God has also promised to express appreciation to those who are faithful (2 Timothy 4:8; Luke 6:35; Ephesians 6:8).

For many years, Pastor Rick has spent his Friday morning commute to church focusing upon just one question: "Who am I grateful for today?" As he prayerfully considers this question, the Holy Spirit brings names and faces to Rick's mind. Recently, Rick has expressed gratitude for each of these: George, a faithful member of the church body who serves as "greeter" for each worship service; Margaret, the saint of all children's workers; Millie, a friendly hospital nurse who, in spite of not being a "church-goer," is always helpful when Rick makes his weekly hospital visits; and Andrew, a young pastor of a new church that was recently established in their community.

When Pastor Rick arrives at the church each Friday, he spends an hour making phone calls and sending e-mails to each person the Lord has brought to his mind. His messages often contain thoughts such as, "As I drove to the office today, I was reminded of how grateful I am for you. I just called to let you know I was thinking about you and what a blessing you have been to my life." Rick also shares a few specifics about their faithfulness, friendliness, or helpfulness. The recipients of these Friday morning messages are often startled by such thoughtfulness, encouraged in their work or ministry, and in a small way are reminded that they have been cared for by the Lord.

4. **Approval**—The need for approval is met by building up and affirming other people, as well as by acknowledging the importance of your relationship with them. Approval also involves noticing and affirming positive character qualities— praising people for who they are, not just for what they do (Ephesians 4:29).

Jesus frequently expressed approval to various people. He affirmed a generous widow (Mark 12:41–44), Peter (Matthew 16:13–19), Mary of Bethany, who anointed Him with perfume for burial (John 12:2–8), and a grateful leper (Luke 17:11–19).

After highlighting several positive character qualities from the Book of Proverbs, youth leaders at Calvary Church led high school students in a meaningful exercise in approval. Leaders described character traits such as diligence, truthfulness, humility, loyalty, generosity, and boldness. They then encouraged students to find a positive trait that they could see in one another. A time of group sharing followed where each student received two or more affirmations from the group: "I am impressed by your boldness. I see that character trait when you talk in class about your faith." "Our group benefits from your sensitivity. You are careful to include others and notice how people are feeling." The group was then challenged to live out this example in all their relationships and reminded that "man looks at the outward appearance, but the Lord looks at the heart" (1 Samuel 16:7).

> **5. Attention**—The need for attention is met by conveying appropriate interest, concern, and care for other people. We meet people's need for attention when we take thought of them, particularly when we enter into their "world" (1 Corinthians 12:25 NASB).

Jesus did not spend all His time with the masses. He gave individual attention to people such as Zacchaeus (Luke 19:1–10), Nicodemus (John 3:1–21), and the Samaritan woman (4:4–26). Jesus met our need for attention by leaving His world and entering ours. He became like us so that we could know Him and have a personal relationship with Him.

Each member at Trinity Church can count on several friends "taking thought" of them on their birthday. Each Friday, a community e-mail is sent out to the church family (except for members who have a birthday that week) reminding them of next week's birthdays and giving contact information for each person who has a birthday coming up. Members are then surprised by phone calls, voice mails, e-mails, and personal contacts from Pastor Lewis and other members of the Trinity family.

> **6. Comfort**—The need for comfort is met by responding to a hurting person with appropriate words, feelings, and physical touch. Comfort involves hurting with another person and expressing care and sadness for his or her grief and pain (Romans 12:15; Matthew 5:4; 2 Corinthians 1:3, 4).

Jesus comforted people throughout His earthly ministry, often identifying with others' hurt so much that He wept with them (John 11:35; Luke 19:41). Even on the eve of His death, He comforted His disciples as He sensed their sorrow and anxiety (John 14:1, 18; 16:33).

Care teams from Good Shepherd Church make regular visits to the emergency waiting rooms of local hospitals. Tragedies, accidents, and violence fill the waiting rooms with family members and friends as they wait anxiously for news about their loved one. Care team members are careful not to give advice or exhortation, but simply comfort those they meet. After brief introductions and conversation, team members share gentle, empathetic words from their heart. They might pray with a family member or simply sit, listen, and hold a hand. Hospital attendants have come to trust the care teams and see them as an extension of the hospital's desire to provide care and healing.

---

7. **Encouragement**—The need for encouragement is met by urging other people to persist and persevere toward their goals, and by stimulating them toward love and good deeds (1 Thessalonians 5:11; Hebrews 10:24).

During His earthly ministry, Jesus continually encouraged His disciples and those who were downcast and discouraged. The Pharisees even criticized Jesus because He regularly met with those who were struggling spiritually and emotionally (Matthew 9:10–13).

A recent worship service at Freedom Fellowship focused on "Our words that minister grace." The texts were 1 Thessalonians 5:11: "Therefore encourage one another and build each other up," and Ephesians 4:29: "Do not let any unwholesome talk come out of your mouths, but only what is helpful for building others up according to their needs." The contrast between edifying and unwholesome words was clearly articulated, and the pastor led members to see the wonder of our ability to minister divine grace through our words. Then church leaders led the congregation in a time of experiencing the text.

The congregation stood and was challenged in each of the following areas: Who around you might be discouraged and need a word of encouragement? Who has been a good friend and might benefit from a word that stimulates them toward more good deeds? Who has inspired you? Impressed you? Blessed you by their persistence or perseverance?

The praise team began to sing, and church members were challenged to move around and talk with one another. They were challenged to encourage one another right there in the auditorium, immediately experiencing 1 Thessalonians 5:11.

> **8. Respect**—The need for respect is met by communicating value or giving honor to other people. It also involves regarding others highly and treating them as important (Romans 12:10; 1 Peter 2:17).

Jesus ignored all the social prejudices of His society by showing respect to tax collectors, Samaritans, the poor, lepers, and women. He treated all people as having infinite value, regardless of their status.

The pastoral team and church council of Grace Church meet together twice a year for a special time of "Leadership Listening." After a brief time of worship, the members who are present spend time in personal prayer and reflection in the spirit of 1 Samuel 3:9: "Speak, Lord, for your servant is listening."

First, they listen to the Lord concerning this statement: "I believe the Lord is especially pleased with our. . . ." Participants pray and discern how they might finish the sentence.

Following this time of personal prayer, each person gives their response to the sentence completion. Then the pastor leads everyone in a time of praise-filled rejoicing.

A second period of personal prayer focuses on this statement: "I believe the Lord may want us to consider. . . ." The participants share their impressions from the Lord concerning this second sentence, then close in worship. Decisions and actions are addressed at other times; this meeting is dedicated solely to hearing from the Lord and respectfully listening to what God has birthed in the hearts of those around them.

> **9. Security**—The need for security is met when we establish and maintain harmony in relationships. We also meet the need for security by providing freedom from fear or threat of harm (Romans 12:16, 18).

During His earthly ministry, Jesus offered security to those who were close to Him by unconditionally meeting their needs. Christ provided for the disciples' physical, relational, and spiritual needs without condition or demand. At times, He even performed miracles to meet people's physical needs, such as the need for food (Mark 6:30–45, 8:1–9).

The Moms and Mentors Ministry at Westlake Community Church provides the perfect environment for single moms to become connected with other women and their families. These moms come to feel less alone as they are paired with another Westlake family, which provides the security of fellowship, counsel, discipleship, and practical support. The women meet together weekly for "girls' night," where they find mutual encouragement and polish practical skills in parenting, budgeting, and goal-setting. Experts from the community are always present in order to give help with housing decisions, car repairs, insurance challenges, and career options. On regularly scheduled "Family Fun Days," single-parent families come together with mentor families to enjoy fun activities. These times provide the opportunity for friendships to be formed among the kids and allow for the positive influence of male role models from the mentor families.

---

10. Support—The need for support is met by coming alongside someone who is struggling or has a problem and providing appropriate assistance (Galatians 6:2).

Jesus invited the multitudes to "Come to me, all you who are weary and burdened, and I will give you rest" (Matthew 11:28). He consistently provided physical, emotional, and spiritual support for people who were struggling.

Grace Fellowship sponsors a monthly "Parents' Night Out" as a ministry to their own members as well as an outreach opportunity. One specific night was dedicated to supporting parents in two neighborhood housing projects. An Adult Bible Fellowship and the youth department teamed up to welcome 40 children and teens to a local park for a night of games, contests, food, and activities. Fliers were posted in the neighborhood, and an announcement was printed in the community paper. This event was designed to support and serve those couples in the neighborhood who needed a "date night" without the expense of childcare and single parents who could benefit from a night of "personal time."

NEW METHODS ARE NEEDED FOR THIS FRESH MESSAGE.

In order for us to live out a message of relevant love in the coming decades, our ministries may need to look significantly different from the way they look now. It is crucial that any necessary restructuring or altering of methods be dictated by ministry objectives driven by both the Great Commission and the Great Commandment.

A growing network of churches around the world has begun to undertake such changes, thereby forging a relevant and fruitful approach to Christian ministry. They have moved beyond merely hosting meetings and conducting services where people come together, take good notes, and walk away saying, "Wasn't that a fine sermon?" or "Wasn't that a great lesson?" The fresh message these church leaders proclaim is affecting the traditional structure of ministry, and it demands fresh methodologies.

> **In order for us to live out a message of relevant love in the coming decades, our ministries may need to look significantly different.**

New Birth Church provides a good example of this relevant and relational approach. The church became concerned about the rising crime rate among the youth in the area. As church leaders considered the problem, they acknowledged that the young people were not just juvenile offenders; they were kids with deep, unmet relational needs. They had not experienced Great Commandment love. New Birth decided to help at the level of deepest need.

The church worked out an arrangement with law enforcement authorities to assign youth offenders to church families. These families, trained to identify the relational needs of the young people, began to minister to their aloneness by loving them as their special "neighbors." Classes were offered to equip neighborhood parents to remove the aloneness and meet the relational needs of their own children. Together, the church and families provided an abundance of loving attention, comfort, and care for these love-starved youth.

To date, the families of New Birth have ministered to hundreds of these young people and their parents. Many have made personal commitments to Christ, and an astounding 90 percent of the kids cared for in this way have not been arrested again!

Several new ministry objectives may be needed to create this type of relevant relational ministry within your own congregation.

Meet people at their point of need.

The church must be more than just the defender and propagator of truth. It must be a place where biblical relational needs are met—not just talked about. We all have relational needs, such as acceptance, attention, respect, approval, and comfort, and there is no better place to experience the mutual addressing of these needs than at church. As Christ's body, we freely receive of His acceptance, love, and comfort, and we have a responsibility to freely give these things to others in turn. The church should not only positively impact our mind by thoroughly grounding believers in the absolute truth of God's Word, but should also equip and lead us to express God's Great Commandment love in our own relationships.

The church should not only positively impact our mind by thoroughly grounding believers in the absolute truth of God's Word, but should also equip and lead us to express God's Great Commandment love in our own relationships.

This prioritizing of relational needs should also affect our approach to evangelism. Instead of merely trying to get people to believe what we believe, we must lovingly represent to them a God who cares for them and wants to meet their needs, including their need for the forgiveness of sin, which makes a meaningful relationship with Him possible.

Prioritize relationships.

We can often get so wrapped up in the busyness of the Christian life that we neglect to prioritize knowing God personally and intimately. We read the Bible in order to prepare for Sunday's lesson, but how often do we meditate on Scripture solely to know God's heart? We focus on facts about God and the programs of the church, but how much time is spent hearing His heart? As church leaders, we must reprioritize our own commitment to know Him—not just learn about Him.

For ministry to be relevant and authentic, we must also encourage healthy relationships in the home. The church must prioritize family relationships and provide the tools necessary to strengthen them. The concentric circles of ministry as presented in Acts 1:8—Jerusalem, Judea, Samaria, and the ends of the earth—must be applied not only to our evangelism, but also to our witness of love, beginning with those nearest to us: our spouse if we are married, or closest family members if we are single (Jerusalem), our children if we have them, or other close family members (Judea), our close friends (Samaria), and then everyone else (the ends of the earth).

Churches must offer ongoing relational ministries for singles, couples, parents, and families that equip individuals to meet relational needs and foster growing intimacy. Such relationship-centered ministry is proving to be invaluable in reaching postmodern culture, in which relationships are valued above rational arguments. It is the sharing of God's love with one another that removes aloneness and challenges us to live out that which we claim to know and believe. It is this authenticity that the Spirit builds upon to draw others unto the Son.

Create an atmosphere of vulnerability.

People are more likely to be affected by relational ministry when church leaders foster an atmosphere of openness and vulnerability. Vulnerable self-disclosure communicates, "We all need God, and we all need one another." This encourages people to humbly acknowledge their own needs and allow God to meet those needs directly and through others.

> **People are more likely to be affected by relational ministry when church leaders foster an atmosphere of openness and vulnerability.**

We must resist the common misconception that people in ministry are to be self-reliant and guarded, carefully concealing imperfections and needs. Church leaders who hold to this false notion contend that the flock will not follow a shepherd who struggles, fails, and hurts as they do. In reality, people are inspired when they see God's strength made perfect in the weakness of their leaders (2 Corinthians 12:9). Honest, humble sharing of our struggles and needs as leaders is powerfully effective and refreshing. One layman commented, "When my pastor shared that he was struggling to be more patient when things get out of control, it not only helped me see my need for help in that area, but it raised my respect for him." Genuine accountability and encouragement can flourish in an environment where leaders are appropriately open about their needs.

The primary model for vulnerability in leadership comes from Christ Himself. God became vulnerable, approachable, and knowable as the Word became flesh and dwelt among us. Jesus, the Great Shepherd, modeled vulnerability by humbling Himself and leaving heaven. He then not only became a man, but a servant. Though sinless, He experienced the pain of rejection, loss, disappointment, and loneliness so He could empathize with our struggles.

What is God presently at work to change in your life? Do you have a ready answer for that question? If you and your message are to be relevant to the needs of people, vulnerable self-disclosure of your needs is vital. What better way to open yourselves to others than to verbalize how God is at work in your life to bring you into conformity with His likeness?

Take a moment to experience this principle of relevant ministry. Take advantage of this opportunity to become vulnerable with your own imperfections.

An Experience With God's Word

"Speak, Lord, for your servant is listening" (1 Samuel 3:9).

Spend a few minutes in quiet prayer before the Lord. Ask God to speak to you, assuring Him of your willingness to hear His words and yield to His will. Ask Him to show you how He might want to change you so that you might more effectively meet the needs of other people, including your family, friends, church members, and those who do not know Christ. Ask Him to reveal how He might want you to change your approach to ministry.

Review this list of ten needs as you pray. Does God want you to become . . .

more accepting?
more affectionate?
more appreciative?
more approving?
more attentive?
more comforting?
more encouraging?
more respectful?
more committed to the security of others?
more supportive?

I might need to become more . . .

An Experience With God's People

"This is the confidence we have in approaching God: that if we ask anything according to his will, he hears us. And if we know that he hears us—whatever we ask—we know that we have what we asked of him" (1 John 5:14).

Now pray with a partner or small group. Ask God to make these changes in you, knowing that it is His will. Thank Him in advance for doing what you have asked. Your prayer might sound like the following:

Heavenly Father, do in my heart and life whatever You need to do. Help me to accept and address the changes that need to be made. Thank You for hearing my prayer and accomplishing Your will in my life. In Jesus' name, Amen.

Our world needs relevant, vibrant bodies of believers who will serve as shelters in the storm, places of refuge from the pressures of life, sanctuaries of hope where hurts can be healed and spiritual needs can be met. Christ is the answer—we sincerely believe it. But this needy world has every reason to question the relevance of the answer if our lives and ministries fail to convey the necessity of both a relationship with Him and relationships with other people. Let us hold fast to this relational foundation and commit to experiencing renewed relevance as we live out God's command to love Him and one another.

For Further Study

NEEDING BOTH GOD AND OTHERS

"He took Peter and the two sons of Zebedee along with him, and he began to be sorrowful and troubled. Then he said to them, 'My soul is overwhelmed with sorrow to the point of death. Stay here and keep watch with me'" (Matthew 26:37, 38).

Relational relevance is lost when we misunderstand man's need by claiming he only needs God. When we deny our need for meaningful relationships with one another, we begin to exalt self-reliance as if it were maturity. When we proclaim the incomplete message that "You only need God" rather than the good news that "We need God and one another," the church becomes irrelevant in a world that is already plagued by disconnectedness and isolation.

When Jesus was in the Garden of Gethsemane, He expressed His need for Peter, James, and John to keep watch with Him. If we had been present, we might have argued, "Jesus, do You not know that You already have God? You do not need anyone else!" Of course, Jesus did know that He had His Father's presence and provision, but in His humanity, He also expressed His need for others. If Jesus, the Son of God, needed both His Father and others, why should we think that we do not need both?

Consider these passages of Scripture:

- In Luke 2:52, Jesus grew in favor with _____.

- In Philippians 4:19, the apostle Paul says that "God will supply all your needs," and in verse 18, he acknowledges that God met some of His needs through

  _____.

- In 2 Corinthians 1:3, Paul exalts the God of all comfort, but in verse 4 he reminds us that we are often comforted so that we can _____.

- In 1 Corinthians 12:21, Paul says that every believer is a member of Christ's body and that we need each other. It would be absurd to say, "I do not _____."

- In Revelation 3:16, the apostle John rebukes the Church of Laodicea because they have become "lukewarm" (irrelevant), and in verse 17, specifically confronts the exalted self-reliance of those who declare, "I am rich; I have acquired wealth and

  _____."

Why Did God Create Us With Needs?

The Father could have created us so that we did not need food to eat, air to breathe, or comfort when we are hurt. But He chose to do otherwise. Let us consider the manifold wisdom of God making us as He did.

Needs Remind Us of Our Dependency and Call Us to Humility.

Jesus revealed His total dependence on the Father when He said, "The Son can do nothing by himself; he can do only what he sees his Father doing" (John 5:19). Jesus also taught us how dependent we are on Him when He said, "Apart from me you can do nothing" (15:5).

Since God created us to be needy, humility is prompted within us. In this state of humility, we may receive His abundant grace (James 4:6). Furthermore, our journey toward being conformed to His image must include the pursuit of humility because Jesus Himself was humble (Matthew 11:29).

Needs Remind Us of the Father's Loving Care and Call Us to Exercise Faith.

Our needs also stimulate our faith. If we did not have needs, there would be no opportunity for us to exercise faith. Scripture tells us that we were created for God's pleasure (Revelation 4:11), but without faith, God cannot be pleased (Hebrews 11:6). It thus becomes clear that the interaction between our neediness and our faith is an essential component in fulfilling the purpose for which we were created.

If and when we admit that we have needs, we will be faced with a critical decision: will we selfishly "take" in order to have our needs met, or will we exercise faith that we will receive from the giver of all good gifts (James 1:17)? If we are fearful of not receiving, we will be tempted to selfishly take from God and others. In attempting to take eternal life and a relationship with God, man exalts religious ritual and good works, thus missing the simplicity of receiving these gifts through childlike faith (Titus 3:5).

When man was created, everything he needed to survive—air, food, water—already existed. Before man needed redemption, the Savior was available in the Creator's eternal plan. Jehovah Jireh, God the provider, can be trusted with our needs. He alone is worthy of our faith.

Needs Remind Us of Our Worth to the Father and Call Us to Gratitude.
As we exercise faith at the point of our need, we experience the caring involvement of the One who knows everything about us yet still loves us. It was God who declared us worthy of the gift of His Son, even while we were still sinners (Romans 5:8); but even in the face of God's overwhelming, unmerited favor, some of us are self-condemning, rejecting the available righteousness of Christ. We would do well to remember that, because of His lavish grace, "There is now no condemnation for those who are in Christ Jesus" (8:1).

Jesus reassures us of our worth in His discourse on the birds of the air and the lilies of the field (Matthew 6:25–34). Just as God feeds the birds and clothes the flowers, He is ever attentive to our needs. Reflecting upon the certainty of God's provision moves us to respond with sacrifices of praise to Him (Hebrews 13:15).

Reflect on these three dimensions of the Spirit's deepened work—humility, faith, and gratitude. Could you benefit from a deepened expression . . .

- of humility in your walk with Him?
- of faith in His provision?
- of gratitude toward Him?

Pause now and ask the Lord to bring about any needed changes in you.

HOW TO GIVE TO MEET THE NEEDS OF OTHERS

In this section of further study, we are going to focus on meeting other people's needs within our congregations. We will be exploring ways in which we can experience these verses:

> "Do nothing out of selfish ambition or vain conceit, but in humility consider others better than yourselves. Each of you should look not only to your own interests, but also to the interests of others" (Philippians 2:3, 4).

"Share with God's people who are in need" (Romans 12:13).

"If anyone . . . sees his brother in need but has no pity on him, how can the love of God be in him" (1 John 3:17)?

Listed below are the ten biblical relational needs we examined earlier. Often, we might approach such a list by asking, "Which of these needs are most important to me, and how are they being met?"—a legitimate question (and one which you can explore by using the Relational Needs Questionnaire in the Appendix). But understanding these needs also presents us with the opportunity to be blessed (and be a blessing) by giving to meet the needs of others (Acts 20:35).

Jesus had needs that He vulnerably expressed to others: "My soul is overwhelmed with sorrow to the point of death. Stay here and keep watch with me" (Matthew 26:38). But it is significant that He also said, "The Son of Man did not come to be served, but to serve" (20:28). How well do we express this attitude of Christ?

Listed below are some practical ways we can give to others to meet each relational need. After reading each group of statements, use the scale below to assign the score that you think best reflects your church or ministry team's consistency in giving to meet each need. Indicate a score for each sentence, then add up the total score for each relational need and write it on the appropriate line.

Not at All	Very Little	Neutral	Some	A Lot
-2	-1	0	+1	+2

Acceptance

_____ We go out of our way to welcome people who may not look, believe, or act like we do.

_____ When we are with a group of people, we try to spot anyone who may feel uneasy or alone and initiate conversation in order to make him or her feel welcome.

_____ We look beyond people's faults and minister to their needs.

_____ We accept people, not just when they are "up," but also when they are "down."

_____ When someone "blows it," "messes up," or offends us, we are quick to forgive.

Total score for Acceptance _____

Affection

_____ We generously offer appropriate, physical gestures of love and tenderness.

_____ We often tell people, "I love you" or "I care for you."

_____ We welcome people into our church by initiating warm greetings and demonstrating caring concern.

_____ We are vulnerable in sharing our heart with others, expressing, at times, that they are "very dear to us" (1 Thessalonians 2:8).

_____ We strive to be mindful of how others may or may not wish to receive affection.

Total score for Affection _____

Appreciation

_____ We commend others for doing well or putting forth effort.

_____ We write notes thanking others for what they do for us.

_____ We notice special times in people's lives when they should be commended (ball games, recitals, big projects completed, graduations, and other similar occasions).

_____ We focus on what people do that is right more than on what they do that is wrong.

_____ We have learned how others prefer to receive appreciation: public vs. private, written vs. verbal, and so on.

Total score for Appreciation _____

Approval

_____ We are able to view people through God's eyes—to separate who they are (valuable, important, and significant) from what they do (sometimes good, sometimes bad).

_____ We look beyond a person's activity and performance and caringly affirm their character, heart, and spiritual maturity.

_____ We are quick to commend people when they have displayed Christlike character and attitudes.

_____ We are particularly careful to affirm those for whom we have particular responsibility (children, employees, co-laborers) when they have done well, and give specific focus to the character qualities (diligence, sensitivity, honesty) that contributed to them doing well.

_____ We go out of our way to tell others how blessed we are to be in relationship with them.

Total score for Approval _____

Attention

_____ We spend time with individuals, finding out about their struggles, joys, and dreams.

_____ We strive to initiate care for one another, letting others know that we have been thinking of them.

_____ We try to enter into other people's emotional world by seeking to discern their emotional state, striving to gain understanding, and empathizing with them.

_____ We demonstrate good listening skills by giving good eye contact, offering appropriate feedback, and seeking to hear fully before we respond.

_____ We spend time with people, doing what *they* enjoy doing.

Total score for Attention _____

Comfort

_____ We notice when people are hurting, anxious, frustrated, or emotionally "down."

_____ We have moved beyond spiritual platitudes and developed an appropriate "comforting vocabulary" in order to communicate our care and concern for hurting people.

_____ We have learned how to sense God's compassion for others and enter into their emotional pain.

_____ We know how to respond to hurting people with a gentle touch and affirming words.

_____ When people are hurting, we first express feelings of sadness and hurt for them rather than giving them advice or exhortation.

Total score for Comfort _____

Encouragement

_____ We try to anticipate times and situations in which people may be discouraged so that we can encourage them.

_____ We often go out of our way to call, write, or visit someone who is discouraged, disappointed, or struggling.

_____ We encourage others toward positive vision and realistic goals and then help support them in their journey.

_____ We faithfully pray for people, both privately and with them.

_____ We encourage others by expressing sincere confidence and belief in God's work in and through them.

Total score for Encouragement _____

Respect

_____ Before making a decision, we solicit input from those whose lives will be impacted by the decision.

_____ We have a high regard for others people's ideas, opinions, and perspectives, even though they may differ from our own.

_____ We initiate times of listening to the hearts and needs of those we are seeking to serve.

_____ We treat everyone with dignity and courtesy regardless of their race, lifestyle, or socio-economic status.

_____ We are careful to be on time to appointments and meetings.

Total score for Respect _____

Security

_____ Those whom we are closest to never have to wonder about where our relationship stands. We are open and transparent in sharing our heart, care, and concern.

_____ We pro-actively attempt to maintain health in all our relationships. If a relationship is strained, we attempt reconciliation quickly.

_____ We make decisions based on the well-being of those we love and care for, not just our own well-being.

_____ We are self-controlled. Others around us do not fear outbursts of temper or impulsive decisions from us.

_____ We can be counted upon to think and speak the best of others.

Total score for Security _____

Support

_____ We are known for our availability and our desire to help people in times of need.

_____ We often attend weddings, funerals, recitals, sports activities, and other events, just to show our love for someone.

_____ We often use personal resources to help support others.

_____ We willingly defer our plans, agenda, and schedule in order to be available for others.

_____ We do not stand at a distance and give advice, but willingly help others bear their burdens.

Total score for Support _____

In which areas were your ministry's point totals highest?

_____

_____

_____

_____

Which were lowest?

_____

_____

_____

_____

Others might be blessed as we work on being more sensitive to meeting needs such as:

_____

_____

_____

_____

What practical steps could your church or ministry take to become more sensitive to people's needs?

_____

_____

_____

_____

Additional Resources

Robert Benson, *The Broken Body: Answering God's Call to Love One Another* (New York: Doubleday, 2003).

Robert E. Fisher, *The Joy of Relationship* (Cleveland, TN: Pathway Press, 1996).

Linda Riley, *The Call to Love* (Wheaton, IL: Tyndale House Publishers, 2000).

Chapter 5

Seeing People as Both Fallen and Alone: Our Foundation of Anthropology, Part 2

God revealed a second dramatic principle as I studied in the Bodleian Library years ago. This revelation centered on the order of events in the early chapters of Genesis. I was shocked to realize that God said that something was "not good" in the Garden (Genesis 2:18) several verses **before** man fell into sin (3:6). God's declaration about the "not good-ness" of man's aloneness actually preceded the Fall into sin. Aloneness came before fallenness.

Everything within me reacted to this truth. Reflecting back, I recall that my heart was filled with a mixture of shock and anger. "Why haven't I seen this before? Who's been keeping this from me?" All of my training, mentoring, and education had convinced me that God's declaration regarding man's condition was only and always a result of the Fall.

Until that day in the Oxford library, I was convinced that all of the "not good" in man's condition could be attributed to sin. The order of events in the early chapters of Genesis seemed to argue for a different perspective. Something was "not good" before sin ever entered the Garden. The Lord began to solidify the significance of this revelation within my heart. He began to impress me with the importance of seeing man's true condition.

> I was convinced that all of the "not good" in man's condition could be attributed to sin. The order of events in the early chapters of Genesis seemed to argue for a different perspective.

The Book of Genesis recounts the day that mankind lost fellowship with the Creator. Genesis 3:1–24 details how Adam and Eve fell from their position of perfect communion and harmony with God to one of animosity and strife. As a result of these events, mankind is now fallen, sinful, and in desperate need of a Savior. We must, however, look back to the second chapter of Genesis. Before Adam's fallenness, God declared his state of aloneness, and described it as "not good." Our Creator is acutely aware of man's condition: we are both fallen **and** alone. If we as the leaders of Christ's church hope to reach the world for Him, our ministries must reflect this same relational foundation. We must see people as Christ sees them—both fallen and alone.

A Sharp Contrast in Perspective

Imagine this scene from John chapter nine: it is a warm Sabbath morning in Jerusalem, and we are strolling with Jesus and His disciples. Having visited the temple, we follow the Master through the narrow, bustling streets. Jesus stops suddenly. The disciples whisper questions among themselves:

"What's going on?"
"Why are we stopping?"
"What's the Master doing?"

We approach Jesus in order to inquire about what has attracted His curiosity. We are quickly silenced by the intensity in His eyes. Following His gaze into a shadowy corner, we discover the object of His rapt attention: a blind beggar huddled alone beside the teeming river of humanity.

The people who jostle past the beggar are as blind to his presence as he is to them. But Jesus notices him. The Savior's brow furrows with concern, but his face radiates compassion. We are gripped by the love pouring from His eyes.

> **God's heart is captivated by human need, while God's people are too often preoccupied with human sin.**

But before the Master moves to touch the needy, blind beggar, one of the disciples shatters the tender moment. "Master, whose sin caused this man's blindness? Did he do something wrong, or were his parents at fault?"

We are struck by the contrast. The Master is thinking, "How will I minister to this precious child of God? How can I alleviate the loneliness He must feel?" But the disciples' only focus seems to be finding fault and assessing sin.

Within this biblical story lies a significant insight into Christlike living, as well as a partial explanation for the irrelevance of the 21st century church: God's heart is captivated by human need, while God's people are too often preoccupied with human sin.

If we are to live out a testimony of Christ's life and love with those around us, we must begin to see people as both fallen and alone. Our churches must see people as sinful and in need of a Savior, yet at the same time we must also recognize their desperate need for relationship. God seems to be challenging His people to embrace His perspective of our sin. We all know that God is burdened by our sin because He is a holy God. But what we often miss is that God's heart is also burdened by our sin because sin is what keeps His children alone, separated from Him and from one another.

Additionally, as we come to truly understand His complete provision for sin at Calvary, we are challenged to consider this question: upon which of these two issues (sin or aloneness) can we actually make an impact? When Christ cried out, "It is finished!" He was declaring that He, and He alone, had made provision for our sin. But we have the privilege of joining Him in removing a measure of the aloneness in people around us. God seems to be challenging His church to first see people as both fallen and alone, and then to take initiative to remove people's aloneness. All the while, He remains quite capable of and wholly responsible for addressing man's sin.

> **Upon which of these two issues (sin or aloneness) can we actually make an impact?**

My Personal Journey

Almost 20 years ago, my heart was broken over my own tendency to look for people's sin rather than their needs. It often seemed that I was focusing only upon identifying areas of fallenness, never considering or addressing people's aloneness.

A friend had invited me to make pastoral visits with him at a community AIDS clinic. This was in the early days of the epidemic, and medical professionals were just determining the different ways of contracting this horrible disease. The pastor briefed several of us on the day before our visit. He warned us that we would see babies who were born with AIDS and were slowly dying. We would see healthcare workers who had contracted the disease through the simple conduct of their duties. There would be some who had become infected through a transfusion of contaminated blood (prior to the screening process now in use). There would be some with a history of drug abuse who had been exposed to AIDS through the use of contaminated needles. Finally, there would be those who contracted AIDS as a result of a homosexual lifestyle or promiscuous, sexual behavior. Every individual in this clinic faced impending death, and we were going there to be ministers of the Gospel of Christ.

On the following day, we went to the clinic and began to enter the rooms of these terminally ill patients. Painfully, I found inside of me a response much like the disciples as they encountered the man born blind. As I walked into many of those rooms, the first questions in my mind were, "I wonder how he caught it? I wonder how she contracted this disease?" My response was just like the disciples in the Gospel of John. I wanted to know who had sinned. The coldness of my own response broke my heart. I did not like that part of me that focused on people's sin, but it was definitely there. I knew I wanted to be moved with Christ's compassion for these people who were dying. I was convicted as I reflected upon the fact that Christ would have walked into every one of those rooms already knowing how the person contracted the disease, yet His heart would have been moved with compassion, ministering grace to those in need.

As God began to reveal how He saw the people around me, I came to see that my experience in the AIDS clinic was not an isolated occurrence. God began to show me how I had often missed seeing my own wife's aloneness. I focused on her imperfections instead of her feelings, concerns, or needs. Similarly, I often focused on my children's sin. I was careful to bring attention to the fact that chores were not done or beds were not made. But too often, I was totally insensitive to any aloneness in their hearts.

An Experience With God's Son

"Yet the Lord longs to be gracious to you; He rises to show you compassion" (Isaiah 30:18).

Imagine the scene described in Mark 5:24–34. A large crowd is following Jesus around the Sea of Galilee. Citizens of the community have come to see the One who is rumored to have healed a man possessed by demons. Reports of the Savior's other miracles have circulated through the local towns, bringing hundreds of people to see the Lord. As He works His way through the crowds, Christ's progress is slowed by the hustle and bustle of so many people. Scripture tells us that they "pressed around Him" (v. 24).

A quiet, desperate woman makes her way through the crowd. She is suffering greatly from the pain of an illness that no doctor has been able to cure. The years of physical pain are no match, though, for the emotional and spiritual suffering of this woman. Perhaps on this day she hears someone in the crowd murmur, "That's the woman with the rare blood disease. We can only guess what sinful behavior has brought about that kind of punishment." These whispers of contempt serve only to fuel the flames of her own uncertainty about God and His care for her pain.

But on this day near Galilee, this desperate woman has a reason to hope. Because of the miraculous reports she has heard concerning Jesus, the woman concludes that just by touching Christ's clothes, healing could occur. While the shame of her illness does not allow her to ask for healing, she hopes to stealthily obtain a drop of mercy for herself. In the midst of the rough-and-tumble crowd, she inches her way forward. She pushes past onlookers and reaches toward the Savior. As she comes up behind Him, she discreetly touches the edge of His cloak. Immediately, she feels the health return to her body. A surge of joy mixed with relief flows over her spirit, soul, and body.

At once, Jesus realizes that power has gone out from Him. He stops, looks around, and asks, "Who touched Me?" Others watch as the woman falls at Christ's feet, trembling with fear. With a voice of compassion, Jesus lovingly offers reassurance: "Daughter, your faith has healed you. Go in peace and be freed from your suffering" (v. 34).

Jesus stopped and noticed the need of the one who touched Him that day. The Savior did not focus on any sin that might have been associated with the woman's illness; He concentrated instead on her loneliness and suffering. Christ looked deep into the heart of the woman and was moved with compassion. He saw her physical suffering, the shame she had endured, and the many hopeless nights she had spent in prayer. He chose words that were tender and that conveyed the compassion in His heart: "Daughter . . . go in peace." Christ's words were not only meant to bring reassurance to the woman. They also served as a proclamation of her restoration to the community. Jesus addressed her physical, mental, emotional, spiritual, and social needs, bringing complete healing to her situation.

Take a moment to express your gratefulness to Jesus for His heart of compassion. Praise Him for being the kind of God who not only has a burden for your sin, but compassion for the sufferings of your heart. Give thanks to Him for noticing your needs and being gracious to you.

Jesus, I want to thank You for Your heart of compassion. I feel _____ as I reflect on . . .

Thank You for having both a burden for my sin and compassion for the sufferings of my heart. I am especially grateful as I reflect on . . .

Pause now, and consider your relationship with the people in your own life. Reflect first upon those who are nearest to you: your spouse, children, family members, and closest friends.

Who might benefit from a change in your perspective? Who might need for you to see beyond their faults or imperfections and see the aloneness in their hearts?

Take the next few moments and ask God to reveal any changes that may need to be made. Ask Him to help you see your spouse, children, family member, or friend as He sees them. Ask Him to give you His perspective—one that sees beyond a person's fallenness and wants to remove their aloneness. Finally, ask God to show you one or two people that might especially benefit from a change in your heart.

My _____ could benefit from a change in my perspective. I know he/she needs for me to look beyond his/her faults and see the aloneness of his/her heart.

How does it make you feel to reflect upon your relationship with each of these people? Does it sadden your heart to know that your "nearest ones" may have sensed your concern for their fallenness, but rarely felt your compassion for their aloneness?

As I reflect upon my relationship with _____, I am saddened as I realize . . .

Now consider those to whom you minister: your congregation, fellow church members, those who have left their faith, or individuals who are not yet followers of Christ.

_____ could benefit from a change in my perspective. I know he/she needs for me to look beyond his/her faults and see the aloneness of his/her heart.

What does it do to your heart to reflect upon your relationship with each of these people? How does it make you feel to know that they may have sensed your concern for their fallenness, but rarely felt your compassion for their aloneness?

As I reflect upon my relationship with _____, I am saddened as I realize . . .

As you complete these sentences, share your responses with your partner or small group. Pray together, asking God to open your eyes and heart that you might see His people as He sees them, so that you might love them as He loves them.

CULTIVATING CHRISTLIKE COMPASSION

A pastor and his wife approached me during a break in one of our conferences. They wanted to talk about Rachel, a woman in their church they had been counseling for months. As a little girl, Rachel had been sexually abused by her father. Anger and resentment were eating her life away.

"David, we have tried everything we can think of to help her forgive her father, but she will not let go of her bitterness," the pastor lamented. "We remind her that God has forgiven her for things she has done, so she must forgive also. We tell her that forgiving is for her own freedom and that it does not mean that what happened to her was right in any way. We have gone through all of that and more, but nothing works. She is as bitter as ever."

"As you have come to understand Rachel's pain from her past," I said, "what feelings have you had for her?" The couple's response was classic: "Feelings? Just as we said, we feel she needs to forgive her father." "Yes, Rachel needs to forgive," I agreed. "But what do you feel **for** Rachel as you consider the painful trauma she has experienced?"

I received blank stares, so I rephrased the question: "Can you imagine what God might feel toward Rachel, given all that she went through? This innocent, little girl was betrayed and violated by someone she trusted. She probably lay awake countless nights dreading her father's appearance at the door of her room. What do you think God must feel toward Rachel, knowing that this defenseless, little girl was physically and emotionally wounded?"

The couple stood motionless for a moment, God's insight and revelation flooding their hearts. The pastor's wife spoke first: "I imagine that God feels incredible sadness for her. He must feel great compassion for the pain she's endured." The pastor then echoed: "Oh yes, I imagine that God must feel great sorrow for her. He must be brokenhearted over the devastation the abuse has had on her life."

I let a few seconds pass, then left the couple with this assignment: "If God feels sadness and compassion for this young lady, maybe you could come to feel the same. Could you let the Lord impact your heart with what He feels for Rachel, and then share those feelings with her? Rachel might need to sense that she's not alone in her pain before she can receive your exhortation. The next time you are with her, simply share something like, 'Rachel, we just want you to know that God has sorrowed our hearts for you. We have been saddened by all that you have been through. We are so sorry that you were hurt in such significant ways because we have grown to really care for you.'"

> **Reaching a pain-filled world with the relevant message of the Gospel is going to require a change in the way we see people.**

Several weeks later, I received a note from the pastor. It was brief and to the point: "It worked!" As this couple moved beyond their focus on Rachel's "sin" and unforgiving heart, they encountered God's compassion and ministered His love at the point of her aloneness. Rather than continue to be preoccupied with human sin, they changed their perspective as they were moved by God's concern for human need. That change in perspective is what made the difference in Rachel's response, allowing many years worth of bitterness to be released.

Reaching a pain-filled world with the relevant message of the Gospel is going to require a change in the way we see people. The church of Christ is going to have to see people as both fallen and alone. We must cultivate the compassionate heart of the Savior. Jesus' ministry in the Gospels is the believer's model for compassionate ministry. While others around Him responded out of fear, judgment, or legalism, Jesus was moved with compassion and acted out of love.

Christ related to people in the Gospels with a heart that was both gripped by the burden of man's sinfulness and moved with compassion because of man's aloneness. He consistently demonstrated concern for the aloneness of people as well as the sin that kept them separated from God and one another.

Recall that when the blind man came to Jesus for healing, the disciples wanted to know whose sin had caused the blindness. Jesus was moved with compassion and miraculously healed the blind man. Jesus never specifically called attention to the man's sins, but Christ's concern for the man's aloneness clearly made a spiritual impact because he boldly declared his faith in the One who had healed him (John 9:38).

> **We must be moved with compassion by people's need for relationship as well as their need for redemption.**

We also see evidence of Christ's heart of compassion on the occasion when the disciples picked grain on the Sabbath (Matthew 12:1–8). The Pharisees condemned them for not adhering to man-made laws, but Jesus was moved with compassion because of the hunger of His followers. Christ's focus was upon the needs of people instead of the church's religious rituals.

Christ's exhortation to the religious leaders of the 1st century is still applicable today: "If you had known what this means, 'I desire compassion, and not a sacrifice,' you would not have condemned the innocent" (Matthew 12:7 NASB). If we, as Christ's followers, desire a relevant, relational church, we must be concerned about the pain and aloneness of people as well as their sin and fallenness. We must be moved with compassion by people's need for relationship as well as their need for redemption.

Let us review some of the practical ways that churches around the world have begun to develop this heart of compassion and concern for the aloneness of others.

St. Stephen's Church is in a small, Texas town near the state penitentiary. Hundreds of families have moved to the town in order to be closer to loved ones who are serving lengthy prison sentences. The leaders of St. Stephen's were moved with compassion as they watched families deal with the stress, anger, and shame of having a loved one incarcerated. Rather than pass judgment on these families, St. Stephen's began a ministry of support and acceptance. They provide mentors for the children, financial assistance for the families, and transportation to the jail on visiting days. Even more remarkable, church leaders have partnered with state and prison officials to provide marriage seminars inside the prison facility. They minister to inmates and their spouses who want to preserve their marriage in the face of horrific stress. This church has seen countless inmates and family members come to Christ as a result of their ministry. It is a ministry of compassion, one in which church members are concerned for both the sin and aloneness of hurting people.

Unbelievers who enter the church's doors, who occupy the cubicle next to ours, or who live near enough to borrow eggs and sugar, often live pain-filled lives. Multitudes of the men, women, teens, and children we encounter during the week are victims of one or more of the plagues of 21st century culture: broken homes, abandonment, neglect, physical violence, sexual abuse, and addictions in the home. Yes, these people must eventually deal with their own sin in order to receive God's forgiveness and experience new birth. But will they be drawn to the Savior more effectively by our condemnation of their sin or our compassion for their pain? Christ's example compels us to share the Good News with these people through the doorway of compassion.

Fellow believers who worship alongside us also need to be treated with Christlike compassion. Even those who lead our worship often need the ministry of Christ's love. Recently, a denominational leader was moved with compassion as he reflected on the vast number of clergy leaving the ministry because of moral and ethical compromise. Rather than abandon these ministers and their families, or "write them off" as simply unfit to hold their office, the denomination's leaders appointed a unique team of individuals to address these issues. Their task is to take proactive steps to restore clergy to health in marriage and family relationships, as well as work toward the reinstatement of ministry roles when appropriate.

Local churches with a unique heart and calling are also being trained to become "churches of refuge" where fallen ministers and their families can be supported in their healing journey. Church leaders who struggle to live out the truths they believe are now being mentored through steps of reconciliation, instead of being faced with devastating loss alone.

These examples of compassionate ministry illustrate a change in perspective. These leaders were convicted that they needed to share God's view of people. In order for relevant, relational ministry to occur, they had to see people as both fallen and alone. Only as we see people as God sees them can we love them as He loves them.

You may wonder if we are suggesting that churches simply overlook the sinful heart of man. You may feel concern about advocating a "soft position" on sin. It would certainly be a mistake to discount the serious nature of our fallen condition. Must each of us give an account to God for the testimony of our lives? Absolutely. Do all of us need God's forgiveness and grace for the sins that so easily entangle us? Certainly. But will we be more effective at living out the Gospel by communicating condemnation and judgment within the body of Christ? No. Christ's example compels us to extend His mercy and grace to our fellow believers. A relevant church lives out the glorious truth that it is only the wonder of God's grace that empowers us to live rightly before Him.

> **Only as we see people as God sees them can we love them as He loves them.**

CHRIST'S PRIORITIES IN MINISTRY

Ask yourself this question: How **did** Christ address the fallenness of others? Did He ignore their sin? Of course not—He is the Holy Lamb of God. No, Jesus did not let people just get away with their sin. He addressed the sins of the people that He encountered, and because of their experience with Christ, lives were changed and souls were saved. We know that Jesus pointed out the sin of the woman at the well. Christ revealed that the man she lived with was not her husband. Jesus also identified the sin of the woman caught in adultery. He commanded the woman to go and sin no more. Finally, Christ did not let Zacchaeus' thievery and embezzlement go without notice. Because of his encounter with Jesus, the tax collector made restitution for all he had done and became a follower of Christ.

> **Jesus addressed these people's sins only within the context of ministering to their relational needs.**

It is important to notice, however, that Christ did not criticize, lecture, or judge any of these individuals concerning their sin. He did not try to use condemnation, chastisement, or shame to coerce people into becoming His followers. Instead, Jesus addressed these people's sins only within the context of ministering to their relational needs. To the woman at the well, Christ offered friendship and acceptance **before** He discussed her sin. To the woman caught in adultery, Jesus provided protection, security, and comfort in the midst of her accusers **before** He commanded that her behavior change. To Zacchaeus, Jesus presented an opportunity for loving fellowship **before** any discussion of sin and restitution. This order is critical to Christ's impact on the lives of each of these people. He ministered to their aloneness in order to provide a relational context for addressing their fallenness.

Relevant, relational ministry requires seeing and responding to the aloneness in a person's heart, rather than simply urging them to change their beliefs or behavior. It compels us to look beyond people's faults to see their needs. We will now focus specifically on the story of Zacchaeus and the way in which it further illustrates Christ's priorities for ministry.

The Zacchaeus Principle

As an agent of the Roman government, Zacchaeus reached deep into Jewish purses for Roman taxes, and whatever else he could possibly extort from the people, he likely kept for himself.

> **Relevant, relational ministry requires seeing and responding to the aloneness in a person's heart, rather than simply urging them to change their beliefs or behavior. It compels us to look beyond people's faults to see their needs.**

The Jews typically regarded tax collectors with contempt; they were considered deceitful traitors and thieves. The people of Jericho would have felt especially betrayed by Zacchaeus since he was not only a cheating tax collector, but a fellow Jew. Since his Jewish neighbors must have despised him, Zacchaeus probably felt rejected, guilty, fearful, and alone on a daily basis.

When Jesus traveled into Jericho that day, Scripture tells us that He stopped to speak to Zacchaeus, who was short of stature and had climbed to the top of a tree to gain a better view. As Jesus looked up into the sycamore tree, He knew all about the sinful behavior of the man peering down at Him. It is notable, however, that Christ did not say to him, "Zacchaeus, you lying, cheating thief, get down here right now and stop your sinful behavior." Rather, he said, "Zacchaeus, come down immediately. I must stay at your house today" (Luke 19:5). Jesus offered to enter this man's home and, as was the custom, eat out of the same dish with him. He could hardly do anything more accepting! Indeed, the Pharisees' frequent complaint was that Jesus actually ate with tax collectors and sinners. Zacchaeus' response demonstrated the impact of Jesus' offer: "He came down at once and welcomed him gladly" (v. 6). How thrilled Zacchaeus must have been to know that the popular, miracle-working rabbi wanted to be with him! We can be certain that Zacchaeus felt the same satisfying sense of fulfillment that we all experience when our spouse, a friend, or even a stranger ministers to us at a time when we are feeling alone.

Jesus did not ignore the fact that Zacchaeus was a lying, cheating thief who needed to love and obey God with heart, soul, and mind. He verbalized His concern for Zacchaeus' fallenness later in the conversation: "The Son of Man came to seek and to save what was lost" (v. 10). Jesus sought Zacchaeus at a relational level, taking time to visit with this lonely, rejected, insecure man. As a result, Zacchaeus' spiritual needs were addressed quite naturally in the context of this relationship. Scripture records that "Zacchaeus stood up and said to the Lord, 'Look, Lord! Here and now I give half of my possessions to the poor, and if I have cheated anybody out of anything, I will pay back four times the amount.' Jesus said to him, 'Today salvation has come to this house, because this man, too, is a son of Abraham'" (vv. 8, 9).

What happened in Jesus' incredible encounter with Zacchaeus? When the love of Christ touched Zacchaeus at the point of his need, that love constrained the sinner to confess his sin and make things right. In other words, Christ's love ministered to the man's deepest need, and Zacchaeus responded to the Holy Spirit's prompting to deal with his faults.

Had Jesus simply rebuked Zacchaeus in the tree for his sinful behavior and gone on His way, would the results have been the same? Probably not. Zacchaeus had undoubtedly been rebuked regularly by the religious leaders of the day. They must have communicated consistent rejection since they were not about to "defile themselves" by fraternizing with Zacchaeus. Jesus, however, discerned the tax collector's needs as well as his dishonesty. Like everyone else, Zacchaeus needed attention, acceptance, and respect, but he was seeking to meet those needs in sinful ways. Once he experienced Christ's loving acceptance, Zacchaeus was ready to receive the truth about his sinful behavior. Jesus' ministry and message addressed both his need and his sin, both his aloneness and his fallenness. That is relevant, relational ministry.

My Personal Journey

One of my first encounters with the loving acceptance of God came through a godly grandfather. I got into a lot of trouble growing up. I rebelled against most any authority during those years: parents, school officials, and local law enforcement. My most valued possession was a car—a drag-racing car that could do at least 160 miles per hour on the open road. I am not proud to admit it, but I got six speeding tickets in six months and almost lost my license. As you can imagine, this did not impress my father, who was a retired, Marine drill instructor. I cannot count the number of family arguments that resulted from discussions about my car and those speeding tickets. But in the midst of this family turmoil over my behavior, my grandfather sought me out. He did not approach me by giving lectures or preaching sermons. Instead, I remember him saying, "David, I hear you're about to lose your license, and I've come up with a plan that will help you keep driving and maybe even outsmart the police." Now, if you are a teenage rebel and somebody comes up with a plan to scam the police, you are thinking, 'Boy, this is going to be good!' He said, "I think the problem is that the police know this car of yours, and every time they see you leave the driveway, they just radio ahead and tell their buddies to watch for you on that 30-mile stretch from here to the junior college. So I think you need to quit driving your car and start driving my pickup. That way, they won't know it's you."

I could not believe my good fortune. I was thrilled by my grandfather's plan! The next morning, I got in his pickup and headed off to college. As soon as I hit the highway, I pressed the pedal to the floorboard, intent on speeding toward the school and outsmarting the police officers along the way. That's when I realized that my grandfather knew something about the pickup that he had not told me. The pickup had a governor on it—it could not go over 50 miles per hour! Amazingly, I did not get angry, but smiled as I had this thought: "My granddad was not going to enable my sin, but he was not going to reject me like so many other people had." I remember thinking, "If there is a God in heaven, He must be a lot like my grandfather."

I did not realize it then, but the Lord was involving my grandfather in ministering to my need for acceptance. My granddad looked beyond my fallenness and saw the aloneness of my heart. He accepted me in the midst of my sinful behavior. As a result, my heart was drawn to ask,

"How was my grandfather able to respond in such a loving manner?" Years later, I came to realize that the source of his loving response was his relationship with an accepting, gracious, and merciful God.

Ministering acceptance and removing a person's aloneness does not mean that we condone sin. Rather, it means that we look deeper in order to see people's needs. God has given the Holy Spirit the task of convicting of sin. He does so in order to keep us in fellowship with God and other people. It stands to reason, then, that we are in a much better position to minister to people's aloneness than to assume the role of the Holy Spirit. It is **His** job to point out a person's sin, not ours! Additionally, we will not be able to see the needs of others if we are preoccupied with judging their deeds. God equips us to be

> **Ministering acceptance and removing a person's aloneness does not mean that we condone sin. Rather, it means that we look deeper in order to see people's needs.**

people of compassion by making us stewards of His grace and acceptance. Our life's calling must include co-laboring with the Lord to minister to people's needs, rather than simply reacting to their behaviors and their sins.

An Experience With God's Word

"Accept one another, then, just as Christ accepted you, in order to bring praise to God" (Romans 15:7).

Take a moment to recall a time when someone looked beyond your faults and saw your needs. When did you receive acceptance in spite of your behavior? When did someone look past your fallenness and see the aloneness of your heart?

Now, share that memory with your partner or small group. Recount both your experience and your feelings related to the acceptance you received.

Someone looked past my fallenness and ministered to the aloneness of my heart when . . .

As a result, I remember feeling . . .

Make certain to give accepting responses to one another as you share. Accepting responses might sound like: "I know that time must have been so hard for you. I'm grateful that you received his/her acceptance," or "I am so sad that you experienced those difficult things, yet I am happy that the Lord brought him/her into your life to show you His acceptance."

Jesus met our need for acceptance by declaring that, although you and I sin, we are more than our sin. Christ's death for us gave evidence of our incomprehensible worth to the Father. The inexpressible joy and wonder of that truth can prompt and empower changed behavior.

We, in turn, are called to be stewards of this amazing grace. As unbelievers are lovingly accepted, comforted, and cared for by the church, they will begin to wonder, "Where did you receive the acceptance, comfort, and care you have shared with me?" At that point, the body of Christ will be ready to give an account of the hope that is within them. They will be prepared to proclaim the good news about the God who accepts us, thus empowering us to accept others.

Likewise, church leaders will begin to relate to their congregation with more of Christ's acceptance and grace, pointing church members to an intimate relationship with the One who has accepted us. Church will become a place to celebrate our relationship with Christ rather than just a place to rehearse His traditions. Ministry relevance will increase as we address people's fallenness within the context of love. Jesus said, "A new commandment I give to you, that you love one another, even as I have loved you, that you also love one another" (John 13:34, 35 NASB). We are identified as followers of Christ by loving as Christ loved. The world will not know we are His disciples simply by observing our religious activities or seeing our commitment to keeping His rules.

GOD'S PROVISION OF RELATIONSHIPS

Throughout this chapter, we have noted that we must come to see people as not only fallen and sinful, but also needy and alone. God's burden for our sin is closely tied to His concern for our aloneness, since sin acts to separate us from Him and from those around us. The good news of the Gospel is that relationships with God and other people are possible because of Christ's provision at Calvary. Sin is what keeps us alone. God-ordained relationships remove that aloneness. God, in His wisdom, has made provision for both our fallenness and our aloneness.

In Genesis 2:18, God declared that He would solve man's dilemma, and He did so by creating another human, someone with whom Adam could be intimate. God said, "I will make a helper suitable for him." Be assured that when God says, "I will," He will. The obvious and profound implication of this declaration of God is that we need each other! Adam not only needed to relate intimately with his Maker, but God created him with a need to relate intimately on a horizontal level, with other people. Therefore, God ordained three divine relationships: marriage (Genesis 2), the family (Genesis 4; Psalm 127:3), and the church (Matthew 16). God was so concerned about our separation from Him that He died on Calvary, and He was so concerned about our separation from one another that He ordained these three divine relationships.

Our lives must now reflect this same concern for the aloneness of others. Let us first reflect on our care for those nearest to us—our spouses, family members, and friends.

My Personal Journey

Married, But Still Alone

For years, my marriage to Teresa was characterized by aloneness. I left her alone by putting ministry before our marriage. Teresa left me alone by prioritizing our children. For years, we struggled to resolve these differences, but we often resorted to pointing out each other's shortcomings and fallenness. Although the church viewed us as the ideal ministry couple, we continued to silently endure the pain of being very alone.

> **Sin is what keeps us alone. God-ordained relationships remove that aloneness.**

I desperately tried to find the balance between ministry and family responsibilities. But what I really needed was to capture the heart of God, who wanted to love my spouse and family through me. As I purposed to do this, I began to see my wife in a whole-new light, as evidenced one night when Teresa and I hosted a Bible study in our home. On this particular evening, we were discussing how our concept of God is often shaped by childhood experiences. I asked everyone to share an early memory about his or her father.

When it was Teresa's turn, she told a story I had never heard before. She told about a home with six kids, and about two parents who did not seem to have enough attention to meet all their needs. To complicate matters, three of the children were hearing-impaired, requiring special attention. So as a child, my wife often craved her father's attention and was disappointed when he had so little left for her.

Teresa told about waking up one morning and realizing that her father did not have to work that day. She wandered through the house looking for her daddy. She found him outside, on top of the house, getting ready to repair the roof. She remembered going up the ladder, climbing it rung by rung until she reached the very top of the house—a very scary feat for a five-year-old. Teresa remembered feeling very scared, but she chose to look past the fear because this was her one chance to receive Daddy's attention. There was desperation in her voice as she recalled the depth of her aloneness.

As Teresa shared her touching story, something profound began to happen in me. I was suddenly aware of her deep need for a loving, attentive husband and the comfort of a compassionate God. I felt the ache of her aloneness, and it broke my heart. That night, I realized that God was as concerned about Teresa's unmet need for intimacy as He had been about her need for forgiveness. I had often prayed for Teresa's spiritual well-being and character flaws, but I had ignored her deep

> **Marriage is intended to be a relationship in which God works through you in order that your spouse might be less alone.**

aloneness. God began to radically reorder my priorities and impressed upon my heart an important purpose of marriage: marriage is intended to be a relationship in which God works through you in order that your spouse might be less alone.

Pause and Reflect

If you are married, does God want to change your perspective as it relates to your relationship with your spouse?

God may want to impress you with this truth: of the six billion people on the face of this planet, no one has been called to minister to your partner's aloneness more than you! Will you be a part of removing the aloneness of your spouse's heart?

Ask God to show you any changes that might need to be made in terms of your priorities or focus. Ask Him to show you any ways in which your spouse is alone and empower you to remove that aloneness.

In a Family, But Still Alone

If we have children, seeing them as both fallen and alone can change the nature of our relationship in significant ways. It is certainly important to teach, train, and provide correction for our children, but in order to restore relevance and intimacy to our relationships with our children, we must also see the aloneness of their hearts.

For too many years, I prided myself on the careful attention I gave to the teaching and training of our children. We assigned chores in order to teach personal responsibility and had rules about making beds and cleaning rooms before playing outside. We discussed principles for godly friendships and dating relationships. We had family Bible studies and completed service projects together in order to build a strong spiritual foundation. My wife and I even made it a special priority to encourage and challenge each of our children regarding specific character qualities, knowing that they needed to continue to grow, change, and mature in individual ways.

Yet as God began to work in my life regarding the priority of removing aloneness, the Holy Spirit began to ask, "David, you know whether or not Eric made his bed today, but do you

know the issues of his heart? You know that Robin spoke disrespectfully to her mother today, but do you know about the joys and sadness of her life? David, you are aware of Terri's need to grow in courage about her convictions, but are you aware of her thoughts, feelings, and needs?" The Lord sobered my heart with those questions, and I asked Him to give me His compassion and concern for the aloneness of my children.

Pause and Reflect

Does God want to change your perspective as it relates to your relationship with your child? Does He want to refocus your heart on removing aloneness instead of only correcting behavior? Does He want you to reprioritize your discovery of your child's feelings and needs?

God may want to impress you with this truth: of the six billion people on the face of this planet, no one has been called to minister to your child's aloneness more than you! Will you be a part of removing the aloneness of your child's heart?

Ask God to show you any changes that might need to be made in terms of your priorities or focus. Ask Him to show you any ways in which your children are alone and empower you to remove that aloneness.

Part of Christ's Church, But Still Alone

Finally, a view of people as both fallen and alone can enrich our friendships within our spiritual community. The church is one of God's special provisions for relationships, and an important means through which He removes the aloneness of His people.

As I shared in an earlier chapter, my wife and I had the privilege of serving on the staff of a large church for several years. After sustaining a series of financial blows, the church had no choice but to lay off all but one of its full-time staff members. The Ferguson family was suddenly without any means of financial support. Teresa and I prayed fervently and sensed the Lord's direction. We decided to continue to serve the church part-time, even without salaries. We were confident of God's provision on our behalf.

Our family was overwhelmed by the ways in which the Lord worked through His people to provide for us. I can recall the day that our friend Gary showed up at our home, bringing barbecue from the restaurant he owned. Gary simply knew of our need and wanted us to know that we were not alone. I remember the creative ways that God involved Christian physicians, condominium managers, and countless friends who gave of their time, finances, and resources to help support our family.

The Lord used this time to provide our family with mighty reminders of His faithfulness. He also began to confirm His work in me. I came to realize that, too often, I had only seen the church body as a group of people who needed conviction and redirection. The congregation that I had wanted to correct through my sermons was the very same congregation that lovingly, unselfishly met our needs. I was grieved by my own view of my friends and fellow Christians. As a church leader, I had offered counsel, advice, sermons and, at times, even condemnation. What I came to realize was that, just as our family had been blessed by the gestures of love that removed our aloneness, I, too, needed to share my life with others. My friends needed my time, not just my advice. My fellow church members needed me to prioritize getting to know them, rather than be preoccupied with training them. The gratefulness I experienced as God involved others to remove my aloneness was used by the Holy Spirit to birth in me a desire to remove the aloneness of others. Because the caring and compassionate members of the body of Christ removed our aloneness, our family remembers those days with joy and gratitude rather than heartache and sadness.

Pause and Reflect

Does God want to change your perspective as it relates to your relationship with your friends, fellow church members, or even non-Christians? Does He want to refocus your heart on removing aloneness instead of only correcting behavior? Does He want you to reprioritize your discovery of your friends' feelings and needs? Will you be a part of removing the aloneness of your friends' hearts?

Ask God to show you any changes that might need to be made in terms of your priorities or focus. Ask Him to show you any ways in which your friends or church members are alone and empower you to remove that aloneness.

God knew that **things** could not remove our aloneness or satisfy our need for intimacy. The aloneness that God spoke of in Genesis 2:18 as being "not good" was intended to be removed through loving, deliberate, intentional giving from within marriages, families, and the body of Christ. As church leaders who are committed to restoring relational relevance to the church, we must lead our congregations toward the priority of relational ministry. Since God's plan was for the church to be one of the primary provisions for removing aloneness, we must give His plan priority in the church's calendar, ministry planning, and overall mission. The church must become a place that removes aloneness!

> **The church must become a place that removes aloneness.**

In addition to encouraging an intimate love relationship with God, relevant ministry encourages God-ordained love relationships among people, beginning with spouse and children and extending to the whole world. Therefore, equipping individuals to develop and maintain loving relationships should be a fundamental priority in ministry. When the relational needs of spouse and children are being met in the family, the church's overall health and relevance in the community are greatly improved. When friendships are marked by vibrancy, vulnerability, and mutual care, our lives serve as living epistles that clearly declare God's grace and love.

A key goal for marriage, family, youth, children, and singles ministries should be to equip individuals to meet relational needs and foster growing intimacy, thus removing aloneness. Ongoing ministry by trained lay leaders and mentors should be the rule, with one-time events supplementing this commitment to equip the saints for this important work of ministry.

How does a church begin to cultivate this heart of compassion for people? How do we begin to change our perspective and develop Christ's heart of love?

LEARNING TO LOOK FOR ALONENESS

"Jesus heard that they had thrown him out, and when he found him . . ." (John 9:35).

If we were to look again at the story of the man born blind, we would see Christ's ministry to the man continue as He stopped and noticed all that the man had experienced. Scripture tells us that Jesus not only healed the man, but upon hearing about the Pharisees' treatment of him, went to find him. Having just been criticized by the religious leaders, abandoned by his family, and thrown out of the synagogue, the blind man most certainly experienced a measure of aloneness. But the compassionate heart of Christ recognized the man's hurt and responded with love.

As we learn to look for the aloneness of others, we must follow Christ's example. We must stop, look, and listen for aloneness in our spouse, children, fellow believers, and those who do not yet know the Savior.

Stop and Notice People. (See Mark 5:25–34—Jesus stopped when He was touched.)

The people who are closest to you—roommates, family members, spouses, work associates, fellow Bible study participants—may feel very alone. Stop and take time for their feelings, needs, and issues of the heart. Caring effectively for others requires learning to give close attention. That is difficult to do if you are too busy with activities, tasks, or even "religious things."

Noticing Aloneness at Home

Teresa and I came home from one of our many ministry trips some years ago. Suitcases in hand, we walked through the living room where our teenage son was sprawled on the floor. We were weary from the trip but had enough awareness to wonder why our very active son was home alone on a Friday night. "Hi, Eric. Good to see you! What's going on tonight?" He used the remote control to flip through the channels as he gave the very solemn reply, "Oh, not too much."

Too often, my wife and I might have simply continued to the bedroom, unpacked our suitcases, and privately reflected on the blessings of our trip. On this night, however, the Lord graciously helped us stop and notice our son's aloneness.

We set down the suitcases and began to talk with Eric. "It sounds like you might be feeling kind of down. We would like to hear about it." Our son began to tell us about a difficult argument with his girlfriend. We were able to care for him, share words of comfort, and leave him feeling less alone. Some of the spark had returned to his eyes before we left the room. He was still saddened over the conflict, but that night Eric was able to say, "I know I'm not alone."

Noticing Aloneness in the Church

Pastor Dale serves as the Senior Pastor at Faith Community Church. His commitment to notice the struggles of his congregation, coupled with his dedication to creating worship experiences that foster intimate encounters with God, have produced a thriving ministry within their community.

During one particular worship gathering, Pastor Dale shared how God was challenging him to "stop and notice" the aloneness in the lives of others. The service began with choruses of praise. Then, as the instruments played softly in the background, Dale said, "Sometimes, even as faithful believers, we are robbed of intimacy with God by self-condemnation. Perhaps you are struggling with that hindrance right now. I know that many of you struggle to see yourselves as God sees you. I know this because of the precious conversations I have had with many of you, the times of prayer that we have shared, and the countless needs that have come to our staff's attention. Perhaps you are struggling with self-condemnation right now. Maybe something happened this week that left you feeling spiritually defeated or worthless. You stand here today under a dark cloud. You feel that God is not interested in your worship because you are just not good enough. You may even have a specific weakness or failure in mind. Is there a particular issue on your heart?"

Pastor Dale waited as the congregation pondered his question silently. Then he said, "At times, we all feel a little like the apostle Paul. He laments in Romans 7:15 that he found himself doing the things he hated to do instead of the things he wanted to do. Even during a time of worship we may find ourselves thinking, 'What a worthless person I am!' Bondage like this blocks our worship, and the Father longs for us to enjoy freedom. But how can that happen?"

> **Worship leaders who stop to notice the aloneness of their people bring relevance back to worship.**

Pastor Dale continued, "Consider with me a liberating truth, and see if it does not set your heart free to gratefully praise God. You may be disappointed by your inconsistencies and failures, but are these lapses a surprise to God? Did He not know about your criticism, impatience, anger, or unforgiveness long before He chose to birth you into His spiritual family? Did He not see all your sins of omission and commission—past, present, and future? Yet He chose to make you His child. Think back to the time when you were born again. Then consider that, at that moment, God knew about all of your weaknesses and sins, yet, by His grace, He extended His life and love to you in spite of them!

"Let your hearts be delivered from condemnation and freed to worship God with deep gratitude. Let this truth bring a smile to your face as you rejoice with the apostle, who exclaimed, 'Thanks be to God—through Jesus Christ our Lord! . . . Therefore, there is now no condemnation for those who are in Christ Jesus, because through Christ Jesus the law of the Spirit of life set me free from the law of sin and death' (Romans 7:25; 8:1, 2). Let us sing our heartfelt praise together."

This kind of corporate worship allows people to find healing for their souls and removes the aloneness of their hearts. Worship leaders who stop to notice the aloneness of their people bring relevance back to worship and encourage an intimate relationship with the One who is the "Ultimate Healer" of our aloneness.

Look for Signs of Aloneness. (See John 5:5, 6—Christ looked at the man beside the pool.)

Notice the symptoms or manifestations of aloneness in their context. People face losses, trauma, broken relationships, or failures, but often face them alone. When pain is faced alone, it may be manifested in symptoms such as withdrawal, anger, control, manipulation, procrastination, or even physical disorders. We must look for the pain of aloneness that may be made evident through such symptoms.

Seeing Signs of Aloneness at Home

A fourth-grade boy named Billy was having some behavioral problems at school. His mom and teacher were quite puzzled because Billy had never been in trouble before. But, suddenly, Billy had begun talking out in class, passing notes, and ignoring the classroom rules. As a consequence, Billy had to stay after school with his teacher.

Billy's mother took him to a counselor in order to sort out this change in behavior. After getting to know Billy and establishing important rapport, the counselor asked him, "When have you recently felt most loved and cared for?" Billy's immediate response was, "When my teacher spends time with me after school, she talks with me! And best of all, she's not getting paid for it!"

The counselor soon discovered the important events that led up to the change in Billy. His father had begun to travel a great deal, and his mom had taken on the responsibility of caring for an aging parent, which often kept her away from home. Billy was feeling alone, and the symptom of his aloneness was his inappropriate behavior in school. Billy needed the adults in his life to stop, look for the signs of his aloneness, and take loving action to remove it.

Seeing Signs of Aloneness through Ministry

The youth and children's ministry of Mount Zion Church is committed to training parents to look for the signs of aloneness in their children. Church leaders do not just encourage good parenting, but **show** parents how to become godly parents for their kids. Part of that training involves challenging parents to look beyond their children's deeds and see the aloneness of their hearts.

Miriam is one of the parents of Mount Zion Church. She has been burdened about her relationship with her 12-year-old son, Joshua. Their conflicts seem to be increasing, and Miriam needs the support of other parents as she looks ahead to the challenges of the teenage years. Miriam shared this account of a recent conflict with Joshua:

"It was a few minutes after six o'clock, and I walked outside to call Joshua for dinner. He had been playing basketball with his friends, but it was time to eat. I called his name several times with no response and finally walked over to the neighbor's yard and insisted that he come home. Instead of complying, Joshua threw a huge temper tantrum. When I finally got him inside, I was so upset that I said some really inappropriate things, which only fueled his anger.

I was furious at that point and demanded that Josh go to his room without dinner. I spent the rest of the evening feeling guilty for my outburst and uncertain how to deal with my son."

Mount Zion has been a place of refuge and hope for Miriam. The youth leaders provide regular classes where parents like Miriam are trained to offer comfort and reassurance to disappointed, fearful, and sometimes-angry children like

> **We must go beyond simply instructing, exhorting, and encouraging parents in church and expecting them to go home and parent effectively. We must provide on-the-job training in the art of looking for the aloneness of others.**

Joshua. One part of the training focused on challenging parents to live out Proverbs 15:1: "A gentle answer turns away wrath." These classes have equipped Miriam with the skills to address Joshua's behavior, help him resolve his anger, and look deeper to the aloneness of his heart. After the parent training, the scene with Miriam and Joshua looks more like this:

Miriam calls to her son from the front porch. Joshua comes over from play, out of breath. "What do you want, Mom?"

"Look at your watch," she says, pointing to his wrist. "It's almost six o'clock. The other night we agreed that playtime is from four until six, and that at six o'clock we begin family time around the dinner table. It will be time to eat in 15 minutes."

"Mom, not now! I'm about to beat my all-time record in free throws!" Joshua laments in an angry tone. "I don't want to come in."

Miriam leans down a little closer to her son. "I know you feel disappointed when you have to stop playing, and I'm sorry that you're sad." Miriam gently puts her hand on Joshua's shoulder. "You can play for the next 15 minutes, and then basketball is over for tonight. You'll be able to play more tomorrow. Family time is important to me, and I think it is important to you. So let me see those free throws for a few more minutes, and then we will go have dinner together."

This gentle, anger-dissipating response is in sharp contrast to Miriam's previous interactions with her son. The ministry leaders of Mount Zion continue to teach Miriam and the other parents how to establish healthy boundaries of discipline and how to minister comfort to disappointed children. Mount Zion has gone beyond simply instructing, exhorting, and encouraging parents in church and expecting them to go home and parent effectively. They have provided on-the-job training in the art of looking for the aloneness of others.

Listen for the pain of aloneness. (See John 4:7–26—Christ listened for aloneness in the woman at the well.)

We must learn to listen for pain beneath the surface. Sometimes, aloneness is revealed in unlikely places. The man who talks incessantly may really be saying, "Please listen and care." The woman who is quick to offer spiritual platitudes may really be disguising a lonely, disconnected heart underneath. At times, aloneness is revealed in the cries, "I don't think I can go on," or "I just don't know what to do."

Listening for Pain One Person at a Time

Andy was a man who had become known for his violent temper and destructive, raging outbursts. I came to know Andy when his pastor brought him to my office. Having been briefed ahead of time about his anger and the problems it had caused in his marriage, I spoke with Andy compassionately but directly. I said, "Andy, I just want you to know that I believe underneath all your anger is a great deal of pain." Andy's countenance softened, and I continued: "As a matter of fact, Andy, I suspect that underneath your anger is a great deal of pain that you have been dealing with alone." Andy's eyes filled with tears, confirming my assumption. Later, Andy would share with his pastor, and then with me, his tragic story. As a nine-year-old boy, Andy took a shortcut through a park one night as he was hurrying home from playing baseball with his friends, and was attacked and sexually abused by several men. When he finally returned home, Andy was punished for being late. He never said a word about the painful, humiliating ordeal he had experienced. Andy had carried this unhealed pain for decades. His anger was actually a symptom of the great depth of aloneness that he had experienced.

As you relate to others at home, at work, or even during this course, make certain that you stop and listen carefully to the needs of the moment (Ephesians 4:29). Look for the pain of aloneness that may be hidden beneath sinful, unproductive behavior. Become a living expression of Christ's love by ministering to aloneness in the lives of people around you, trusting God for His timing and guidance in addressing any fallenness.

Listening for Pain—A Ministry Focus

There is a new church being planted in Florida, and its name says it all. It is called "Church Under the Bridge." This unusual gathering of believers in the city of Miami has a special burden for the homeless men, women, and children in their city. Every Sunday morning, the leaders of this church dress in casual clothing and hold worship services under a bridge in downtown Miami. As the worship leaders and musicians sing and play, countless faces begin to appear from makeshift shelters. The worship leaders are careful to sing choruses that are familiar to most, so that the "congregation" feels a part. Next, church leaders distribute blankets and serve hot coffee and muffins. There are plenty of handshakes and hugs as they model Christ's acceptance and demonstrate His love. Conversations precede sermons in the order of worship because leaders want to get to know these men and women before they discuss spiritual topics. They listen for the pain of abandonment, desperation, or rejection and then demonstrate care. Next, a brief message of hope is shared while the congregation is introduced to a Christ who feels compassion for forgotten people. Finally, church leaders discuss potential job leads with their friends and pass along housing opportunities that have developed within the community. Church leaders and members leave every service of the Church Under the Bridge with a renewed perspective on the God who cares about both fallenness and aloneness.

As your gratefulness abounds at the compassionate heart of Christ, and as you become His co-laborer in removing the aloneness of others, you will need to be able to discern the aloneness in the hearts of those around you. Take a moment now, and read the following experience that I have shared. As you read, imagine that I am actually sitting with you, sharing my story. Ask yourself these questions as you learn to look for aloneness even now: What words might indicate feelings of aloneness? What about this experience might have been difficult or painful? What words of care or compassion might you share?

My Personal Journey

When I was growing up, I had a black cocker spaniel named Inky. Inky's custom was to greet me at the door when I came home from school. I remember coming home one particular day and being puzzled when Inky was not there to greet me. I wondered where he was and felt worried that something had happened to him. I searched each room of the house and called his name in the backyard. Then I remembered that Inky sometimes liked to hide in the crawl space under our house. This hiding place offered comfort and shade from the hot, Texas sun.

That's where I found Inky—under the house with a broken leg. Inky had a habit of digging under the fence and chasing cars in the street. He had apparently been hit by a car, and his left front leg was in tremendous pain. Not knowing what else to do, I crawled under the house with Inky. As I held my dog and tried to console him, I remember feeling completely alone. I knew it would be a couple of hours before anyone else would be home, since both my parents worked. So I just waited by myself under the floor of the house. I remember feeling scared for Inky but also very helpless and alone.

Stop and consider what I have just shared. Did you look for any underlying sadness or pain that I might have felt? Did you listen for the words that reflected my aloneness? What words of care or compassion can you imagine sharing with me?

Complete your own story, prayerfully reflecting upon a time when you were alone.

I remember feeling very alone when _____

_____

_____.

(For example: _I remember feeling very alone when I was not picked for any of the sports teams_, or _I remember feeling very alone when my father died last year. I received the call late at night, and my spouse was out of town at the time_, or _I remember feeling very alone when I graduated from college and neither of my parents attended the ceremony_.)

An Experience With God's People

"Mourn with those who mourn" (Romans 12:15).

In order to be equipped and competent to remove another's aloneness, it is important to have received care for your own experience of aloneness. This exercise will help you focus on the reality of aloneness. It will give you an opportunity to remove a degree of aloneness from one another.

One of the most powerful ways to remove the aloneness of others is to offer words of comfort for their pain. Scripture calls this "mourning with those who mourn." It requires that you reflect upon the aloneness or pain of another person and then minister comfort. Mourning with another requires giving an emotional response. It does not involve words of advice or encouragement (although those may be needed later), nor should it include spiritual pep talks or logical explanations. Mourning with another person means you simply hurt with them, conveying your care and compassion, and sharing what you feel as you reflect upon their pain. (See the Emotional Responding section of the Appendix for further explanation of these principles.)

Take turns sharing your experiences and recollections of aloneness with your partner or small group. As you listen to others share, **stop** and give them your full attention; **look** for the underlying sadness, pain, or loneliness each might have felt; and **listen** for the words that reflect aloneness—even if the story is decades old.

Ask yourself these questions as you reflect upon each story of aloneness:

- What painful emotions did this person possibly experience?

- What does it do to your heart to know that this person experienced such pain?

After you have considered your responses to the questions above, share your feelings with the person who shared. Be sure to offer words of comfort, mourning with each person as they share their experience of aloneness. Your response might be, "Thank you for sharing your story. I'm so saddened by your experience of aloneness," or "Thank you for being vulnerable with me. I'm sorry for the aloneness you felt."

After each person has given and received comfort for their pain and aloneness, pause and give thanks to God for His compassion expressed through other people. Thank Him for being the God of all comfort (2 Corinthians 1:3, 4) and for the blessing that comes when His love is demonstrated through His people.

Churches that are able to effectively remove the aloneness of others are well-equipped in the ministry of mourning and comfort. They will give priority to creating a setting in which people are free to share their inevitable experiences of aloneness, and equipping God's people with the skills to remove that aloneness. As we present an environment in which people are free to be genuine and vulnerable, others will be drawn to Christ by our love (John 13:34, 35). As a church leader who is committed to restoring relational relevance, you will want to lead your congregation in this ministry of mourning and comfort.

Christ's ministry was characterized by first meeting the relational needs of others and then, through His relational connections with people, addressing the sins that kept them alone and disconnected. In our efforts to become relationally relevant, we, too, must learn to minister out of love and compassion, seeing others as first alone and then fallen. This relational foundation is critical to relevance in life and ministry.

For Further Study

EMPOWERING COMPASSION

We have said that God declared Adam's aloneness "not good." But how does God know that being alone is not good? Was this declaration simply based on His intrinsic omniscience, or did God make His pronouncement from an experiential knowledge, having personally tasted the "not good-ness" of being alone?

Some people struggle with the idea that God could personally experience being alone. They might suggest that the triune God has never been alone in all of eternity. After all, Scripture tells us that at Creation, God said, "Let **us** make man in **our** image, in **our** likeness" (Genesis 1:26). The one true God is the perfect unity of Father, Son, and Holy Spirit.

But while this notion of a perfectly unified relationship is absolutely true, we must realize that God is not confined to time and history as we experience it. When He declared in the Garden, "It is not good for the man to be alone" (Genesis 2:18), had He not already experienced the crisis of Calvary? Is Jesus not "the Lamb that was slain from the creation of the world" (Revelation 13:8)? In His eternal existence, had the Father not already heard His Son cry out in agony, "My God, my God, why have you forsaken me" (Matthew 27:46)? Had the Father not already experienced the heart-piercing pain of being separated from His only Son as the One who had never known sin was delivered over to death for our sins (Romans 4:25)?

As I reflected years ago on the truth of Genesis 2:18, I came to believe that He had. This is how God could say to Adam with authority that aloneness is not good. God knew from experience what it meant to be alone. From eternity past, the Father knew the pain and emptiness of being separated from His Son. This may be part of the reason that He compassionately calls you and me to join Him in removing others' aloneness.

As one who hopes to restore the heart of Christ's compassion and relational relevance to the church, will you now pause and reflect on Christ's experience of aloneness? Take the next few moments, and ask God to move your heart with compassion for Jesus. Ask Him to allow you to share in the fellowship of Christ's sufferings. As you are able to share in the sufferings of Christ, you will come to more intimately know Him and will be empowered to convey His compassion to others.

An Experience With God's Son

"I want to know Christ . . . the power of His resurrection and the fellowship of sharing in His sufferings" (Philippians 3:10).

Before you begin this meditation, pause and pray this simple prayer:

Heavenly Father, I desire to know You and Your Son more intimately. I ask You to lead me into a deeper fellowship with Your sufferings. I want to experience Your heart as it is expressed in Your Word in order to better share Christ's love with my loved ones, church members, neighbors, coworkers, and others. I pray this in Jesus' name. Amen.

Jesus Christ was fully man as well as fully God. He had the same needs we have: air, food, water, sleep, as well as comfort, encouragement, and support. He even hurt the way we hurt, yet was without sin.

Imagine Jesus in the upper room, only hours before the atrocities of the trial, the merciless beatings, and the Crucifixion. Cloistered with the 12 men into whom He had poured His life, He breaks bread and says, "Take and eat; this is my body" (Matthew 26:26). Then He lifts the cup and says, "Drink from it, all of you. This is my blood" (vv. 27, 28). Consider His vulnerability, His openness in speaking of His death. He has never before shared with such shocking clarity.

But how do the disciples respond to Jesus' openness and transparency? "A dispute arose among them as to which of them was considered to be greatest" (Luke 22:24). Did such rejection hurt the Savior? He agonizes that His body will soon be broken and His blood shed, while the men he counted as friends argue over their own status. Can you hurt with Him at such insensitivity? Can you find fellowship with His suffering?

After Judas leaves to betray Him, Christ speaks to the remaining 11. He continues to minister out of selfless concern for His friends: "Do not let your hearts be troubled. Trust in God; trust also in me" (John 14:1). Jesus lovingly speaks of preparing a place for His disciples and returning to take them home. It is this unwavering concern for the disciples, even to the very end, that makes their insensitivity and selfishness so painfully cruel. He concludes, "I am the way and the truth and the life. No one comes to the Father except through me" (v. 6).

Philip's response must have slashed through the Savior's heart: "Lord, show us the Father and that will be enough for us" (v. 8).

After more than three years of day-to-day contact with God in human flesh, Philip only wants to see the Father. What rejection! Can you hear the pain in Jesus' reply? "Don't you know me, Philip, even after I have been among you such a long time" (v. 9)?

Next, prayerfully picture Christ at Calvary. He hangs before you on the Cross. He has been tormented, mocked, and beaten. He has taken upon Himself the sins of the world. Suddenly, He cries out: "My God, my God, why have you forsaken me" (Mark 15:34)?

Something happened at Calvary that day that had never happened in all of eternity (nor will it happen again): God experienced aloneness! The Son "became sin" and was separated from His Father (2 Corinthians 5:21). Because of His holiness, God the Father was forced to turn away from His Son. Therefore, on the Cross of Calvary, Christ was utterly and completely alone.

Allow yourself to experience sorrow for the pain that Jesus suffered as His Father turned away. Imagine the Father's sorrow as He averted His eyes from His Son because He could not look upon sin. The powerful impact of these verses may bring tears to your eyes. Imagine the Savior speaking these words from the Cross: "Have I been with you this long and you do not really know Me?" Is your heart stirred to sadness for a hurting Savior? Is your heart moved with compassion for the Son of God as He experiences rejection from both man and His Father—rejection accompanied by immeasurable aloneness?

Tell Christ about your feelings for Him. Tell Jesus what it does to your heart to know Him and sense the pain He must have endured.

Jesus, I am saddened as I reflect on . . .

It hurts my heart to imagine You _____
because I love You!

(For example: *It hurts my heart to imagine You completely alone. I have known the pain of loneliness after the joy of intimacy, but it cannot compare to what You endured. I am saddened by Your suffering because I love You!*)

Close with a prayer of gratitude and empowerment:

Heavenly Father, please remind me often of the pain that You endured. I am so grateful that You loved me enough to face the heartache of this world. Please empower me to share the love that I feel for You because You have first loved me.

It is love for Christ, not rules and commands, that motivates a heart of relevant, compassionate love. Having experienced a measure of fellowship with Christ's rejection and aloneness, may we be more compassionate toward others who are forsaken, rejected, ignored, and alone. Having been moved with compassion for this One who never knew sin, may our hearts be more tender toward those who are alone because of the consequences of sin.

As you enter into the fellowship of Christ's sorrow, something else may begin to happen. You may begin to experience a deeper sense of repentance. Having more intimately shared in the pain of His rejection and betrayal, you will not want to add to Christ's grief with your continued sin. His love will constrain you to walk uprightly with Him. When you have felt a measure of what He has suffered, you will begin to love Him too much to add to His pain. Walking intimately with Him will motivate you to righteous living and compassionate caring.

For Further Study

GOD'S ORIGINAL DESIGN: LOST BUT RESTORED

We know that God's original plan for His relationship with Adam (and, ultimately, with you and me) was disrupted in the Garden of Eden. When Adam and Eve chose to sin, thus breaking the bonds of unity and intimacy with their Creator, shame, fear, and aloneness entered their lives. But what was God's original desire for His relationship with mankind? Both Old and New Testament Scriptures reveal that His original intent was that, in humble dependence and expectant faith, humankind would dwell in grateful communion with God. Let's go back to the Garden of Eden, before man's sin, in order to get a glimpse of this intimacy that God originally intended.

God's Original Design

Humble Dependence

In the Garden, Adam was totally dependent upon his Creator. He must have quickly recognized his needs for such things as water, food, and sleep, and he was deeply aware of the ways in which God abundantly met these needs. Never once did Adam experience a need for something and find no supply. God confirmed man's posture of humble dependence when He declared, "It is not good for the man to be alone." The Creator revealed man's need for companionship and abundantly met that need. As Jehovah Jireh (the God who provides), our Creator provided Adam with a helpmate—the one designed and destined to join the Creator in removing Adam's aloneness. Therefore, the original inclination of Adam's heart was to humbly look to God for His provision.

God's unchanging nature is to reveal man's needs and then abundantly meet those needs. God now confirms this original facet of His intimate relationship with man through the revelation of His Word. The New Testament reveals that God resists the proud but gives grace to the humble (James 4:6). This **humility** of heart in response to God's gracious provision was one crucial part of the Creator's original intent for His relationship with man.

Expectant Faith

Next, imagine talking with Adam immediately after God declared his aloneness. The conversation might have gone something like this:

"Adam, how are you doing?"
"Not good."
"What's wrong?"
"I'm alone."
"But Adam, what does that mean?"
"I don't really know, but it's not good."
"How do you know it's not good?"
"Because God said so."

Adam's heart was originally inclined to trust God and exercise expectant faith because of his confidence in God's Word. Adam was able to trust God since everything God said was certain to occur. Everything the Creator promised came to pass. When God said, "I give you every seed-bearing plant on the face of the whole earth and every tree that has fruit with seed in it. They will be yours for food," Adam promptly received God's provision (Genesis 1:29). When God declared Adam's dominion over the birds of the air and the beasts of the field, it was so (1:26, 28; 2:19, 20). When God showed Adam all the animals and there was not a suitable helper among them, Adam, by faith, received God's provision. Adam could exercise faith since the faithful Creator had promised to provide a helpmate for him. Just as Adam exercised faith because of his certainty in the word of his Creator, we, too, must learn to demonstrate this same trust in God and His Word. If we are to be a part of God's original design for His relationship with man, we must exercise faith that comes from hearing God's Word (Romans 10:17) and boldly trust in His provision. In so doing, we can be confident of an intimate relationship with our Creator. Thus, another element of God's original design was for us to please Him with the demonstration of our **faith**, for "without faith, it is impossible to please God" (Hebrews 11:6).

Abundant Gratitude

Finally, after God set Adam and Eve in the Garden of Eden, He personally blessed them (Genesis 1:28), gave them authority and dominion over all that they could see (vv. 28, 29), and pronounced the whole scene "very good" (v. 31). God provided for their every need with extravagant abundance and bestowed great trust upon Adam and Eve by giving them authority over this garden of delight. It is not hard to imagine the gratefulness that must have overwhelmed Adam and Eve as they experienced the abundance of God's provision. Their hearts must have been filled with gladness before the Tempter introduced insecurity and doubt. The Creator's plan was to abundantly supply every need of His people, and as they offered thanksgiving for their provision, the path would be paved for a relationship with Him. This **gratitude** in response to God's lavish gifts and undeserved grace was the third element of God's original design for His relationship with His creation, and it is this grateful love that can come to constrain our lives and ministries as it did the apostle Paul's (2 Corinthians 5:14 KJV).

Man's Fall From Grace

God planned to provide abundantly for Adam's needs and entrust him with the care of His work. In turn, Adam was to relate to God with humility, faith, and gratitude. We know this plan was altered after the sin of Genesis 3, but what specific changes occurred? We know that God stayed the same, so what changed within the heart of man?

As a result of the Fall, all descendants of Adam now enter the world with a corrupt nature. Inclinations and passions that were once directed toward God are now directed away from and even against Him. Thoughts that were once pure and God-focused are now wicked and unsettled. Willful obedience has given way to blatant rebellion. All mankind is now by nature dead in transgressions and sins, and our only hope lies within the redemption that is offered through the last Adam who will become our "life-giving spirit" (1 Corinthians 15:45).

As we study the Fall of Adam and Eve in Genesis 3, we gain insight into the strategies of Satan and the tendencies of our own corrupt nature. Sinful behavior can be traced back to its roots in three expressions of the Fall: self-reliance, selfishness, and self-condemnation.

The Pain of Self-Reliance

After the Fall, rather than exhibit a humble dependence upon God and His provision, man became prone to prideful self-reliance. Instead of approaching God with humility, many of us now may deny our needs or even claim to be able to meet all our needs on our own. Just as Christ was tempted by Satan to meet His own needs in the desert (Matthew 4:1–4), many of us are tempted to rely upon our own strength, abilities, or determination as we try to meet the God-designed needs of the human body, soul, and spirit.

The Pain of Selfishness

Second the Fall resulted in man's tendency toward selfishness and "fearful taking." Rather than exercising faith in God to meet our needs, man is now tempted to selfishly take from others. Instead of trusting God to abundantly provide, many of us now demand, manipulate, or self-gratify because of a fear that our needs will go unmet, rather than receiving God's grace by faith. We may even seek to take from God, demanding His blessings based on our own "good works." Just as Christ was tempted by Satan to take from God and demand His protection in the desert (vv. 5–7), many of us are tempted to selfishly take from God and other people. For some of us, our fallenness is most often expressed in behaviors that gratify ourselves.

The Pain of Self-Condemnation

Finally, the Fall rendered man vulnerable to self-condemnation. Instead of expressing thanksgiving and gratitude for the gracious provision of God and acknowledging God's inherent declaration of our worth (worth the gift of His Son), man is now prone to question his worth and live in doubt about the validity of his needs. This tendency may leave us vulnerable to feelings of discontentment, a sense of unworthiness, or the loss of our joy and hope. Just as Christ was tempted by Satan to surrender His true identity in the desert (vv. 8–10), many of us are tempted to question our own identity as the beloved of God. Rather than expressing thankfulness for God's provision, we are often tempted to question our worth and deny our inherent value as declared by God.

Pause and Reflect

As you reflect on each of these results of the Fall of man, ask yourself the following question:

To which of these three tendencies am I most prone? Selfishness? Self-reliance? Self-condemnation?

I have a tendency to be _____(selfish, self-reliant, or self-condemning).
This tendency may result in . . .

Pause now, and pray for God to remove this tendency from you. You may wish to pray with your partner or small group. Ask for His sanctifying work regarding this area of fallenness. Ask that the Spirit might bring forth humility, causing self-reliance to give way to total dependence. Ask that the Spirit might bring forth faith, causing selfishness to give way to confident trust. Ask that the Spirit might bring forth praise-filled gratitude, causing self-condemnation to give way to the wonder of God's love.

Additional Resources

David G. Benner, *Sacred Companions: The Gift of Spiritual Friendship and Direction* (Downers Grove, IL: InterVarsity Press, 2002).

Larry Crabb, *Connecting: Healing for Ourselves and Our Relationships* (Nashville, TN: Word Publishing, 1997).

David Ferguson, *Never Alone* (Wheaton, IL: Tyndale House Publishers, Inc., 2001).

Josh McDowell, *See Yourself as God Sees You* (Wheaton, IL: Tyndale House Publishers, Inc., 1999).

Chapter 6

Rediscovering Church: Our Foundation of Ecclesiology

More than a decade ago, God began to shake my understanding of the church. He did so during a conference on racial reconciliation in the southern United States. I had just concluded the opening session at the conference and had explained that all members of Christ's church share a common faith and have received the same mandate to go forth and make disciples. But before the next session, God's Spirit intervened to teach me something else about the church. God orchestrated certain events that enabled us to experience His words to the church at Ephesus: we were "being built together to become a dwelling in which God lives by his Spirit" (Ephesians 2:22).

Prior to this time, I viewed the church as a group of individuals who had received the same grace, the same forgiveness, the same Spirit that I had received. From my perspective, the church was made up of those people who had received the gift of salvation; we were all individual recipients of divine grace. It was also my understanding that we had each received particular gifts from the Holy Spirit. Yet with all of this biblically accurate knowledge, I had no experience of what Paul meant when he said that "there are many parts, but one body" (1 Corinthians 12:20). While I was attending this particular conference in Mississippi, God began to change all of that.

Jonathan, an elder statesman among the African-American ministry leaders at the conference that week, stood unannounced to address the group. "I have a sense from the Lord that He wants to take us deeper into reconciliation than we thought. And for Him to do so, we must truly know one another's souls." Jonathan then began to share the story of his own childhood— a childhood marked by poverty, abandonment, and abuse.

Jonathan grew up as one of the few African-American children in a predominantly white neighborhood. He initially spoke of his childhood years with great fondness. His three best friends had no prejudices; they saw no racial differences among them. The four boys just played together, learned together, and had fun together. Some of his best memories were of their morning carpool to school. One boy's parents had a big van and would take them to school each morning with lunchboxes, backpacks, and plenty of banter in tow. Jonathan recalled the jokes and laughter that were shared; he smiled as he recounted the sweet memories of fun-loving boys. But Jonathan's countenance changed as he relayed a final memory:

> All of that changed on the first day of fifth grade. I went to the same street corner where my friends and I had waited each morning for five years. I waited with anticipation for my buddies to meet me. I waited for our ride to school, but my friends never came. I stood there wondering, "Did my mother send me to school a day early? Did I misread the time? Have all my friends overslept?" Realizing that I would soon be late, I ran the 20 blocks to school that morning. Upon arriving late to class, I found my three friends. They reluctantly shared the reason for leaving me behind. They awkwardly explained why the carpool had gone on without me: my friends' parents had decided that since we were now in the fifth grade, they should make friends with "their own kind."

> **We are not just separate persons embracing a common faith; we are all members of one body, connected by one Spirit and saved by one Lord. If relevance is to be restored to the 21st century church, we must acknowledge and live out this connection to one another through Jesus Christ.**

As Pastor Jonathan recounted his story, tears began to fill his eyes. The memory of the rejection and betrayal was clearly etched in his mind and heart. As I heard his words and reflected on the pain he felt, I fell to my knees and began to weep, heartbroken for a man that I had met only the day before. How was that possible? How could I be feeling such compassion for a man I barely knew? The Spirit of God said to my heart, "David, when one part of the body suffers, the head, Jesus Christ suffers. When this dear child of God experienced hurt and rejection, the God of all comfort was touched deeply with compassion. And the same Jesus that hurts for Jonathan is in you. My Spirit is in you, and it is in Jonathan. David, I have just broken your heart for this man because you are both members of one body."

What God began to birth in me that day was a renewed vision for His church. We must see the church as more than individual recipients of divine grace and the Holy Spirit's gifts. We are not just separate persons embracing a common faith while trying to negotiate our differences and reconcile our misunderstandings. We are all members of one body, connected by one Spirit, and saved by one Lord. If relevance is to be restored to the 21st century church, we must acknowledge and live out this connection to one another through Jesus Christ.

THE MYSTERY OF CONNECTION

One body, made up of many parts, which are connected to one another and connected by the Spirit to one Lord: could this be a fresh vision for what the church ought to look like? If we could see into the spirit world, we would see Christ, the head of the church, connected to every member of His body. We would then notice that the Holy Spirit of God connects Himself to one follower of Christ, and then to another and another.

We might refer to this mysterious image of the church as the "Holy Ghost Octopus." While this name might seem unspiritual at first, it is helpful in visualizing the relationships of the church. Imagine Christ as the head of the octopus. The Spirit descends from heaven and attaches Himself to every believer, thus creating hundreds of millions of "tentacles." In this way, each member of the body is attached both to the head and to each other (see 1 Corinthians 12:12–20). Join us now as we look at several blessings that await those who come to truly experience this connection with Christ and one another.

Since We Are Connected to Christ, We Will Be Moved to Demonstrate His Heart for Others.

As we come to sense our connection with the Head, Jesus Christ, we will often be moved with the same feelings that He has and prompted by the same heart that is in Him. We will sense that His heart is broken when those He loves experience rejection, abandonment, and loneliness. In response, we will be moved with the same brokenness and will want to demonstrate the same compassion. This renewed vision of the church gives fresh meaning to Paul's words in 1 Corinthians 12:26: "If one part suffers, every part suffers with it."

Consider my encounter with Pastor Jonathan. Jonathan was filled with sorrow that day, but because he was attached by the Spirit to the Head, Jesus was moved with compassion. God then ministered comfort to him, and His Spirit began to engage other parts of the body. When I wept with Pastor Jonathan, my heart was being "pulled on" from heaven. The Holy Spirit was attached to my spirit, moving me with Christ's heart of compassion.

> **This mystery of our union with Christ and with all believers in Christ must pervade our churches today.**

Every time one part of the body of Christ suffers, the Holy Spirit wants to move in our hearts so that we will be saddened and moved to compassion by the fact that another part of the body is hurting. In our own homes, lectures, advice, pep talks, and empty prayers will be replaced by true comfort from above. In our churches, we will find less judgment, comparison, and criticism, and more compassion. As we live out this connection with Christ, we will extend His loving care to a pain-filled world.

Similarly, because we are connected to Christ, we will also sense His heart of joy when one part of the body is honored, and our response will mirror His. When one part of the body receives commendation, we will rejoice in what the Lord has done. We will leave behind any feelings and attitudes of jealousy, envy, comparison, or contempt, and will instead glory in the ways in which Jesus is honored when a part of His church is honored. As we come to experience this connection with Christ, we will sense the Holy Spirit moving in our hearts, prompting us to rejoice. This was what the apostle Paul had in mind when he said, "If one part is honored, every part rejoices with it" (1 Corinthians 12:26). This mystery of our union with Christ and with all believers in Christ must pervade our churches today.

Since We Are Connected to Christ, Our Divisions Will Decrease Because of Our Care for One Another.

"So that there should be no division in the body, but that its parts should have equal concern for each other" (1 Corinthians 12:25).

A second blessing will occur as we come to experience this connection with Christ: our churches and homes will be places of unity and harmony rather than enmity and strife. If relevance is going to be restored to our lives and ministries, we must ask ourselves a critical question: "Does the Jesus in me love the Jesus in you?" Our answer must be an unequivocal "yes." We may be members of different races or cultures. We may represent varying Christian traditions, denominations, and theological persuasions. We may disagree with one another about issues of eschatology, eternal security, ordination, local-church autonomy, and apostolic authority. But if we are true followers of Christ, parts of one body connected by His Spirit, then the Jesus in me **will** love the Jesus in you, regardless of any superficial or substantial differences between us.

> **If relevance is going to be restored within life and ministry, we must come to ask a critical question among Christ's believers: "Does the Jesus in me love the Jesus in you?"**

This unity of spirit was one of the significant dynamics in the ministry of the 1st century church. *The Evangelical Dictionary of Theology* notes that "the unity in the fellowship of the early church was not based upon uniformity of thought and practice, except where limits of immorality or rejection of the confession of Christ were involved" (Elwell, 2001). It was not conformity of rational belief, but rather simple, childlike faith that brought these believers into loving connection with one another through the One who is love (1 John 4:16). The oneness that declares to the world that we are His disciples does not come through complete conformity of belief, but through the loving connection of both your heart and my heart to His (John 13:35).

Since We Are Connected to Christ, We Will Desire to Know and Care for Those He Loves.

Third, our connection to Christ will motivate us to know and care for those within the body. We will want to experience the same depth of love within the church that Christ experienced with His Father.

A few hours before He went to the Cross, Jesus prayed to the Father for those who would believe in Him, asking "that all of them may be one, Father, just as you are in me and I am in you" (John 17:21). In Christ's closing prayer before He was faced with the agony of crucifixion, He made this request on our behalf. He did not ask for us to be strengthened, to be given courage, or to be granted great faith. Instead, Jesus prayed that we would experience oneness in our relationships, that we would be unified in heart and spirit, just as He is one with the Father. Our unity and oneness of spirit was of such importance to Christ that He gave it priority in the last hours of His life.

What does Jesus desire for our lives and ministry? "That all of [us] may be one." To clarify the quality and depth of relationship that Christ hoped for, He prayed that all those who believe in Him would experience intimacy with each other to the same extent that the Trinity experiences intimacy: "that they may be one as **we** are one" (v. 22). Imagine the impact that we might have on a watching and conflicted world by living out this oneness in our marriages, families, friendships, and churches!

> **We will want to experience the same depth of love within the church that Christ experienced with His Father.**

Experiencing the oneness described in Christ's prayer involves more than sharing common beliefs, visions, purposes, strategies, and programs. The Father, Son, and Holy Spirit certainly have these things in common, but their oneness transcends these elements, stemming instead from the fact that they deeply know and care for one another even as they are one. Because we are all parts of one body, we will also want to know and care for one another.

Knowing One Another

"No one knows the Son except the Father, and no one knows the Father except the Son and those to whom the Son chooses to reveal him" (Matthew 11:27).

In this passage, and throughout the Gospels, the Son of God expresses His confident understanding and deep, intimate knowledge of His Father. When people questioned whether or not Jesus was really the Messiah sent from heaven, He claimed, "I am not here on my own, but he who sent me is true. You do not know him, but I know him because I am from him and he sent me" (John 7:28, 29).

The Scriptures not only provide us with ample proof that the Son of God knows the Father, they also give evidence that God knows us intimately. The Hebrew word *yada* means "to know; to have an intimate knowledge of another person." The Lord assured Jeremiah that "Before I formed you in the womb I knew (*yada*) you" (Jeremiah 1:5). In Psalm 139, David meditates upon the mystery of God's all-encompassing knowledge of him. Like Jeremiah and David, we have a God who knows us, inside and out. He knows our strengths, weaknesses, secrets, failures, and deepest desires. He takes interest and delight in us. Our God wants to know about our joys and our sorrows because He cares for us (1 Peter 5:7).

As we gain an experiential understanding of our connectedness with Christ, we will come to value the experience of truly knowing others in the same way that Jesus knows the Father and that God knows each of us. This will mean getting to know people deeply and intimately. It will require gaining insight into their strengths, weaknesses, hurts, needs, interests, and even failures. It will include spending time with one another in both casual and formal settings, fun get-togethers as well as church-related activities.

Too often, our knowledge of one another lacks depth and intimacy. We may know a person's talents and strengths, their shortcomings, and even their sins. We may know their profession and job title, and can discern their economic status by observing their attire, their home, or the car they drive. But do we really know them as a person? Do we know them as God knows them? Do we take the time to know each individual as one who is created in His image, declared worthy by Him of Christ's sacrifice?

Knowing One Another at Church

Recently, several homeless men entered our church midway through a worship service. They wore tattered clothes and ragged shoes, and looked as if they carried all of their earthly belongings in their backpacks. As they made their way across the worship center, they crossed in front of Teresa and me. My heart was stirred by my wife's response. She watched intently as they made their way toward a few empty seats. As the men were approached by one of the church ushers, Teresa anxiously whispered a few words. I am confident that only God and I overheard her whisper, "Oh, sir. Treat them right. Please treat them right."

Teresa's anxiety was born out of her concern for those men. She was anxious for the church usher to treat them well. She hoped that the saints they sat beside would respond to the men with the heart of Christ. She desperately wanted her fellow believers to **know** these men, rather than judging them by how they looked or what they wore. She wanted the church to recognize the men as ones for whom Christ chose to die. The words were Teresa's, but the heart was His! My wife's anxiety was soon replaced with joy as the church members graciously accepted these men.

Imagine what it would be like to go to a church where others truly sought to know and understand you. Picture an environment in which genuine fellowship is prioritized and time for relationships is paramount to church life. Consider the sense of connection you might experience if leaders and other church members kept up with your interests, your spouse, and your children.

> **Imagine what it would be like to be able to go to church and tell others how you are really doing.**

Think about how blessed you would feel if your church leader remembered your birthday, anniversary, or another significant event in your life. Consider how freeing it would be if others in the church knew of your struggles and failures, yet offered no judgment, only care and support. Imagine what it would be like to be able to go to church and tell others how you are **really** doing.

My Personal Journey

Having been in ministry for more than 20 years, I had preached countless sermons on 1 Corinthians 13, and knew how to speak eloquently about the biblical characteristics of love. I had taught numerous classes on living a Spirit-filled life. But on one particular day, God broke my heart over the irrelevance of my own life.

While sitting in my office preparing for a sermon, I overheard a conversation between my secretary and another member of our ministry team. He spoke excitedly about how his daughter had recently received several academic recognitions from her school. He was thrilled to share how the Lord had blessed her efforts and seen her through several challenges that semester. Suddenly, I had a painful thought: "I have served with this colleague for several years, and I do not even remember his daughter's name."

The Spirit impressed me with these words: "David, I know every detail of your life. I have noticed your interests and have entered your world. I take note of your joys and sorrows, and respond with care. Could you now give that same priority to knowing those closest to you?" My heart was first broken and then touched with gratitude for how the Lord has known and taken interest in me. The Holy Spirit brought conviction and began to empower my efforts to better know my wife, my children, and those I am privileged to serve alongside.

As we relate this characteristic of "knowing one another" to the church, we must ask ourselves these questions: How well do people know one another in our church? Do they delve beyond doctrine, ministries, and events to discuss issues of the heart? To what extent do church members genuinely share their lives with one another? Do they dwell only on the positive aspects, or do they feel the liberty to talk about the sad, painful areas? How well is the church balancing the two critical roles of "sharing the gospel" and "sharing our lives" (1 Thessalonians 2:8)?

In previous chapters, we have taken the time to briefly assess the relevance of our personal lives and ministries. The following assessment tools will allow us to take a more comprehensive look at the extent to which our church members are experiencing relationships that allow them to deeply know one another.

Personal/Ministry Assessment

How are we doing at knowing one another?

1. We prioritize, encourage, and give time for relationships and interpersonal sharing.

Strongly Disagree	Disagree	Neutral	Agree	Strongly Agree
1	2	3	4	5

2. People are made to feel welcome and accepted, regardless of their "spirituality" or how well they fit in.

Strongly Disagree	Disagree	Neutral	Agree	Strongly Agree
1	2	3	4	5

3. There is a visitor-friendly atmosphere within our ministry.

Strongly Disagree	Disagree	Neutral	Agree	Strongly Agree
1	2	3	4	5

4. I am being an effective role model by seeking to know others more intimately.

Strongly Disagree	Disagree	Neutral	Agree	Strongly Agree
1	2	3	4	5

What improvements may be needed in the area of knowing one another?

1. We have implicit messages, program formats, time constraints, or preaching/teaching methods that contradict or undermine the experience of knowing one another at church.

Strongly Disagree	Disagree	Neutral	Agree	Strongly Agree
1	2	3	4	5

2. We need to adjust schedules in some of our areas of ministry to allow time for more one-on-one sharing and relationship-building.

Strongly Disagree	Disagree	Neutral	Agree	Strongly Agree
1	2	3	4	5

3. We need additional leadership development, resources, or curriculum to re-train leaders in relationship-building.

Strongly Disagree	Disagree	Neutral	Agree	Strongly Agree
1	2	3	4	5

4. We need more creative ways of bringing individuals, couples, and families together through classes or small groups, so as to facilitate deeper knowing of friends, spouses, and family members.

Strongly Disagree	Disagree	Neutral	Agree	Strongly Agree
1	2	3	4	5

Pause now, and discuss your responses with your partner or small group. Be sure to give consideration to how you might contribute to any areas of needed improvement.

The Challenge of Vulnerability

Knowing one another requires vulnerable self-disclosure. Once again, Jesus is our model—the Father was vulnerable with Him, and He, in turn, was vulnerable with the disciples: "I have called you friends, for everything that I learned from my Father I have made known to you" (John 15:15).

The biblical concept of vulnerability is related to the Hebrew word *sod*, which means "to reveal; disclose." God not only reveals His existence through creation and circumstances, but also discloses His thoughts, feelings, and character through His Word and the life of His Son, thus allowing us to know Him more deeply. The wise sage used the word *sod* when he noted, "[God] is intimate (*sod*) with the upright" (Proverbs 3:32 NASB). God allows those who have been connected to Him by His Spirit to share in the very depths of His love.

Since our heavenly Father is vulnerable with us, we will want to allow others to know us deeply. We should even have some relationships in which we are comfortable sharing our sins and failures. Church must become a safe place where people are accepted by one another, just as they have been accepted by Christ (Romans 15:7). Imagine the blessing of feeling free to share the burdens of your heart without fear of criticism or condemnation. Think about what it would be like to belong to a church where you felt free to "be real" and trust others with the issues of your heart. Consider how wonderful it would be to experience a church environment in which even the leaders shared their weaknesses and their needs. Such vulnerability would prompt a measure of security and a feeling of connection as you came to know one another in a deeper way.

You will now have the opportunity to assess how well your church or area of ministry is doing at "vulnerable communication." Consider how well the members of your "body" are doing at creating a safe place for knowing each another.

Personal/Ministry Assessment

How are we doing at communicating vulnerably?

1. We encourage and model personal disclosure of God's workings in individual lives.

Strongly Disagree	Disagree	Neutral	Agree	Strongly Agree
1	2	3	4	5

2. Our church/ministry is a safe environment where people feel free to share areas of weakness as well as strengths.

Strongly Disagree	Disagree	Neutral	Agree	Strongly Agree
1	2	3	4	5

3. We move beyond spiritual clichés to real-life issues and pain.

Strongly Disagree	Disagree	Neutral	Agree	Strongly Agree
1	2	3	4	5

4. Our preaching, teaching, and discussions focus on "God, me, you, and others" instead of "us versus them."

Strongly Disagree	Disagree	Neutral	Agree	Strongly Agree
1	2	3	4	5

What improvements may be needed in the area of vulnerable communication?

1. There has sometimes been an over-emphasis on imparting truth rather than imparting life.

Strongly Disagree	Disagree	Neutral	Agree	Strongly Agree
1	2	3	4	5

2. The church/ministry leaders need to more effectively model vulnerability by sharing more of their own struggles, weaknesses, and failures.

Strongly Disagree	Disagree	Neutral	Agree	Strongly Agree
1	2	3	4	5

3. There has been an over-emphasis on one-way communication rather than mutual sharing in relationships.

Strongly Disagree	Disagree	Neutral	Agree	Strongly Agree
1	2	3	4	5

4. We need to provide more time and opportunities for structured sharing among church members at various gatherings.

Strongly Disagree	Disagree	Neutral	Agree	Strongly Agree
1	2	3	4	5

5. We have at times (explicitly or implicitly) displayed judgmental attitudes in reaction to people's struggles, weaknesses, or failures.

Strongly Disagree	Disagree	Neutral	Agree	Strongly Agree
1	2	3	4	5

6. Our ministry environment has been more characterized by fears (of failure, rejection, or inadequacy) than by love and acceptance.

Strongly Disagree	Disagree	Neutral	Agree	Strongly Agree
1	2	3	4	5

Pause now, and discuss your responses with your partner or small group. Be sure to give consideration to how you might contribute to any areas of needed improvement.

Rejoicing With One Another
We hope that you have come to better understand what it means to know one another and be vulnerable with one another in the body of Christ. During the following exercise, you will have the opportunity to know others in the church, as well as letting them know you. It will be important to show acceptance to others as each of you verbalizes your responses. Group members will need to sense that you receive them unconditionally. You will need to do your part to create a safe place for vulnerable sharing. To create such an environment, give appropriate eye contact, listen attentively without interruption, and respond with caring words. Celebrate with others as they share about positive things that have happened. Your rejoicing responses might sound like, "I am so glad you shared that with us! What a terrific blessing," or "I am thrilled for you. I can see why you are grateful to the Lord," or "Thank you so much for your vulnerability. I feel privileged to hear how you have experienced love."

An Experience With God's People

"Rejoice with those who rejoice" (Romans 12:15).

The following exercise is a way to begin the process of knowing one another on a deeper level, and to increase vulnerable communication. Take turns sharing your responses to the following sentences. Be sure to respond to one another, rejoicing when a group member vulnerably shares something positive in their life.

My name is . . .

My family consists of . . .

The best thing I did during the past year was . . .

I am currently feeling grateful for . . .

I feel loved and cared for when . . .

Now that you have experienced the opportunity to know other believers in Christ and increased your sense of connection to them, you will be more inclined to care for one another, more moved with compassion for other members of the body of Christ. This loving care is another essential characteristic of those who are connected to Christ by His Spirit.

Caring for One Another

Scripture gives evidence of the deep care that exists between Father and Son within the mysterious relationship of the Trinity. When Jesus was baptized, His Father proclaimed deep feelings for

Him: "This is My Son, whom I love, with him I am well pleased" (Matthew 3:17). These words were not prompted by the Son's performance; He had not yet preached a sermon or performed a miracle. The Father simply expressed His joy and delight in His Son and their relationship, feelings that He reaffirmed later at the time of Jesus' Transfiguration (17:5).

Likewise, Jesus felt deeply for His Father. At the age of 12, Jesus declared to His earthly parents, "I must be about my Father's business" (Luke 2:49 KJV). When Christ witnessed money-changing and the sale of sacrificial animals in the temple, He was angered that His Father's house had been dishonored: "How dare you turn my Father's house into a market" (John 2:16)! As His death approached, Jesus prayed that the Father would allow the disciples to experience the same love with which He was loved, "in order that the love you have for me may be in them and that I myself may be in them" (17:26). The Father and Son are one in essence, and, therefore, expressions of care flow easily from Father to Son and Son to Father.

Since we are connected to the Father and His Son through the Person of the Holy Spirit, we must ask ourselves: "Is the church of today, the adopted sons and daughters of our heavenly Father, experiencing the same, deep care for one another that we see evidenced in the Trinity? Are we experiencing the kind of mutual love that is shared by Jesus and His Father?"

First Corinthians 12:25 defines what this mutual care and concern will look like: "so that there should be no division in the body, but that its parts should have equal concern for each other." To be concerned about others is to express the very heart of God. It would be contrary to the nature of God for Him to be unconcerned. So it should be for those who have become partakers of His divine nature (2 Peter 1:4 NASB). It is critical for the body of Christ to demonstrate care and concern at the most fundamental level. We should be able to rejoice when one part of the body is lifted up, without feeling jealous or threatened. We should be able to mourn when one part of the body suffers, never celebrating because of another's suffering (Romans 12:15). Through this kind of caring responsiveness, the church will be able to clearly communicate: "Now [we] are the body of Christ, and each one of [us] is a part of it" (1 Corinthians 12:27). Because the Spirit connects us to Christ, we can experience the intimacy of mutual, heartfelt care. Just as the psalmist speaks of God's caring involvement in our lives (Psalm 139:3), so also we are called to be lovingly involved in the lives of others. Therefore, equipping individuals to develop and maintain loving, caring relationships should be a fundamental priority of church ministry.

What Happens When the Church Does Not Express Care for One Another?

Several times in the Scriptures, God's faithful people, in moments of pain, isolation, and confusion, cried out, "Why, God?" or "God, where are You?" Could it be that some of this confusion about God's character and questioning of His ways sprang from a failure to live out His love in relationships with others? Could it be that one reason **we** might, at times, question the love of God is because our marriage, family, and church relationships have failed to consistently embody His love?

The Book of Job tells the story of one man whose faith was tested through incredible trials. In his time of loss, Job's friends failed to effectively offer care or comfort. Instead, they confronted his impatience (Job 4:5), told him that sin was the cause of his difficulties (8:3–7), and tried to convince him that repentance was his greatest need (11:13–15). These men struggled to demonstrate the care of God to Job. Consequently, Job responded with the heartfelt cry, "For the despairing man there should be kindness from his friend; so that he does not forsake the fear of the Almighty" (6:14 NASB). The absence of such kindness on the part of Job's friends in the face of their fellow believer's hardships was evidence that the spiritual community was not functioning as it should have.

> **It is critical for the body of Christ to demonstrate care and concern at the most fundamental level. We should be able to rejoice when one part of the body is lifted up, and mourn when one part of the body suffers.**

Jeremiah, the weeping prophet, wrote, "O Lord, you deceived me, and I was deceived; you overpowered me and prevailed. I am ridiculed all day long; everyone mocks me" (Jeremiah 20:7). The first part of this verse reveals that Jeremiah clearly had doubts about God's love. The second part of the verse clarifies the situation further by showing that the prophet's uncertainties were voiced in the context of a potential community of support that had broken down. Could Jeremiah's doubt and confusion have been lessened or removed if God's people had come alongside the prophet and removed his aloneness? Perhaps his cry was less a commentary on the character of God than a commentary on the spiritual community that had been called to receive and share His love.

Our failure to consistently demonstrate care for one another may be a major reason why the church of today has lost relevance within our culture. God has always intended for the "divine commodities" of love, forgiveness, and acceptance (various forms of His grace) to be received by His people and then shared with others (1 Peter 4:10). God longs for us to experience His love in community with others, as well as receiving it directly from Him. The question, "God, where are You?" is answered not only by the wonder of His personal presence and provision, but also by His declaration, "I am in those around you."

Take a few moments to reflect on your church's ability to care for one another. Carefully assess how well your church or ministry is reflecting the loving care of Christ.

Personal/Ministry Assessment

How are we doing at caring for one another?

1. The attitude of "What am I getting out of church?" has been replaced with "How am I caring for others? How am I gratefully giving of His love to others?"

Strongly Disagree	Disagree	Neutral	Agree	Strongly Agree
1	2	3	4	5

2. The spontaneous initiative to minister out of Christ's constraining love has replaced pleading and guilt-ridden promptings.

Strongly Disagree	Disagree	Neutral	Agree	Strongly Agree
1	2	3	4	5

3. The priority of becoming servants and caregivers has replaced endless activity and competitive performance.

Strongly Disagree	Disagree	Neutral	Agree	Strongly Agree
1	2	3	4	5

4. Relationships and friendships for couples, families, and single adults, rather than calendared events, have become the focus of ministry.

Strongly Disagree	Disagree	Neutral	Agree	Strongly Agree
1	2	3	4	5

What improvements can be made as we learn to better care for one another?

1. There is an over-emphasis on "believing right," which hinders us from being humble, gentle, and caring people.

Strongly Disagree	Disagree	Neutral	Agree	Strongly Agree
1	2	3	4	5

2. Leaders need to do a better job of modeling care for others by giving appreciation, attention, and comfort in various ministry settings.

Strongly Disagree	Disagree	Neutral	Agree	Strongly Agree
1	2	3	4	5

3. We have sometimes emphasized faults and fallenness and neglected to minister to people's neediness and aloneness.

Strongly Disagree	Disagree	Neutral	Agree	Strongly Agree
1	2	3	4	5

4. We have sometimes confused the giving of truth with the giving of oneself.

Strongly Disagree	Disagree	Neutral	Agree	Strongly Agree
1	2	3	4	5

5. We need more learning exercises and experiences where members are allowed to practice caring for one another, so that they will know what giving care looks and sounds like.

Strongly Disagree	Disagree	Neutral	Agree	Strongly Agree
1	2	3	4	5

6. We need more frequent times to focus on and share gratefulness for the abundant blessings
we have received, expressing our thanks for God's care of us.

Strongly Disagree	Disagree	Neutral	Agree	Strongly Agree
1	2	3	4	5

Pause now, and discuss your responses with your partner or small group. Be sure to give
consideration to how you might contribute to any areas of needed improvement.

God wants us to experience the abundance of His manifold love. What better way to experience
His love than through His church? Join us now as we discover how to increase the relevance
of the 21st century church. Let us look at what may be missing from our sermons, lessons, and
relationships within the body of Christ.

AS HIS LOVE IS REVEALED, RELEVANCE IS RESTORED

The Curtis family discovered that their teenage daughter had cancer. They suffered with her through
months of chemotherapy, radiation, and all the associated difficulties of treatment. They watched
her hair fall out and her weight decline. Tears flowed. Prayers for healing were fervently offered.
Mr. and Mrs. Curtis began to wonder if God was on their side. They even began to question whether
He really loved them. While attending church on one occasion, the Curtises heard their pastor
deliver a sermon on suffering that, although it was applicable to their situation, only seemed to
bring more pain. Although the minister's words were spoken with sincere confidence and the
purest of motives, they left the Curtis family with feelings of emptiness. Here is what he said: "You
must always see that behind your suffering is the cross of Jesus Christ. God's love for you was once
and for all demonstrated on the Cross. The Cross, the death of Jesus Christ, and His resurrection
are God's final, total, and complete expression of His love for you."

Everything the pastor said was true, but was it the entire truth? Did God mean for us to cling to
the Cross as His final and only demonstration of love for us? On the contrary, the Scriptures
tell us that Calvary opened the floodgates of heaven for God's continued, abundant, and sacrificial
loving provision. The apostle Paul seemed almost transfixed by this truth when he said, "He

who did not spare his own Son, but gave him up for us all—how will he not also, along with him, graciously give us all things" (Romans 8:32)? After reading Paul's words, we can say with confidence that since God gave the supreme gift of His Son to save us, He will certainly give us whatever we need to bring to fulfillment His promise of abundant life (John 10:10 KJV).

If it is true that God will graciously give us all things, how does He plan to do that? The answer lies in the picture of the "Holy Ghost Octopus" that we described at the beginning of this

> **God's love reaches its fullest expression when we love one another.**

chapter. The God who gave us the gift of His Son, and connected us to Him by His Spirit, desires for us to be conduits of His love, mercy, and grace to one another. Just as we are connected to Jesus Christ, the Head, we are connected to one another as members of the same body. Therefore, as Jesus feels love and compassion for members of the body, we are to be channels through which that love can flow. As Christ feels sorrow or joy for parts of the body, we are to be His hands that show kindness, His voice of compassion, and His arms of support.

Relevance Vs. Irrelevance

That is God's desire for the church—but what happens when His church falls short? You are undoubtedly well-acquainted with the results of God's church failing to express His love. We have all experienced the same kind of emptiness as the Curtis family. Have there not been times when you were struggling in your faith, and, although God's truth was shared, you walked away with emptiness and an unchanged heart? Can you remember the hollow feeling of hearing what you knew was truth, but sensing little or no help, benefit, or impact? That feeling of emptiness, that hollowness in your heart, is what we would describe as irrelevance. Your church experience was simply irrelevant to your need.

Now imagine how different that same time of struggle would have been if part of the body of Christ had first cared about your pain. What if someone within the church had taken the time to know you, been careful to hear and understand your struggle, and then communicated deep compassion for you? Consider how different you would have felt if another member of the body of Christ had shared God's comfort with you rather than only sharing God's truth. What a difference the love of Christ would have made!

Likewise, imagine the difference that might have been made in the lives of Mr. and Mrs. Curtis had they been met in the church parking lot by a compassionate saint who said something like the following: "As I reflected this morning on Christ's suffering and loneliness at Calvary, I was reminded of your situation. I cannot imagine the depth of your sorrow and the pain of your journey, but I want you to know that God gave me deep compassion for you this morning. I am so sorry. I really care for you and your daughter."

This picture of a loving church is what the apostle John was hoping to communicate in 1 John 4:12: "No one has ever seen God; but if we love one another, God lives in us and his love is made complete in us." In other words, since our source of love is God's love, His love reaches its fullest expression (is made complete) when we love one another. The God whom no one has ever seen is seen in those who love because God lives in them. It is this expression of love that, if consistently displayed within the body of Christ, will bring relevance back to the church.

Mourning With One Another
During the exercise that follows, you will have the opportunity to know and care for others in the family of believers (Galatians 6:10). You will have the chance to share the multi-faceted grace of God with those around you (1 Peter 4:10). Each participant will have the opportunity to complete several sentences. As they do, you will want to share God's love with each person. Scripture tells us to "Mourn with those who mourn" (Romans 12:15). When we hear another child of God expressing sorrow or emotional pain, we are called to mourn with, feel sad with, and express compassion for that person. Refrain from responses that minimize the pain of another person. Advice, pep talks, and analysis do not convey the compassionate heart of the Savior. Trying to explain the situation or solve the problem does not foster love or connection. True compassion involves simply hurting with another person as God's Spirit, the Comforter, moves within us.

As a member of the body of Christ, pause now and ask God to give you His heart for the people who are about to share. Ask His Spirit to touch your heart with the compassion of Christ. Just as Christ was moved to mourn with Mary after the death of Lazarus, so the Spirit longs to move us with compassion for other people (John 11:33–36). Ask Him to help you experience what He feels for each member of the body. When you are ready to respond, express the feelings you have discovered. Tell each person how it impacts your heart to hear what he or she has to say. Your responses might sound like, "My heart is saddened to hear you say . . ." or "It hurts my heart to know . . ." or "I am so sorry that . . ." or "I feel great compassion for you because. . . ." Above all, allow the Holy Spirit to direct your words and prompt your heart with the compassion of Jesus.

An Experience With God's Word

"Mourn with those who mourn" (Romans 12:15).

Take a few moments to reflect on how you might complete the sentences below.

I feel sad when . . . (or I recently felt sad when . . .)

God would seem more real to me if . . .

My biggest regret this year was . . .

I sometimes fear that . . .

Share your responses with your partner or small group. As each person shares, respond with care and compassion. Allow the Lord to express His love through you. His love is best communicated by living out the verse above. As group members share, ask yourself, how does this person feel? How might Christ's heart respond to this person? How can I express God's comfort and care for this person?

(For example: *It broke my heart when I heard you say that God would seem more real to you if you could sense His care, or I am so sorry that you have experienced such incredible heartache and regret, or My heart is sorrowed that you have felt so afraid about the death of your father, or I felt compassion when I heard you talk about the sadness you felt because of conflicts in your family.)*

"Now that you have purified yourselves by obeying the truth so that you have sincere love for your brothers, love one another deeply, from the heart" (1 Peter 1:22, 23).

Now that you have "obeyed the truth" of Romans 12:15, is your heart prompted to love one another? As you experienced the heartfelt care of those around you, could you sense an additional measure of connectedness? Did you deepen your love for your fellow brothers and sisters in Christ? We would suggest that what you have just experienced is the epitome of true biblical fellowship, or *koinonia*.

REDISCOVERING GENUINE FELLOWSHIP

As we strive to bring relevance back to the church, we will encounter significant challenges. Sadly, some of our most formidable obstacles may arise from within the church itself, as it seems that the Western church now tends to prioritize "getting things done" over knowing and caring for people. This is a dangerous departure from the approach of the New Testament church, and explains, in part, the irrelevance of our churches today.

In Acts 2:42, Luke observed the following about the early Christians: "They devoted themselves to the apostles' teaching and to the fellowship, to the breaking of bread and to prayer." Do we experience all of these characteristics as they were practiced among the early believers? Reflect on your most recent church experience. Was the Word of God preached? Undoubtedly. Did you pray together with other Christians? Of course. Was communion observed (or, depending upon your tradition, will it be duly observed in the near future)? Almost assuredly. But now a very important question must be asked: did you experience genuine fellowship (*koinonia*)? Did you come to more intimately know another part of the body of Christ, or did everyone focus only on activities and responsibilities? Was priority given to creating a safe place where God's people could be real with one another, or was there pressure to wear masks of self-protection? Was the Spirit allowed to lead people into intentional and genuine care for one another? If we define true fellowship in this way, most of us would have to voice a resounding "no" to the *koinonia* question. Tragically, many of us would have to admit that we have apparently missed this special fellowship with other believers without even realizing it.

The purpose of this section is to explore some key elements of genuine fellowship and caring connectedness. We will unravel this mystery of fellowship and see how caring for one another in special ways will impact our lives, homes, and ministries. Join us as we discover how true fellowship can restore relevance to life and ministry.

As We Rediscover Genuine Fellowship, the Real God Will Be Experienced.

A devotion to fellowship and commitment to experience true connection within the body of Christ refines our image of the real God. If our churches are marked by painful relationships and hurtful experiences, it may be difficult for us to conceive of God as "the Father of compassion and the God of all comfort" (2 Corinthians 1:3). Seeing God as critical, distant, or rejecting hinders those within the church from loving Him with all of their heart, soul, mind, and strength (Mark 12:30), and hinders the unchurched from coming to trust Him. But the fellowship of God's love, shared through our lives, allows His Spirit to transform people's perception concerning who He really is. God will only be seen as accessible, available, attentive, and accepting if those characteristics are lived out through us, His church.

> **We must ask ourselves, "Are the people that make up our small group, ministry team, or church body living and loving in a way that enables us to 'see God' in one another?"**

When we show unconditional **acceptance** to a church member who has failed, we let others see the accepting heart of the real Jesus (Romans 15:7). When we offer **comfort** and consolation to a brother or sister who has shared a life struggle, we enable them to know the God who longs to be gracious and rises to show them compassion (Isaiah 30:18). When we demonstrate **care** to a friend who is lonely, we give testimony to a God who "makes a home for the lonely" (Psalm 68:6 NASB). Each time we gather together in worship or in honor of our Lord, we have an opportunity to let others see God by allowing His love to be perfected in us as we become living epistles of Christ's care.

We must ask ourselves, "Are the people that make up our small group, ministry team, or church body living and loving in a way that enables us to 'see God' in one another? Are we enabling the world to see God for who He really is?" If we see a God who is only concerned about right behavior or right beliefs, a God who is judgmental or inspecting, or a God who is harsh and condemning, then those attitudes will most likely be expressed in our ministry. But as we connect together and experience the real God, we will be able to partner together for the purpose of expressing the real Jesus to our fellow believers and those outside the household of faith.

As We Rediscover Genuine Fellowship, We Will Create an Environment of Safety.

Genuine fellowship within the body of Christ is only possible when we know one another. This requires going beyond academic discussions, spiritual comparisons, and event-driven conversations. When we truly want to know one another, we will share the critical issues of our heart, the joys and sorrows of life, the victories as well as the failures. We must work to create church environments that are safe and conducive to this type of sharing.

Church leaders will have to take the first steps toward creating this environment by being vulnerable with those they serve. Imagine going to a worship service where a leader is vulnerable with personal challenges and shares his or her struggles in living the Christian life. Consider what it would be like to have a leader who is honest about his or her need for support, one who trusts you with issues of the heart and spirit. Think about how approachable that kind of leader would be. How much more would you want to follow such a leader? Would such vulnerability not prompt a certain level of security and feeling of connection? Would you not want to know that leader and let yourself be known in return?

Many leaders have bought into a damaging half-truth about their relationship with the church. They have believed, "As a good shepherd, you must know your flock, but you must not allow the sheep to know you." In reality, vulnerability in ministry is a two-way street. If we expect members of our churches to be open about what is happening in their lives, we as leaders must (within appropriate boundaries) be open about what is happening in our own. People must sense our approachability and availability. We want others to sense that our church, our offices, and our classrooms are safe places to come and be real with one another. If we are prioritizing relationships, connecting with one another in meaningful ways, and experiencing the real God, then others will be drawn to the safety and security that we have to offer.

We will now look at several ways to assess the level of "safety" within our churches. Let us delve deeper into this critical element of fellowship:

> **If we are prioritizing relationships, connecting with one another in meaningful ways, and experiencing the real God, others will be drawn to the safety and security that we have to offer.**

- A safe place is created when churches cultivate an ever-expanding ministry of compassion toward needy people.

Every Christian leader and church seems to have a "comfort zone" within which care and concern for others is relatively easy. This comfort zone may relate to people's socio-economic strata, ethnicity, education, or profession. A relevant church, however, will not be content to minister within their comfort zone, but will make purposeful decisions and take active steps toward cultivating a ministry of compassion to needy people. A predominantly affluent church might ask the Lord to show them practical ways in which they could minister to the needs of the homeless and unemployed. A church located in the suburbs of a large city might be impressed to begin a ministry to the children of an inner-city apartment complex, or to help out with an urban restoration project.

- A safe place is created when church leaders make clear distinctions among personal preferences, personal convictions, and biblical absolutes. **Personal preferences** (such as the style of worship music you enjoy most) should be held lightly and relinquished at times to accommodate the needs of others and prevent division. **Personal convictions** involve an individual's sense of God's special direction for his or her life. These are not biblical absolutes, but specific, God-directed beliefs unique to each believer. A couple's belief about how best to educate their children (in a public school, private school, or homeschool setting) is an example of a personal conviction. Leaders should honor such convictions as God's standards for their personal behavior, but should also allow others the freedom to hold differing convictions because, as Scripture tells us, "Where the Spirit of the Lord is, there is freedom." **Biblical absolutes** are God's undeniable truths concerning salvation and right living. They must be presented boldly and without apology, but with loving motives.

- A safe place is created when people feel free to participate in church activities instead of feeling coerced to attend. Jesus allowed people to make choices about following Him. Was He concerned that if He gave people the freedom to participate, they might not attend? Of course not. When He challenged His followers regarding their involvement and commitment, it was always from a heart of love. When we gain the freedom to be real and genuine within the church, we allow for a mutuality of giving and receiving. This opportunity to both give and receive produces a heart of gratitude for God's provision. It is that gratitude that will cause us to **want** to attend, participate, and take an active role in the ministries of the church.

As We Rediscover Genuine Fellowship, We Will Be Empowered by Gratitude.

Gratitude must empower and pervade our ministry efforts. The apostle Paul shared the secret of the 1st century church's relevance and effectiveness when he declared, "Christ's love compels us" (2 Corinthians 5:14). What was so attractive about the early church? What enabled them to add thousands of members in one day? The answer is simple—the Holy Spirit's outpouring of Christ's love. The relevant church is compelled to right living and service to others by the Spirit's prompting of joy and gratitude for Christ's love. True fellowship with one another produces a sense of gratitude that prompts us to say, "I am **privileged** to co-labor with Jesus. I am so thankful that I get to share in the ministry of connection with Him."

As we look into the lives of the early Christians, we see the powerful impact of gratitude. We read of Peter's failures and his denial of Jesus (Matthew 26:69–75), yet we find that the resurrected Christ accepted Peter and entrusted him with ministry (John 21:15–19). In a similar way, when we promote true fellowship and provide a safe place for people to be real, there will be times when our vulnerability exposes personal faults and failures. At such times, we will be startled as God's accepting love manifests itself through others. As we receive His grace, we (like Peter) will be touched and empowered by gratitude.

> **The relevant church is compelled to right living and service to others by the Spirit's prompting of joy and gratitude for Christ's love.**

Peter's gratefulness was revealed when he wrote about being filled with "an inexpressible and glorious joy" (1 Peter 1:9).

We also see the impact of gratitude on the life of the apostle Paul following his transformation from a persecutor of Christians to a champion for the cause of Christ (Acts 9:1–31). Paul told the Galatians, "For you have heard . . . how intensely I persecuted the church of God and tried to destroy it" (Galatians 1:13). But he also reminded his fellow believers at Rome: "Since we have been justified through faith, we have peace with God through our Lord Jesus Christ, through whom we have gained access by faith into this grace in which we now stand. And we rejoice in the hope of the glory of God. Not only so, but we also rejoice in our sufferings" (Romans 5:1–3). It was Paul's gratitude for the love and grace of Jesus that empowered his commitment, his effectiveness in ministry, and his ability to rejoice in the midst of suffering.

My Personal Journey

I have shared in previous chapters about the crisis my family faced when I was laid off from my ministry position just as we were moving into a new home. During this time of transition, God challenged my ability to receive from others. Our family budget was tight to begin with, but after I lost my job we were forced to rely completely upon the Lord for His provision. I can clearly recall the feelings of discomfort I had when one of the deacons of our church brought several sacks of groceries to our house. It felt awkward and uncomfortable to be the recipient of such generosity. Those same feelings occurred the night that a fellow church member brought us barbecue from his restaurant in town. God seemed to be challenging me to be "real" and to gratefully receive from others within the body of Christ. I came face to face with my own self-reliance and my tendency to take care of things myself. I knew we could not make it through this financial crisis alone, but I was sure going to try! Fortunately, God's plan was to provide for the needs of our family, both directly and through others. My self-reliance was replaced with gratitude as I humbly received from the Lord, and from the members of His body that He had prompted to care for us.

Cultivating Gratitude

Grateful hearts can be cultivated in several ways:

- Gratefulness is cultivated as believers embrace their identity in Christ. At each church gathering, leaders can promote gratefulness within the body by emphasizing at least one aspect of God's boundless love for His children. As these truths of God's love are emphasized, gratefulness is produced. Believers come to understand and embrace their identity as the "beloved of God." Worship in the relevant church should be a constant reminder of, and grateful response to "who we are," "whose we are," and "where we reside." As people are guided to reaffirm their spiritual identity and heritage, their focus is shifted to a personal and grateful encounter with a loving, heavenly Father.

- Gratefulness is cultivated as the church takes time to recount God's blessings. Church leaders must regularly provide time for the body of Christ to gratefully remember the blessings of the Lord (Psalm 103:2). The tribulations of this life can quickly rob us of our joy and gratitude, so we must go beyond sharing prayer requests and recounting our difficulties to recalling the numerous blessings and benefits we have received from the God who gives "every good and perfect gift" (James 1:17).

As We Rediscover Genuine Fellowship, We Will Become Focused on Relationships.

Effective, relevant ministries will undergird their commitment to right beliefs and right behaviors with a focus on loving relationships. While believing and behaving right are essentials of the Christian life, they are not sufficient in and of themselves. As we rediscover the transforming power of deep, intimate relationships with God and with one another, we will begin to prioritize relationships over religion. It is only through a relationship with the Redeemer that a life can be changed, and it is through relationships with God and others that aloneness is removed. As we rediscover the mystery of fellowship, it will be of the utmost importance for us to equip the body of Christ to love God and each other.

As the church seeks to become relationship-focused, we will want to give special emphasis to the divinely-ordained relationships of marriage, family, and the church. For example, in addition to weekly, on-going ministry for couples, families, and single adults, a church might highlight God's plan for marriage during the week of Valentine's Day, or focus on family life during the time between Mother's Day and Father's Day. The critical role of the church and the special calling of each member of Christ's body could be emphasized during the celebration of Pentecost.

My Personal Journey

I have the privilege of enjoying times of fellowship with various denominational leaders across the United States and overseas. During a recent trip, my wife and I were blessed to come to know one of the single adult leaders who serves with one of our denominational partners. Yvette spoke of her feelings of aloneness, even in the midst of a busy ministry. She recounted the disconnection she experienced as a result of relocating far away from family and childhood friends. Yvette had these feelings of isolation in spite of the fact that she was making valuable contributions to ministry leaders around the world. As we listened to her share, we took the opportunity to express our sadness for her and reassure her of our care. We prayed that God would bring additional, caring relationships into her life.

A week or two later, as I was looking over my notes from that time of fellowship, I was reminded of Yvette's aloneness and need for care. At the next opportunity, I placed a call to Yvette at her office in the denominational headquarters. I told her that I just wanted to call and let her know that I was thinking about her and was still praying on her behalf. I reaffirmed my appreciation of her vulnerability and told her that I had been blessed by our time of fellowship.

Yvette responded with a mixture of feelings. She felt a certain degree of disbelief that I had no other purpose behind my call. She also experienced a measure of gratitude. I heard the emotion in her voice as she thanked me for demonstrating care. God has since prompted me and other members of our team to call Yvette, just to let her know that she was on our hearts and minds. It was the genuineness of our fellowship together that prompted us to prioritize our relationship with this sister in Christ.

The Priority of Fellowship

As we give renewed priority to the mystery of fellowship and connection with one another, we will become better equipped in the "how to's" of intimate living with God and others. In a day when Christian marriages and families are just as much at risk as those without Christ, we must employ practical correctives that address our relationships. First, we must restore the priority of intimate fellowship to our own marriages and families. Then, we as church leaders must equip husbands and wives to love one another with the love of Christ. We must restore the heritage of passing on the faith, as parents re-embrace their intended role as the primary source of discipleship for their children. We must correct the fearful avoidance of relationships and the compromising behaviors that ruin the lives of so many single adults. Such corrections will be accomplished as we connect with one another in true biblical fellowship, gaining encouragement, equipping, accountability, and comfort from our brothers and sisters in the Lord.

Take a few moments now to reflect on your own connection with Christ, the Head of the church. Pause and consider your relationship with Him. Ask the Holy Spirit to help you reconnect to Jesus, deepen your knowledge of Christ, and express your compassion and care for Him.

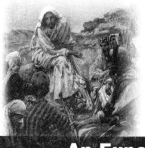

An Experience With God's Son

"This is my Son, whom I love. Listen to him" (Mark 9:7)!

We will now take the opportunity to reflect on the experiences of Jesus. Let us see if the Spirit might stir each of our hearts with additional compassion for Christ and, in turn, for one another. In the next few moments, we will come to know Him more intimately through the "fellowship of sharing in his sufferings" (Philippians 3:10).

Picture the Lord Jesus traveling with His three closest disciples to the top of the Mount of Transfiguration. They wind their way through the steep rocks and past the tree line, and finally rest at a quiet place on top of the mountain. Jesus goes a short distance to find a place to pray. As the Savior looks ahead to the agony of the Cross and His impending separation from the Father, He asks God for strength to face the days to come.

As we look closer, we notice the face of the Savior. Christ's countenance is shining with the splendor of heaven. He is encircled with waves of light; beams of sunshine seem to envelop the entire mountain. Jesus, who was until now known to those around Him only as a human, reveals His divinity.

Looking again, we recognize two other faces. They see not only the face of their Master, but those of Moses and Elijah as well. The great lawgiver and the great prophet stand beside Christ, offering encouragement, consolation, and support. The two Old Testament saints have been sent from heaven, commissioned by the Father to strengthen and encourage the One who will save and redeem us. This moment is sacred. This mountain is now holy ground. If we look closely, we can see the face of Jesus. He is enraptured by the words of the saints. His heart is inspired by eternal purpose.

But where are the ones whom Christ invited to join in this glorious event? Exhausted by the journey, the disciples have fallen asleep (Luke 9:32). After they awake, Peter shatters the joy of the moment further by offering to build three tabernacles to commemorate the event. Then a voice from heaven speaks: "This is my Son, whom I love. Listen to Him!"

Jesus is beaming with hope and filled with excitement as He receives hope and comfort from heaven. But on this most glorious day of His earthly ministry, the disciples first go to sleep, and then, when awakened, demonstrate a lack of understanding by offering to build shelters. The Savior, in some sense, rejoices alone.

What must that have done to the heart of Jesus? How does your heart respond to His? How does it make you feel to see how those closest to Jesus left Him alone? Do you feel sorrow for the Savior? Are you saddened by the insensitivity and ambivalence of His friends? Pause now, and tell Jesus about the reflections of your heart.

Jesus, I am saddened as I reflect on how You . . .

It hurts my heart to imagine that You . . .

Take turns sharing your prayers with your partner or small group.

After you have prayed with one another, consider these questions: is there a part of you that wishes you could have been there on the mountain? Perhaps there is something inside of you that says, "If only I could have been there! If I could have seen the Savior's joy, I would have expressed my joy for Him."

You may also recall that, at the saddest hour of Christ's earthly ministry, these same disciples slept in the Garden of Gethsemane, even after Jesus' pleas for them to join Him in prayer. Remember His pain-filled words: "My soul is overwhelmed with sorrow. . . . Could you men not keep watch with me for one hour" (Matthew 26:38, 40)? Is there something within you that longs to make up for what the disciples missed? Perhaps there is something inside you that says, "If only I could have been there with Him, to comfort Him." But what if you still can?

Imagine the Savior drawing close to you and, with a smile, whispering just loud enough for you to hear, "When you do it unto the least of these, you do it unto Me. When you rejoice with your brother, you rejoice with Me. When you mourn with a fellow believer, you mourn with

Me" (see Matthew 25:40). Consider the wondrous truth that, in some mysterious way, when we rejoice with, comfort, and support one another, we also do it unto Him. As we express care to the various parts of His body, we also offer care to Christ, the Head.

Close this time of reflection by praying again with your partner or small group. Express your gratitude for the Savior who has felt the pain of loneliness and the sorrow of disconnection. Thank Him for the body of Christ that is an expression of His loving presence. Praise Him for the privilege of sharing His life and love with others, and for the wonder that, in some way, He is loved and blessed when you do so. Ask Him to create in you a renewed compassion for Him and for those whom He loves.

For Further Study

TAKEN CAPTIVE BY HIS LOVE

Scripture is filled with references to the pervasiveness of our captivity. As unbelievers, we once "walked according to the course of this world, according to the prince of the power of the air" (Ephesians 2:2 NKJV). The Greek word *sunecho,* which is used in 2 Corinthians 5:14 to describe the captivating, constraining love of Christ, is also used to describe being held captive by fear (Luke 8:37), by the crowd (8:45), and by enemies (19:43). Paul used the same word to describe his dilemma of being "hard-pressed from both directions"—wanting both to be with Jesus and to remain with the Philippians (Philippians 1:23 NASB). It seems that captivity is inevitable. But by God's grace, we can choose our master. Will fear, the crowd, our enemies, or the course of this world control us, or will we be constrained by the love of Christ?

Captivity is not an intellectual exercise or mental process. It is first and foremost an experiential truth, a reality that impacts one's total being. So it is with the constraining love of Christ. It involves more than seeking to comprehend the vastness of God's love, only to be frustrated by our finite humanity. It is more than choosing to tell others about this great love in the hope of maintaining motivation.

What does it mean to be constrained by His love? To better understand and experience such constraint is to better comprehend true love. True love is an issue of God's heart and nature rather than an issue of rational truth alone. The declaration that "love is from God" (1 John 4:7 NKJV) is a certain and secure rational truth. But personally experiencing that "the love of God was manifested in us, that God . . . sent His Son to be the propitiation for our sins" (vv. 9, 10 NKJV) makes it an issue of relationship, an issue of the heart.

The word *sunecho* gives insight into the fullness of this constraint. This word describes the believer's heart response to the Father's unbounded love. It is often translated "to hold, to secure, to control, or empower." Thus, we may make the following observations:

- Thanksgiving for God's unmerited love holds us in grateful obedience, freeing us from the pull of our sinful nature.

- Praise for His loving character reminds us of our secure future, freeing us from the fear of losing His love.

- Worship of the God who is love empowers our grateful stewardship of His love, freeing us from selfish preoccupation.

Be certain to notice that thanksgiving, praise, and worship are not passive intellectual musings, but experiences of the heart and spirit.

Consider how you might respond to each of the following questions, and share your responses with your partner or small group. Allow the Spirit to reveal God's love to you directly and through those whom He loves.

- As a believer in Christ, you have been, are, and always will be loved by your Creator. How does your heart respond?

- In what particular area of struggle do you need the constraining love of Christ?

- What facets of His unmerited love might hold you in grateful obedience? Ask His Spirit to reveal His love to you in new and amazing ways, and express your thankfulness.

- What aspects of God's character remind you of your security in Christ and the fact that you will never lose His love? Ask His Spirit to demonstrate His true character to you in startling ways, and respond in praise.

- In what fresh ways might you worship the God who is love? Ask His Spirit to surround your heart with amazing, irresistible demonstrations of God's love. Ask Him to open your eyes and heart to the infinite ways in which God shows His care for you. Then worship the Lord with your whole heart.

Additional Resources

Gilbert Bilezikian, *Community 101* (Grand Rapids, MI: Zondervan Publishing House, 1997).

Walter A. Elwell, ed., *Evangelical Dictionary of Theology* (Grand Rapids, MI: Baker Books, 2001).

Gene A. Getz, *Loving One Another* (Wheaton, IL: Victor Books, 1980).

Michael C. Mack, *The Synergy Church* (Grand Rapids, MI: Baker Books, 1996).

Wes Roberts and Glenn Marshall, *Reclaiming God's Original Intent for the Church* (Colorado Springs, CO: NavPress, 2004).

Ray C. Stedman, *Body Life* (Grand Rapids, MI: Discovery House Publishers, 1995).

Chapter 7

Imparting Not Only the Gospel, but Our Very Lives: Our Foundation of Apologetics

P reach the gospel at all times. If necessary, use words."—St. Francis of Assisi

As you and I pursue life and ministry relevance, we will want to continue to experience change in how we see God and how we relate to Him through His Word. As our relationship with God becomes more intimate, we will see other people with His eyes of compassion and heart of love. We will come to more deeply cherish God's church and revel in our ability to bring Him glory as we demonstrate care for one another. Finally, this restoration of relationship with God, His Word, and His people will impact our view of those outside of Christ. We will live out the Great Commission with renewed power. We will share our faith with greater conviction and demonstrate immeasurable influence on our world.

In this chapter, we will discuss one final relational foundation and explore the critical principles of sharing Christ with an unbelieving world. We have discussed loving our neighbors as ourselves, examined the need to prioritize relationships with family and friends, and highlighted the importance of intimate relationships within the church. Now, let us focus upon demonstrating love to those outside of Christ by sharing the Gospel.

GREAT COMMANDMENT LOVE EMPOWERS GREAT COMMISSION WITNESS.

A familiar story from the tenth chapter of Luke sets the stage for our discussion of a relational apologetic, or argument for following Jesus. It reveals how the Great Commission must be empowered by the Great Commandment.

A Jewish leader asked Christ how he could inherit eternal life. Jesus invited the man to

> **Jesus began to paint a picture of what Great Commandment love looks like—it is defined not by limits, but by radical and startling power that brings glory to God.**

answer his own question from the Scriptures. The leader responded with what we know as the Great Commandment: that you must love the Lord with all your heart, soul, strength, and mind, and love your neighbor as yourself. Jesus affirmed the man's response. But the expert in the law had another question: "Who is my neighbor" (Luke 10:29)?

The religious leader sought to define the limits for the love he should be expected to demonstrate. But Jesus reframed the man's question, transforming it from one that suggested limits of duty to one that reflected deep care, grace, and compassion. Rather than "Who **is** my neighbor?" Christ posed the question, "Who **was** a neighbor?" Within the context of this introduction, Jesus began to paint a picture of what Great Commandment love looks like—it is defined not by limits, but by radical and startling power that brings glory to God.

The Parable of the Good Samaritan

> **We must learn to live out a relational apologetic that reflects both Great Commandment love and Great Commission passion.**

Jesus told the man a parable that we have come to refer to as the story of the Good Samaritan. Christ's words revealed that Great Commandment love is made manifest as we become good neighbors to those around us. It is this kind of radical, startling love for others that the Holy Spirit can use to draw them into a relationship with Jesus. It will be our unexpected love for the "unlovable" that will point a lost world to the One who loves them. The story of the Good Samaritan affirms the necessity of a relational argument for the faith. If the body of Christ hopes to change the world for Christ, we must learn to live out a relational apologetic that reflects both Great Commandment love and Great Commission passion.

The Connection Between Commandment and Commission

The pages of Scripture reveal that the Great Commandment is actually hidden within the Great Commission. As His days on Earth drew to a close, Christ said to His disciples, "Go and make disciples of all nations . . . teaching them to obey everything I have commanded you" (Matthew 16:19, 20). We can imagine that the disciples might have been somewhat perplexed by these instructions. They might have looked to one another and said, "Jesus taught us so many things. Now we are supposed to not only tell people about all of His commandments, but also teach others to actually live them out. Where should we begin?" The answer to this question comes from Christ's earlier teachings. He had already told the disciples "where to begin." They were to begin with the greatest of all commandments, which is really two-fold: love God and love one another. The Great Commission must begin with the Great Commandment, and truly living out the Great Commandment leads to fulfilling the Great Commission. In fact, the two are inseparable.

GREAT COMMANDMENT LOVE RESTORES RELEVANCE TO THE GREAT COMMISSION.

Could it be that the loss of relevance the church has experienced as we have tried to share our faith is due to our inability to sense this critical connection between the Great Commandment and the Great Commission? Could it be that we have separated these two hallmarks of Scripture and, in so doing, hindered our impact on the lives of unbelievers? Sadly, it is apparent that the struggles of many people have been made worse by a form of religion that is neither helpful nor relevant.

A 1st Century Example

Christ illustrated the irrelevance of 1st century religion as He related the story of the Good Samaritan:

> A man was going down from Jerusalem to Jericho, when he fell into the hands of robbers. They stripped him of his clothes, beat him and went away, leaving him half dead. A priest happened to be going down the same road, and when he saw the man, he passed by on the other side. So too, a Levite, when he came to the place and saw him, passed by on the other side. But a Samaritan, as he traveled, came where the man was; and when he saw him, he took pity on him. He went to him and bandaged his wounds, pouring on oil and wine. Then he put the man on his own donkey, took him to an inn and took care of him (Luke 10:30–34).

Jesus carefully distinguished the compassion of the Samaritan from the insensitivity of the priest and the Levite. The person that Jesus commended was neither the religious official nor the lay associate, but a foreigner who demonstrated a love that knew no cultural boundaries. In some ways, the actions of the religious leaders in this parable foreshadowed the pervasive irrelevance that plagues many ministries today.

A 21st Century Crisis

There are lonely and hurting people lying across the road from us. If we look carefully, we will see that fragmented relationships, feelings of abandonment, struggles with addictions, and

> **Sadly, we can see that the struggles of many people have been made worse by a form of religion that is neither helpful nor relevant.**

painful abuse have taken a terrible toll on our society. Neglect, materialism, and selfishness are widespread. But do Christ's followers actually engage these pain-filled people with compassionate care, or do we simply preach against the evils that brought the pain? Is our witness for Christ mainly confined to the security of our own institutions? Do we pass by those who are hurting and leave them to suffer alone? Do we keep a safe distance from anyone who might be struggling or wounded? Do we shout sermons across the road and loudly pronounce our commitment to prayer, all the while staying within our places of religious comfort? We have been rationally equipped to share the good news of the Gospel, but many of us lack the courage to actually live out the Gospel.

A Needed Work of His Spirit

Our busyness and self-focus often hinder us from noticing the plight of others, thus interfering with the Spirit's attempts to prompt within us a compassionate response. We, as the body of Christ, must ask the Lord to do a work in our hearts so that as we encounter hurting individuals along life's road, we will notice, stop, provide relevant care, and share the Gospel message that will change their lives. Let us not be believers, churches, or ministries that pass by on the other side. May we learn to reach the world for Christ by taking notice of people's pain and providing compassionate care.

Great Commandment ministry must be the context within which we fulfill the Great Commission. The effectiveness of our outreach will be proportionate to the depth of our love. This is the final relational foundation for relevant, meaningful ministry. During this course, we have emphasized the importance of our relationships with God, with our "near ones," and with our fellow believers. We must now address our relationships with those who do not know Christ. We have focused on seeing the real Jesus, seeing those around us as He sees them, and seeing the church as He sees it. Now we must commit ourselves to seeing a hurting world as He sees it—with eyes of love and a heart of compassion.

My Personal Journey

When I became a follower of Jesus at the age of 21, my life was radically changed. But I struggled with knowing how to share my faith with others. During the "Jesus Movement" of the 1960's, I was involved in ministry to other university students, seeking to help them come to know Christ.

> **May we learn to reach the world for Christ by taking notice of people's pain and providing compassionate care.**

Although God had used several caring people to demonstrate Christ's acceptance for me through my relationships with them, I impatiently wanted to get on with the business of fulfilling the Great Commission. Activities and events that were designed to reach students with the message of the Gospel were my priority. It seemed more efficient to present large numbers of students with the message of Christ than to invest in the slower, more personally challenging process of sharing my life with them. Many students made "decisions" for Christ, but even so, little true spiritual fruit grew out of my efforts.

As the pressure to do bigger and more frequent events increased, God began to reveal to me the tragedy of seeking to fulfill the Great Commission apart from the Great Commandment. Gradually, His Spirit took me back to the priority of relationships as the foundation of evangelism. Relevance, gratitude, and true discipleship returned to my ministry, and more importantly, God was surely pleased.

HOW DID JESUS PRESENT AN ARGUMENT FOR THE FAITH?

If we hope to see a child, family member, friend, neighbor, or co-worker come to Christ, we must look to the One who embodies relevance and impact. If we hope to restore relevance to our own lives and ministries as we share the Gospel with others, we must ask ourselves the following questions: How did Jesus present the Gospel? How did He reveal Himself to people? Did Christ offer the Jews rational arguments as to why they should believe He was the Messiah? No. Did He depend upon elaborate performances and costly productions to bring people the message of hope? Hardly. Did Jesus seek out opportunities to debate with political leaders and the religious hierarchy in order to disprove their theories and shed the light of truth upon their misguided philosophies? Evidently not. So how **did** Jesus present a defense of the faith?

A Relational Witness

The answer is revealed across the pages of the New Testament: Christ did not just impart the truths of the Gospel; He lived them out. Jesus did not offer isolated, rational arguments about the tenets of our faith. Rather, He consistently modeled the character and behavior that His teaching encouraged. Christ did not merely present a system of truthful propositions, but revealed Himself as Truth. The Savior did not just talk about the Gospel; He ultimately gave His very life. Christ's most effective and unequivocal defense of the faith came as He shared His life with those around Him, then gave Himself to all generations through His death.

People became convinced that Jesus was the Messiah as they witnessed His tears for a friend, His acceptance of an outcast, and His compassion for the infirmed (John 11:33–36; Luke 19:1–10; 18:35–42). Others were drawn to the Messiah by His supportive presence and unconventional demonstrations of love (John 9:1–41; Luke 17:11–19). Christ's miraculous healings and displays of supernatural power were never performed for the sake of gaining notoriety or simply validating His identity. They took place only within the context of relationships, as means of ministering to the needs of those around Him. Jesus Christ did not merely present a rational or propositional apologetic. He lived out a relational one.

> **People became convinced that Jesus was the Messiah as they witnessed His tears for a friend, His acceptance of an outcast, and His compassion for the infirmed.**

The church of the 21st century must take heed to this contrast in perspective. Just as Christ did not rely primarily upon rational arguments, grand events, or miraculous productions, we, too, must embrace an alternative approach to presenting the Gospel. We must become living epistles of our faith by embracing a relational apologetic.

The apostle Paul reinforced the need for a relational apologetic as he shared this powerful insight for presenting the Gospel: "We loved you so much that we were delighted to share with you not only the gospel of God but our lives as well" (1 Thessalonians 2:8). Paul seems to be saying, "Share the written letter (the gospel), and share the living letter (your life). The two make a powerful combination." Elsewhere in the same epistle, Paul reminds the Thessalonians that "our gospel came to you not simply with words, but also with power, with the Holy Spirit and with deep conviction. You know how we lived among you for your sake" (1:5). These passages confirm Paul's commitment to a relational apologetic and underscore our need for the same. Such a relational approach to the Gospel is even more important in our postmodern culture, where the prevailing question is not: "Are these propositions true?" but rather, "If these propositions are true, then what?" It is only as we impart our lives along with the Gospel that this important question will be answered.

One cautionary note must be given here. If we as Christ's church hope to adopt a relational apologetic, we must recognize that there is a price to be paid. Sharing one's life with another person requires a deep, costly commitment because only as our "walk" matches our "talk" will we have an effective,

> **Only as we offer supportive involvement, caring concern, and practical help will we give witness to the God who bears burdens.**

contagious witness for Christ. Only as we impart His life and love in spite of others' faults and failures will we give witness to a Christ who longs to accept us (Romans 15:7). Only as we offer supportive involvement, caring concern, and practical help will we give witness to the God who bears burdens (Galatians 6:2). Only as we demonstrate compassion and comfort when others are hurting will we give witness to a Christ who is both acquainted with sorrows and grief (Isaiah 53:3 NASB) and moved with compassion for others (John 11:35). The supernatural and sacrificial love of God demonstrated through His people will draw others to Christ and bear fruit that remains. We must be willing to allow God to make the necessary changes in our lives. We must continue to cooperate in His work of shaking our relational foundations so that our lives might be transformed into lights that shine for Him.

Relevance Will Return as We Love Like Jesus Loved.

We live in a world of hurt and emotional isolation. Our communities are filled with people desperate to find healing for broken relationships, a sense of meaning to replace the emptiness of their lives, and peace in the midst of chaos and insecurity. The crises are innumerable; the pressures can be overwhelming. Consequently, our world needs a relevant, vibrant body of believers who will serve as a shelter from the storm and a place of refuge from the stresses of life. People need a place where hurts are healed and hope is restored. They need the body of Christ to cross the road like the Good Samaritan and give relevant, helpful care. If we hope to reach our world with the Good News, we, as the called of God, must show that we are "good neighbors" by our demonstrations of His love. Prayerfully read these pertinent words, penned by Chuck Swindoll more than two decades ago:

> "Churches need to be less like untouchable cathedrals and more like well-used hospitals, places to bleed in rather than monuments to look at . . . places where you can take your mask off and let your hair down . . . places where you can have your wounds dressed. . . .

"Stop and think. Where does a guy go when the bottom drops out? To whom do we Christians turn when stuff that's embarrassing or a little scandalous happens? Who cares enough to listen when we cry? Who affirms us when we feel rotten? Who will close their mouths and open their hearts? And even though we deserve a swift kick in the pants, who will embrace us with understanding and give us time to heal without quoting verses? Without giving us a cassette tape of some sermon to listen to? Without telling a bunch of other Christians so they can "pray more intelligently"?

"Who can you turn to if you just got fired? . . . Or you just got out of jail? . . . Or your 15-year-old daughter told you last night that she was pregnant? . . . Or you beat your kids and you're scared and ashamed? . . . Or you can't cope with your drug habit any longer? . . . Or you need professional help because you're near a breakdown?

"Do you know what you need? You need a shelter. A place of refuge. A few folks who can help you, listen to you, introduce you, once again to 'the Father of mercies and God of all comfort, who comforts us in all our affliction'" (2 Corinthians 1:3, 4 NASB) (Swindoll, 1983).

> **The church will be viewed as a safe place only when people sense that we are more burdened about meeting their needs than judging their deeds.**

Dr. Swindoll's words remind us that relevant evangelism in a postmodern world will involve ministering in love to unbelievers at the point of their need, rather than just urging them to believe what we believe. The church will be viewed as a safe place only when people sense that we are more burdened about meeting their needs than judging their deeds.

> **We ought to be known as "friends to sinners."**

Does this mean that sinful behavior is never confronted? Absolutely not. It simply means that sin is addressed within the context of an accepting relationship, not apart from it. It means that we leave the work of conviction to the Holy Spirit, and that any needed words of reproof are Spirit-prompted, "according to the need of the moment, so that it will give grace to those who hear" (Ephesians 4:29 NASB). Jesus never condoned sin or shied away from identifying it, yet He was known as a "friend of tax collectors and 'sinners'" (Matthew 11:19). Likewise, as we seek to restore relevance to our lives and ministries, we ought to be known as "friends to sinners."

Optimum ministry relevance will only be possible when we fully display love for God and for our neighbors. It will be God's heart of love, expressed through His people, that will draw a searching world to ask about the Source of such love. In our postmodern world, life meaning is

> **Surrounding the unbeliever with Great Commandment love opens the door for Great Commission sharing.**

more often being sought through relationships than through rational systems that emphasize what is acquired, achieved, or accomplished. As unbelievers are lovingly accepted, comforted, and cared for by believers, they will begin to wonder, "Where did you receive all the acceptance, comfort, and care you have shared with me?" At this point, well-equipped believers will be ready to give an account of the hope that is within them (1 Peter 3:15 NASB). In essence, surrounding the unbeliever with Great Commandment love opens the door for Great Commission sharing.

An environment that is conducive to Great Commission sharing may take many different forms, such as the following:

- **Worship services where the unchurched sense acceptance, and where God's truth is experienced and practically applied to everyday life.** Canyon Creek Church encourages and equips individuals who come to their services to enrich their relationships by rejoicing and mourning with one another. As unchurched people attend services and small group meetings, they inevitably ask about the source of these simple yet profound relational principles. Church leaders are then able to introduce these seekers to the God of the Bible and the wisdom of His Word.

- **Classes or support groups offered to the community on topics such as substance abuse recovery, marriage enrichment, and parenting skills.** Each group focuses on experiencing and applying biblical truth. Pastor Ed recently led to Christ a woman who had called in response to a newspaper advertisement promoting a parenting class for blended families.

- **Small groups in homes and other non-church settings where friendships deepen and vulnerable sharing occurs.** First Church of Gainesville regularly sponsors a Sunday-morning marriage class at a nearby hotel. On average, 40–60 unchurched people attend, with 60 percent remaining active in the church after the seminar ends.

- **Backyard barbecues or neighborhood picnics where people demonstrate the relevance of God's love in the midst of everyday life.** David and Beth, a lay couple in California, regularly hold neighborhood events that attract families with young children. Easter egg hunts, Fourth of July parades, and kite-flying contests allow David and Beth the opportunity to establish relationships with these families. As relational connections grow, they have ample opportunity to share the Gospel with their friends.

- **A youth center where fun, food, fellowship, and caring involvement with unchurched kids provokes their hunger for a need-meeting God.** Four different youth groups in a large metropolitan city get together for "Impact." The leaders of these groups provide students with a venue for playing pool, video games, and music. Students are encouraged to bring their friends, hang out, and enjoy building relationships with positive teens. These weekly gatherings bring together youth from varied cultures, ethnic groups, and socio-economic backgrounds in order that they might experience true fellowship. Youth leaders typically connect with 15–30 unchurched youth each week. Relationships are established, and the Gospel is shared as the students grow to feel that they can be real with the youth leaders.

- **A ministry that provides comprehensive care to a diverse population of needy and pain-filled people.** The members of King's Church in the United Kingdom embrace their identity as "friends of sinners," creating an environment in which homeless people, prostitutes, and addicts experience God's grace and hope. The Caring Hands Center provides food, housing, medical services, and job assistance to numerous individuals and families. Support groups for the abused and addicted apply the healing power of God and His Word in a safe environment of genuine fellowship. Many experience Christ in radical, life-changing ways. Community and business leaders are regularly involved in supporting the ministry, with many of them becoming attracted to these relevant expressions of Christ's life and love.

Ultimately, we can be certain that our culture's problems cannot be successfully addressed by political, social, or economic solutions. The answer to the alienation and aloneness of the human condition can be found only in God's offer of reconciliation through His Son, Jesus Christ. It is because of this truth that God is at work in us, calling a hurting world to Himself.

Since God is in us and we are in Him, we have the awesome privilege of co-laboring with Him to see people establish or renew their relationship with Him and strengthen their relationships with one another. Paul's inspired message to the Corinthian church is as pertinent today as it was then: "Working together with Him, we also urge you not to receive the grace of God in vain . . . so that the ministry will not be discredited, but in everything commending ourselves as servants of God" (2 Corinthians 6:1–4 NASB). God desires that our ministries not be discredited or irrelevant. Let us now take a more detailed look at how we might love as Jesus loved, thus restoring relevance to our lives and ministries.

LOVING AS JESUS LOVED: ACCEPTING OTHERS AT THEIR POINT OF FAILURE

Tears glistened in the eyes of Salvation Army Officer Shaw as he looked at the three men before him. Shaw was a medical missionary who had just arrived in India, and the Army had been assigned to take over this colony of lepers. The three ailing men had their hands and feet bound with chains that cut into their diseased flesh.

Captain Shaw turned to the guard and said, "Please unfasten the chains."

"It isn't safe," the guard replied, "these men are dangerous criminals as well as lepers."

"I'll be responsible. They are suffering enough," Captain Shaw said. He put out his hand and took the keys, then knelt, tenderly removed the shackles, and treated the men's bleeding ankles and wrists.

Sometime later, Captain Shaw had his first misgivings about freeing the criminals. He had made plans for an overnight trip but dreaded leaving his wife and child alone. Shaw's wife insisted that she was not afraid, and that she felt secure in the care of the Almighty. When Mrs. Shaw went to the front door the following morning, she was startled to see the three criminals lying on her steps. One of the men explained in broken English: "We know the doctor go. We stay here all night so no harm come to you."

This was how these "dangerous" men responded to an act of love. Captain Shaw saw the lepers through the compassionate, accepting eyes of Jesus. He did not see them as criminals, but as hurting, lonely men in need of comfort and friendship. One simple demonstration of acceptance brought gratitude to the hearts of men and glory to God.

The Power of Acceptance

Captain Shaw's testimony reminds us of the power of accepting one another as Christ has accepted us (Romans 15:7). We also see evidence of the power of acceptance in the story of the Good Samaritan, who risked inconvenience, misunderstanding, and ridicule to demonstrate compassionate acceptance to the wounded traveler. If we hope to have a significant, evangelistic impact for the cause of Christ, we must begin to look for people who are failing and accept them with the grace of God. It may seem radical or unconventional, but in order to restore relevance to our evangelism, we must seek out the lost, the down-and-out, the outcasts, and the unpopular. As we offer God's grace, the gratitude of these individuals will spark revival in our midst. As we demonstrate the acceptance of Christ, our churches will become places of refuge, and those without a relationship with Christ will be compelled to know the One who empowers such grace.

> **We must begin to look for people who are failing and accept them with the grace of God.**

We see evidence of the power of this relational apologetic in Jesus' interactions with the unbelievers of His day. Christ imparted His life to those around Him by accepting people at their point of failure. Jesus demonstrated the life-changing results of acceptance when He encountered the woman at the well of Sychar (John 4:1–42).

In order to fully appreciate Christ's relational approach to evangelism, we must ask ourselves, "How did the woman at the well become convinced of the deity of Jesus? What was it about her dialogue with the Savior that prompted her to say, 'Come, see a man who told me everything I ever did. Could this be the Christ'" (v. 29)?

What do we know about this woman from reading this passage of Scripture and studying its context?

- From a Jewish perspective, this woman was an outcast, both because she was a Samaritan and because of her reputation in the community.

- This woman, by many accounts, had failed. She had been married five times, and the man with whom she was living at the time of her encounter with Jesus was not her husband (v. 18).

How did Christ demonstrate His acceptance of this woman?

- The woman must have been anticipating a very pious, unwelcoming response from

Jesus. It was significant for a Jew to speak to a Samaritan. It was against social custom for a man to have a lengthy discussion with a woman in public. But it was absolutely unheard of for a Jewish teacher to speak to a Samaritan woman about issues of worship. Everything about Christ's discussion with this woman demonstrated His acceptance.

What were the results of this relational apologetic? What impact did Christ's acceptance have on this woman and her community?

- The woman seemed convinced of the identity and deity of Christ, so much so that she invited others to meet Him (v. 29). She was apparently so touched by the Savior's acceptance that she brought others to Jesus, eventually making a significant impact on her entire town: "Many of the Samaritans from that town believed in him because of the woman's testimony . . . So when the Samaritans came to him, they urged him to stay with them, and he stayed two days. And because of his words many more became believers" (vv. 39–41).

What implications might the account of the woman at the well have for the 21st century church?

- The wonder of Christ's acceptance paved the way for the woman's receptivity to the Savior. As we demonstrate acceptance to others, they may be filled with wonder and, therefore, more receptive to the One who is the Source of such acceptance.

- Since the woman was undoubtedly startled by the accepting love of Jesus, perhaps we should look for ways to startle others with the acceptance of Christ.

- There are certain members of the Christian community who are very outspoken about specific groups of people, labeling them as "failures." Christ's acceptance of the woman at the well should prompt a re-evaluation of this approach and a reformation of heart for these members of the body of Christ.

- Christ's ministry of acceptance made His rational arguments much more credible. Jesus did not stand at a distance and pronounce judgment, condemn, or ridicule. He took intentional initiative to show acceptance to the woman at the well. We can apply these same principles to our own lives and ministries, benefiting from combining a ministry of acceptance with our rational arguments for the faith. We may need to assess our own tendencies to judge, condemn, or ridicule others, and look for ways to take the initiative in showing acceptance instead.

- Christ's ministry of acceptance was as much of an apologetic as any of the declarations He made about His identity. Jesus presented a relational argument for His divinity, which was in stark contrast to the Pharisaical rejection and piety with which this woman might have been familiar. It was undoubtedly Jesus' startling love that caused the woman to take notice of what Christ had to say. Could our lack of acceptance be part of the reason that so many unbelievers are taking no notice of what we have to say?

My Personal Journey

During my early years in college, with the hippie movement well underway, my life was characterized by rebellion and sin. Even though I was married, I lived a predominantly "single lifestyle." I focused on having a good time with my single friends. We all wore sandals, grew shoulder-length hair, and opposed anyone in authority.

Out of loneliness, Teresa began attending a neighborhood church, and soon concluded that I needed to attend as well. After considerable discussion and conflict, I finally agreed to go, but with two conditions: we would sit on the back row, and we would leave before the service was over in order to avoid getting "trapped" at the back door by the preacher.

During my first visit to this church, God miraculously intervened in my life through the church custodian. Brother Paul, as I came to know him, sought me out that day. He shook my hand and became my friend. Paul accepted my skepticism and youthful rebellion. He looked beyond my disinterested demeanor and showed interest in me. Over the next year, we became great friends. We painted swings on the church playground and worked together maintaining the church grounds. Paul lived out an example of genuineness and grace that I had not experienced before. God's Spirit began to draw me into a relationship with the Jesus that Paul had known so intimately. I was being accepted and loved by Paul, and that challenged me to personally embrace the One who is love.

Join us now as we live out the call to accept one another. Pause and pray for Christ's acceptance of you to empower your acceptance of others in order that you might bring praise to God!

An Experience With God's Word

"Accept one another, then, just as Christ accepted you, in order to bring praise to God" (Romans 15:7).

Consider some of the following hindrances to showing acceptance to others. Which of these might be true for you?

I sometimes struggle with . . .

- being so busy with my agenda that I fail to notice people's needs.

- wanting to convince others of the truth of the Gospel to the point that I miss seeing their needs or point of view.

- thinking so much about people's spiritual needs that I overlook their relational or physical needs.

- not being able to see beyond a person's sin or the ways in which they are different from me. I am, therefore, not always sensitive to their need for acceptance.

- being judgmental, critical, or condemning.

After you have identified your areas of hindrance, complete the following sentences:

I might sometimes struggle to accept others because I . . .

I regret this struggle or hindrance because I can see now that . . .

(For example: *I might sometimes struggle to accept others because I cannot see beyond a person's sin or the ways in which they are different from me. I regret this struggle because I can see now that even as I have prayed for several family members to come to Christ, my own lack of acceptance may have kept them from hearing God's truth.*)

(For example: *I might sometimes struggle to accept others because I am so busy with my agenda that I fail to notice people's needs. I regret this struggle because I can see now that there have been several people at my office who have needed my acceptance. I wonder if they might have avoided several mistakes and come to a personal relationship with Christ if they had received more of Christ's acceptance through me.*)

Share your responses with your partner or small group. As you share, give accepting responses to one another. Such responses might sound like, *I can understand how hard that is for you,* or *I am saddened to hear of your regret.*

As you share, keep in mind the promise of Romans 15:7: As we accept one another, thus expressing our gratitude for Christ's acceptance of us, praise is brought to God!

Finally, pray together. Ask the Holy Spirit to help you embody the instruction of Romans 15:7. Pray that God would make the wonder of Christ's acceptance real in your life. Ask the Holy Spirit to enable you to demonstrate that acceptance to others in order to bring praise to God.

LOVING AS JESUS LOVED:
SUPPORTING OTHERS AT THEIR POINT OF STRUGGLE

Have you ever felt beaten by the world?
Have you ever felt that your spirit had been stripped
and left bare to the harsh elements?
Have you ever felt that no one cares about your future?
I have been there.
I was the one lying on the side of the road as many passed by.
They continued on, unconcerned or unaware of my need.

But today I am thankful. I'm thankful for the one
who did stop and reach out.
I am grateful for the one who took the time to bring comfort
to my wounds; thankful for the one who supported me
when I could not stand on my own.
I am grateful for the one who cared enough
to see hope in my future.
I can share this story with you because of one . . . one
who became my "neighbor" and extended the love of God to me.

—The Traveler

This beautiful poem, penned by an anonymous poet, captures the heart of an unbeliever who has experienced the grace of God through the supportive care of another person. We can recall that the Good Samaritan provided practical and caring support to the traveler alongside the road, who was struggling to survive. Likewise, if we hope to restore relevance to our lives and ministries, every believer will have to become "a neighbor" to those outside of Christ and lavishly extend the love of God. In order to accomplish this relational apologetic, each of us must continue to look to Christ, reflecting on how He loved and then doing likewise.

The Power of Support

Christ continued to demonstrate a relational apologetic throughout the Gospels. Following the calming of the storm on the Sea of Galilee, the 12 disciples were more convinced than ever of the deity of Jesus. Christ's loving support during their time of struggle served as a compelling argument for faith in Him (Matthew 8:23–27; Mark 4:35–41; Luke 8:22–25).

What do we learn about the disciples' encounter with the storm from reading this passage of Scripture and studying its context?

- Jesus and the disciples got into the boat to cross the Sea of Galilee. While Jesus slept, the disciples began to panic because of a storm that threatened their lives and safety. They awakened Jesus and, though He noted their limited faith, He ministered support to them. Christ spoke to the wind and the sea, and they were immediately calmed.

- The disciples were struggling with a physical force of nature, possibly struggling against spirits of evil, and struggling to exercise faith in the words of God. Jesus had specifically told the disciples, "Let us go over to the other side" (Mark 4:35). His words were a promise; they were going to the other side!

What did Christ do that caused the disciples to ask, "What kind of man is this" (Matthew 8:27)?

- Christ could have waited on the shore of Galilee as the disciples' faith was tested. He could have watched from a distance as they fought against the storm. He could have left them alone in their struggle. But though He slept, Jesus was in the boat with the 12. Though the disciples were filled with doubt, even to the point of questioning the Savior's care, Jesus showed His support. When His closest friends struggled to believe, Jesus got under the burden with them. He spoke to the wind and the waves, and the raging storm was stilled (vv. 38, 39). In the aftermath of this powerful miracle, Christ was revealed as more than a religious zealot or a great teacher—creation had obeyed its Creator!

What implications might this account of the disciples' struggle have for the 21st century church?

- Just as Christ was with the disciples as they struggled against the storm, we will benefit from more intentional efforts to "be with" others as they encounter life's struggles. We must challenge ourselves to move away from a ministry mindset that invites unbelievers to "come and see" and replace it with one that compels us to "go and share." Relevance will be restored as we look for opportunities to join others in their burdens, reassuring them that they are not alone.

- Even though Jesus noted the disciples' lack of faith, He still offered supportive care. When we notice others who have a lack of faith or stamina in the midst of their struggles, we may pave the way for the good news of the Gospel by "getting under the burden" with them. Countless people around us could be empowered to face their own personal struggles and responsibilities through our sharing of God's supportive love.

- Christ's demonstration of support gave testimony of His deity and solidified the disciples' belief in Him. As we support others in the midst of struggles with their marriages, children, health, and financial issues, the Lord will use those opportunities to reveal His care and draw others to Himself. We need to open the eyes of our hearts to the countless people around us who are overcome by the cares of this life and feel that they are adrift on stormy seas.

My Personal Journey

As my friend Paul lived out an example of Christ's love and grace before me, I was particularly impressed by his supportive, caring heart. He frequently provided food or clothing from the church's "Crisis Closet" to those in need. He supported families who had loved ones in prison, and made frequent hospital visits for prayer and ministry. Paul often invited me to join him on these "Good Samaritan" visits, and I was able to witness the powerful impact of Christ's love, the kind of love that bears the burdens of others (Galatians 6:2). Although my peers spoke of caring compassion, Paul lived it out. Gently, God's Spirit drew my heart to consider the Source behind Paul's supportive love. I soon entrusted my burden of sin and rebellion to Christ.

An Experience With God's People

"Rejoice with those who rejoice" (Romans 12:15).

As you reflect on your own salvation experience and your journey with the Lord, can you recall particular members of the body of Christ who were there to support you? Perhaps a friend helped bear a burden or share a struggle. Was there a special family member who celebrated with you during a time of rejoicing? Was there someone who supported you during a time of struggle? Pause now, and remember a time when the Lord provided His support through the care of another person.

I feel grateful as I remember how God brought _____ *to support me when . . .*

(For example: *I feel grateful as I remember how God brought two special friends to support me when I was having difficulties in my marriage. They cared for me when I felt completely alone and abandoned. I am not sure how I could have survived if they had not been around.*)

(For example: *I feel grateful as I remember how God brought Gary to support me when I first became a follower of Christ. He helped me when I had so many questions about my faith. He was never impatient with me or judgmental concerning my struggles. He gently led me to the answers in God's Word.*)

Share your responses with your partner or small group. Rejoice with one another about God's provision of supportive care through His people. Your words of rejoicing might sound like, *I am thrilled to hear how God sent someone to support you in such a mighty way, or I am so glad that God sent someone to help you bear that burden, or I rejoice with you over God's provision. He brought someone to minister to you in such a special way!*

LOVING AS JESUS LOVED: COMFORTING OTHERS AT THEIR POINT OF PAIN

Samantha's mother asked her to walk down the street to borrow a cup of sugar from a neighbor. Her mother was in a terrible hurry to finish a particular recipe, so she expected her daughter back in only a few minutes. After all, the neighbor lived only three houses down the street. Much to her mother's frustration, Samantha took much longer than expected to return home. Her mother was quite irritated and a little worried, and demanded an explanation for her late arrival. Samantha explained that on her way home she met her friend, who lived next door. The friend was crying because her favorite baby doll had broken. "Oh," said the mother, "then you stopped to help her fix the doll?" "Oh, no," replied Samantha, "I stopped to help her cry."

Reaching a pain-filled world with the relevant message of the Gospel requires the compassionate heart of the Savior. If we hope to reach others with the Gospel, we will first have to move beyond our tendency to "fix" the world for Jesus and, instead, stop to help people cry.

The Power of Comfort

Jesus consistently demonstrated compassionate care as He encountered the lonely, hungry, tormented, and sorrowful. The Savior exemplified the power of a relational apologetic that cares for those who are hurting and weeps for people who are in pain. Jesus' ministry to Mary and Martha at the tomb of Lazarus (John 11:17–44) is an especially poignant example to every believer of His commitment not just to "fix" the circumstances of our life, but to care for us in the midst of life's joys and sorrows.

When Jesus saw Mary weeping after her brother's death, Scripture tells us that "He was deeply moved in spirit, and was troubled . . . Jesus wept" (vv. 33, 35 NASB). Lost and hurting people need the body of Christ to follow His example by noticing their pain and being deeply moved with compassion. They need us to care about their sorrows and weep because of their tears, thus living out the admonishment to "Mourn with those who mourn" (Romans 12:15).

What do we know about Mary and Martha and their encounter with Jesus at the tomb of Lazarus? What do we learn by reading this passage of Scripture and studying its context?

- Jesus could have come to Bethany much sooner but chose to delay His arrival in order to bring praise and glory to God (John 11:1–15). Christ's subsequent testimony to the unbelievers was manifested both in the power of a God who can raise the dead and in the compassion of a God who cries.

- Jesus had the power to save Lazarus without being physically present in Bethany. He could have given the command from afar and Lazarus would have been raised from the dead. But He chose to go to Bethany in order to be with Mary and Martha in their sorrow and comfort them in their pain.

- Christ's prayer to the Father revealed that He knew by faith that Lazarus would be raised from the dead. But in spite of the fact that Jesus knew the story would have a happy ending, He was moved with compassion because His friends were filled with sadness.

What did Christ's response communicate to Mary and to us?

- Just as Jesus hurt when He saw Mary's tears, He also hurts when He sees the sorrows of our lives. Our pain moves Him with compassion (Psalm 103:13; 145:9; Isaiah 30:18).

What were the results of Christ's demonstration of compassion and care?

- The Savior's visible grief and tears of compassion communicated His love for Mary, Martha, and Lazarus. The crowd that watched His response that day was impacted by His love: "Then the Jews said, 'See how he loved him'" (v. 36)! Jesus wept, and even the skeptics perceived it as an expression of His loving compassion.

- Many who witnessed the Savior's compassion and demonstration of power that day came to believe in Him (v. 45).

What implications does Christ's response to Mary and Martha have for the 21st century church?

- As we come to know of sorrowed hearts and painful losses, we should take the initiative to seek out and care for those who are hurting.
- Just as Christ's tears of compassion for His friends caught the attention of many onlookers, we will make a significant impact on our world as we are moved with compassion for the hurts of others.
- Even though we know that "happy endings" are in store for all those who have a relationship with Christ, we must avoid the tendency to "talk others out of their pain."

Instead, we should demonstrate Christ's compassion, allowing others the chance to grieve or feel sorrow, yet reassuring them of our love and care.

- As part of our quest to restore relevance to our lives and ministries, we should pray for God to bring rejected, struggling, hurting people who need comfort across our path.

- When people are hurting, they need the blessing of comfort. Comfort can be expressed effectively with a few simple words like, "It really saddens me to hear you say . . ." or "I hurt for you as I consider the pain you're going through." This simple demonstration of God's comfort will cause others to take notice of our love. We will then have the opportunity to introduce others to the One who has loved and comforted us.

My Personal Journey

My friend Paul's prayer life was one of his more interesting ways of living out the Gospel before me. He would often pray for a homeless man after we had helped him with groceries. When we visited someone in the hospital, Paul would end our time in prayer, asking God for healing and imploring Him to bring an end to the individual's suffering. Paul prayed for me on many occasions as well. He prayed for me as I took exams at the University. He prayed for my wife and children.

One of Paul's particular prayer concerns was for Dr. Samuel. Dr. Samuel and his wife lived next to our church, and the two had been in a near-fatal traffic accident. Paul often prayed with the Samuels, asking God to bring healing. I joined Paul at the Samuels' home several times and was struck by the intimacy of his prayers.

Paul spoke of a God who was saddened by the Samuels' tragedy. I had never imagined a God who was so personal, or One who was so close to us that He hurt when we hurt. Paul's faith and testimony became an example for me, and his prayers helped redefine my view of Jesus. My image of God as One who cares and heals was especially strengthened on the day that Dr. Samuel came walking down the hill toward the church to greet us. With renewed health, Dr. Samuel had come to thank Paul for his prayers!

Our Hope of Sharing Comfort

The only hope we have of ministering God's comfort to others is for the Holy Spirit to work within us. Our natural inclination is not to comfort. It is only the Spirit, the Comforter at work within us, that moves us to hurt with people, comfort them, and pray for God to heal their hurt and draw them to Himself.

The power to be compassionate comes as we experience more compassion **from** Him and **for** Him. As you and I are touched by the sufferings of the Savior, our hearts will also become tender toward other people. One of the significant reasons for including experiences with God's Son in every chapter of this resource is so that our hearts might be softened for God's people and for those who do not know Him. Just as we have learned to hurt for Jesus, so we will learn to hurt for those He loves. We cannot impart our lives to meet the needs of those around us unless we each have an intimate relationship with God. It is only as we come to "know Christ and the power of his resurrection and the fellowship of sharing in his sufferings" (Philippians 3:10) that we will be able to be conformed to the compassionate heart of God.

> **The power to be compassionate comes as we experience more compassion from Him and for Him.**

Reflect again on the story of Mary and Martha at the tomb of Lazarus. These women undoubtedly felt alone. The one person they knew could help their brother had not arrived in time. They were grieving, disappointed, and deeply sorrowed by the death of their brother. Mary's prayers seemed to have gone unanswered. Martha's diligent efforts to care for her brother had little effect. These were some of Christ's closest friends; they must have longed for His comforting presence and hoped for His swift arrival.

Imagine for a moment that we are observing the scene when Christ finally does arrive in Bethany. Word has traveled ahead of Him, and Martha hears that Jesus is near. She rushes out of the house and meets Christ on the dusty road outside of their home. Martha falls into Christ's arms, and they exchange a warm embrace. As they pull apart, we overhear her words of faith and confidence in the Savior's care: "Lord . . . if you had been here, my brother would not have died. But I know that even now God will give you whatever you ask" (John 11:21, 22).

Martha goes back home and tells Mary, "The Teacher is here . . . and is asking for you" (v. 28). Mary leaves the house and hurries to find the Savior. As the One who is the source of life meets the one who has encountered death, their hearts are filled with emotion. Mary falls at the feet of Jesus, overcome by her sorrow yet relieved by the presence of her friend. She, too, in the midst of her grief, affirms Christ's power and identity: "Lord, if you had been here, my brother would not have died" (v. 32).

At this moment, we see a spectacular response from the Savior. As Jesus sees Mary crying, the emotional pain of His friends is so great that He weeps. Jesus' eyes fill with tears, and His Spirit is deeply moved with compassion because of the pain of those He loves. The One who knows the future, who knows that Lazarus' life will soon be restored, is still sorrowed by the tears of His friend. Her aloneness hurts His heart. Her sadness moves Him deeply.

Let us now have one final experience with God's Son. This time, we hope that you will receive an abundant measure of the Spirit's comfort and compassion for **you**. Pray now that the Holy Spirit might allow you to experience God's tender care in new and amazing ways.

An Experience With God's Son

"Praise be to the God and Father of our Lord Jesus Christ, the Father of compassion and the God of all comfort, who comforts us in all our troubles, so that we can comfort those in any trouble with the comfort we ourselves have received from God" (2 Corinthians 1:3, 4).

Take a moment, and reflect on your own experiences and life events. Pause to recall a time when you felt some measure of sorrow, sadness, discouragement, or disappointment, and either no one knew, or no one was able to care for you. Can you remember a particular time of aloneness, either recently or in the distant past? Perhaps you experienced a tragic loss, significant betrayal, or painful rejection.

I remember a particular time of sadness/aloneness when . . .

(For example: *I remember a particular time of sadness/aloneness when our children had moved away from home and I realized that my husband and I did not know one another anymore.*)

(For example: *I remember a particular time of sadness/aloneness when I was on a business trip and got the best news of my career, but there was no one around with whom I could celebrate. The joy of the moment was lost because I was alone.*)

Now, reflect further on this occasion of aloneness. As you recall this time when you were saddened, disappointed, or discouraged, consider the Savior's heart for you at that moment. Could it be that during your time of sorrow, God was caring about your pain?

Pause to reflect on Jesus. Picture Him before you, His heart moved with compassion for you just as it was for Mary in Bethany. Imagine the tear-filled eyes of Jesus as He sees you at your point of pain. The prophet Isaiah spoke of Israel's pain and affliction and declared, "in all their affliction He was afflicted" (Isaiah 63:9 NASB). Consider now that Christ was afflicted, sorrowed, and saddened as He looked compassionately upon you and your sorrow.

Imagine Christ's tender face and gentle embrace as He comes to you at your time of pain. He has made a special trip just to see you. His intent is to show you compassion and let you know He cares. Hear the words Christ speaks to you: "Precious child, My heart is sorrowed as I see you now. I am burdened by your pain and grieved by your loneliness. My heart is deeply moved for you. I am here for you, to love you and to reassure you that I care."

Pause now, and share with Christ what this truth does to your heart. Tell Him of your gratitude. Thank Him for His comfort.

Dear Jesus, Thank You for Your compassion. It means so much to me that . . .

I am so grateful that I have a God who cries for me because . . .

Share your responses with your partner or small group. Relate your experience of aloneness, and allow others to offer words of comfort and compassion. Allow the Holy Spirit to bring healing to your heart and life as others mourn with you and share the blessing of God's comfort. Your words of comfort might sound like, *I hurt for you because you have gone through such pain and felt so alone,* or *I care for you, and it saddens me that you have been alone.*

When we truly experience Christ's Great Commandment love and allow it to empower our Great Commission passion, we will startle the world around us. As we look at Christ's ministry, we clearly see the impact of this startling kind of love. The people of Christ's day were startled by His words, such as "Stretch out your hand"; "Rise and walk"; and "I and the Father are one." People were also startled by what Jesus did. He turned water into wine, walked on water, even ate with tax collectors and sinners! But most important, the world was startled by His love. Jesus startled the woman at the well with His acceptance. He startled the disciples with His support. Christ startled the mourners at Lazarus' tomb with His love. Through these startling demonstrations of His love, people were drawn into relationship with Him.

Our world needs to be startled by such love. People need to see a living model of a person who loves God with all their heart and loves their neighbors enough to tell them about the One who is love. Let us go forth and begin to startle our world with God's amazing love!

For Further Study

THE GOOD NEWS OF THE GOSPEL

"You will be my witnesses . . ." (Acts 1:8).

The Holy Spirit empowers our witness to others concerning the good news of the Gospel. Passionate love for God and grateful acceptance of our identity as the beloved of God will manifest themselves in love for others as we share our faith.

It is good news that . . .

- God is love (1 John 4:7, 8), and He is caringly involved in all our ways (Psalm 139:3).

- we do not need to be alone. Christ has paid the price for sin (which keeps us separated from God and others).

- Christ makes available His gifts of forgiveness and life, in order that abundance can be ours both now and for eternity.

- "everyone who calls on the name of the Lord will be saved" (Romans 10:13).

A possible prayer for those who want to receive this good news of the Gospel is . . .

Jesus, I need You.
I need Your forgiveness and Your love.
I receive Your care and acceptance of me.
I yield to You my life, my future, my all.
I invite Your Spirit to change me in order that I might share You with others.

Additional Resources

David Ferguson, *Relational First Aid* (Austin, TX: Relationship Press, 2002).

John M. Frame, *Apologetics to the Glory of God: An Introduction* (Phillipsburg, NJ: P and R Publishing Company, 1994).

Nicky Gumbel, *Questions of Life: A Practical Introduction to the Christian Faith* (Colorado Springs, CO: David C. Cook Publishing, 2002).

Dann Spader and Gary Mayes, *The Everyday Commission: Discover the Passion and Purpose of Partnering With God* (Wheaton, IL: Harold Shaw Publishers, 1994).

Chuck Swindoll, *Dropping Your Guard* (Waco, TX: Word Publishing, 1984).

Chapter 8

Relational Foundations in Ministry

"Neither do men pour new wine into old wineskins. If they do, the skins will burst. . . . No, they pour new wine into new wineskins, and both are preserved" (Matthew 9:17).

The metaphor of the wine and wineskins was undoubtedly perplexing to those who first heard it, but, little by little, the followers of Jesus came to experience the dramatic impact that the "new wine" of the Gospel had on the "old wineskins" of 1st century Judaism. The fresh message of salvation by grace and faith alone (Ephesians 2:8, 9) shattered the judgmental legalism of the day. With Christ's cry from Calvary, "It is finished," the fresh message of substitutionary atonement rent the temple veil (Matthew 27:51). No longer was the glory of intimacy with God restricted to selected priests on specials days. The crucifixion and resurrection of Jesus ushered in a new covenant, in which Christ was available and accessible to all who called upon the name of the Lord (Romans 10:13). As further testimony of this new covenant, the Holy Spirit gave birth on the Day of Pentecost to a new "temple" in which God's glory would now reside—the bodies of believers (see Acts 2:1–36; Colossians 1:27). Truly, the fresh message of the Gospel demanded fresh methods through which God made Himself known. In a similar way, the restoration of love and relevance to the 21st century church will require fresh perspectives on life and ministry.

> **The restoration of love and relevance to the 21st century church will require fresh perspectives on life and ministry.**

In this closing chapter, we will explore some of the opportunities and challenges of living out a Great Commandment heart and Great Commission lifestyle. As we continue to yield ourselves to the Spirit's call, we will be drawn to a fresh, relational message concerning God, His Word, His saints, and those outside of Christ.

THE CHALLENGE OF RELEVANCE

Twenty-first century Christians often struggle with irrelevance in both their personal lives and their ministries. As believers fall into the traps of relativism, materialism, fragmented relationships, and fleshly addictions, it becomes clear that the salt has lost its savor (Matthew 5:13 KJV), and that our lives are losing their meaning and impact. As Christ's church finds itself struggling to survive, particularly in the Western world, the relevance of our ministry efforts must be questioned. In light of these realities, the need for both a fresh relational message and relational perspectives on ministry seems critical. In order for the 21st century church to reclaim its impact, we will have to employ methods that are relevant and applicable to today's world. Our approaches to life and ministry must be sensitive to the climate of our era, while, at the same time, reflecting a 1st century-influenced, relational perspective.

The Postmodern Challenge

> **The Great Commandment can serve as the fresh message that reshapes life and ministry priorities.**

Cultural historians date the modern era from approximately the mid-16th century to the mid-20th century, roughly from the fall of the Bastille during the French Revolution to the fall of the Berlin Wall, which effectively ended the Cold War. Rational arguments and logical systems of analysis were hallmarks of the modern age, as acceptance of the scientific method grew. Knowledge became equivalent to life relevance. Truth was determined by what could be observed and proven.

In the postmodern era in which we live, significant cultural changes shape our pursuit of life meaning and truth. These changes have the potential to either drastically quicken the pace of the church's decline into irrelevance, or to provide the church with one of its greatest opportunities for evangelism and growth in several millennia.

Current postmodern thought emphasizes the significance of relationships in shaping life meaning and the priority of personal experiences in establishing truth. Therefore, the potential of a relational theology centered on loving God and others and grounded in actually experiencing God's Word is being embraced by many believers around the world. Specifically, there are churches in several countries that draw upon the training and resources available through the Great Commandment Network (GreatCommandment.net). These churches are making a commitment to establish both a message and methodologies that impact the culture of our day.

Lessons From the Wineskins: The Message Shapes the Methods

An important principle can be seen in Christ's analogy of the wine and wineskins: The fresh "wine," or message, shapes the "wineskins," or methods. When you pour a small amount of wine into a wineskin, the skin is slack and flexible. But if we put a large quantity of wine in that same wineskin, it expands, growing large and full. The wine shapes the wineskin. Likewise, our message must always shape our methods.

The relational foundations of the Great Commandment can serve as the fresh message that reshapes the priorities of our lives and ministries. Indeed, the message of the Great Commandment was the basis of the methods that allowed the 1st century church to make such a profound impact on their world. But regrettably, the Western church often violates the principle of "the message shaping the methods." We often work frantically to change every imaginable method in hopes of regaining relevance in an increasingly postmodern world. Hundreds of millions of dollars are spent each year on conferences, courses, strategies, and programs that seek to change church wineskins. Emphases upon becoming more seeker-friendly, blending contemporary and traditional worship, and establishing small groups are each an evidence of our attempts to change ministry methods. While such changes may be needed in certain contexts, the church must recognize that rethinking our methods will do very little good unless we first reevaluate the relevance of our message.

My Personal Journey

Recently, while meeting with a group of leaders, church planters and missionaries who are served by our team through the Great Commandment Network, this wine/wineskins lesson proved to be of paramount importance. Initially, the discussion was centered on the issue of small groups. Several years of training, planning, and conferencing had brought about a major re-orientation of ministry, as churches shifted from a large-group, didactic model of Christian education to a "fellowship" model built around newly formed small groups, which were guided by

> **We often work frantically to change every imaginable method in hopes of regaining relevance in an increasingly postmodern world.**

highly trained and motivated leaders who utilized popular curriculum materials. The cost of this transition in terms of time, energy, and money had been considerable, the resistance to such change had been high, and the results had proved to be discouraging. The analysis of this group of leaders was simple: "We've paid a high price in resources and relationships and have simply multiplied and brought more complexity to an approach that wasn't working from the beginning." They concluded that their small group ministries had created more ministry "units," but had brought about only a small increase in effective evangelism. They noted very little deepened fellowship, and even reported decreased giving and accountability. Through our discussions, we concluded that these leaders had changed their churches' wineskins, but the message that they were putting into these new methods had not been evaluated.

In our first meeting together, our ministry team challenged these leaders to take a closer look at their need for a fresh message. One of our first points of emphasis was that it is critical that we see people as needing both God and others. It quickly became apparent that this idea was missing from many of the small groups in questions. Several of the leaders reported that biblical knowledge was exchanged during small group ministry, but that people rarely shared their lives with one another. Apparently, some groups subtly communicated the idea that if the members would exercise more faith or pray more diligently, they would be able to depend only on God. Needing one another was viewed as a sign of immaturity or weakness.

We went on to encourage these leaders to assess the way their small group members saw one another. Did they view each other just as sinful people in need of a Savior, or as both fallen and alone, in need of both a relationship with Christ and relationships with others? We spent our final hours with these ministry leaders allowing them to experience the impact of a fresh, 1st century message, and helping them to see how it could enrich their relationships. They returned to their homes and ministries with renewed hope and increased relevance.

RELEVANT LIVING AND MINISTRY REDEFINED: FRESH PERSPECTIVES ON FOLLOWING JESUS

Throughout this resource, we have explored how a relational message of loving Christ and loving others demands that we reevaluate and redefine what it means to experience life and life abundant. Christ's promise of life's exceeding abundance flows from experiencing Him as He really is, experiencing Scripture with the One who wrote it, and expressing His love toward our "neighbors" as we come to see them as God sees them. Embracing such a radical message will challenge our definition and understanding of what it is to become a true disciple, or fully devoted follower of Jesus Christ. A commitment to relevant living and relevant ministry will force us to redefine some of our methodologies.

My Personal Journey

As I set out at the age of 21 on my own journey toward becoming a fully devoted follower of Christ, activities, events, knowledge, and disciplines became paramount. Bible studies, devotionals, intercessory prayer hours, and evangelistic forays into the world of unsaved university students became marks of "faithfulness." Scripture memory, fasting, and prayers for the sick regrettably became spiritual "merit badges" rather than Spirit-empowered expressions of Christ's life and love. I attended conferences, acquired notebooks, and listened to countless sermons on tape, all in an effort to develop the testimony and vocabulary of the "truly committed." Faithfulness at church was measured by frequency of participation, utilizing such concrete measuring devices as 1) bringing your Bible, 2) preparing your lesson, 3) paying your tithe, 4) offering your prayers, and (possibly the most interesting mark of a true disciple) 5) being on time!

The irrelevance of such a rational and behavioral perspective on abundant life soon began to take its toll. I grew weary in well-doing, and what began as the glorious wonder and privilege of receiving Christ was, over time, replaced by dutiful conformity. My Christian life became a huge "got to" rather than a glorious "get to." Mercifully, the Lord led me on a journey of brokenness and spiritual dryness, only to refresh my heart and spirit with the fullness and wonder of experiencing His life from above. Over time, a new definition of what it means to be a true follower of Christ emerged. I no longer embraced a purely rational or behavioral devotion to Christ, but came to experience an intimate and Spirit-prompted relationship with the One who saved me!

> **Moving beyond the modern age's focus on what we acquire, accomplish, and achieve, this journey in life and ministry relevance places priority on character formation, divine calling, and kingdom cooperation.**

Abundant Life in Christ Is Relational!

As God's Spirit continues His "shaking" and conforming work in order to restore to Christ's followers the relevance of a relational message, a new definition of being a fully devoted follower of Jesus emerges. Believers in this Great Restoration move of God are embracing the powerful simplicity of finding life meaning and effective ministry through relationships. Moving beyond the modern age's focus on what we acquire, accomplish, and achieve, this journey in life and ministry relevance places priority on character formation, divine calling, and kingdom cooperation.

In the section to follow, we will explore the relational destination to which we have been called. As we do so, listen for the Spirit's revealing as He challenges your character, your calling, and your cooperation. Only as He is free to convict and conform your life will you be freed to go forth and make disciples as He intended (Matthew 28:19).

> *Maturity* **will be defined as "Humble servants with expectant faith, who are empowered by gratitude, giving priority to ministry to the Lord, ministry of the Word, ministry of His love to others, and the ministry of reconciliation."**

Reference has been made in earlier chapters to the significant work of God in the Great Reformation, which returned grace, faith, and the Scriptures to the forefront of personal and community experience. However, one of the unfulfilled hopes of the Reformation was the "loosing of the laity," through which it was hoped that each believer, as a unique part of Christ's body, would live out a testimony of His character, fulfilling their individual calling and becoming more and more constrained by kingdom priorities. If the Great Restoration (which we pray is occurring even now) is to bring to fruition what the Reformers began, a relational message of "loving God and loving others" will need to find expression in fresh ways among God's people. A redefinition of discipleship will need to be experienced as God's Spirit transforms His saints for the work of ministry. Join us now as we explore specific ways in which God may want to change our character as we learn to love Him and others more deeply.

In the sections that follow, we will offer a renewed definition of spiritual maturity, taken from the New Testament. Rather than defining *maturity* in terms of knowledge acquired or activities attended, we describe it as follows: "Humble servants with expectant faith, who are empowered by gratitude, giving priority to ministry to the Lord, ministry of the Word, and ministry of His love to others, thus becoming ministers of reconciliation." As we explore this relational definition of maturity in considerable depth, we will also suggest the need for a relational ministry approach that is in contrast to many current approaches to ministry. The relational theology that has been discussed throughout the seven previous chapters can only be contained by and expressed through a relational ministry, which is to say that this new wine will necessarily create newly shaped wineskins.

Devoted Followers of Jesus Are Humble Servants.

"I am among you as one who serves" (Luke 22:27).

"Take my yoke upon you and learn from me, for I am gentle and humble in heart" (Matthew 11:29, 30).

Have you ever considered that in your journey of being conformed to the image of Jesus Christ, you are headed toward becoming a humble servant? It is your choice whether to cooperate with or resist the Spirit, but it is certainly His goal and desire to transform you into a willing servant. The Spirit that is within us longs to serve and serve well. Therefore, a devoted follower of Christ will become a humble servant who serves those around him or her. Success will then mean serving more and more people over the course of our life.

Imagine the scene of the Last Supper. Pause to consider Christ bowing before His followers in the upper room. Only hours before His own betrayal and torment, Jesus girds Himself with a towel, takes a basin of water, and begins once more to serve those He loves. He concludes this tender time with these words: "Now that I, your Lord and Teacher, have washed your feet, you also should wash one another's feet" (John 13:14).

> **Are you known as a servant among those who know you best? Would your spouse, children, friends, and those who work alongside you describe you as humble?**

Scripture also emphasizes the need for humility among God's people: "God opposes the proud but gives grace to the humble" (James 4:6). Furthermore, God's Word warns us that self-reliant pride hinders the supernatural flow of God's grace, but a humble heart yields an exalted life: "Humble yourselves, therefore, under God's mighty hand, that He may lift you up in due time" (1 Peter 5:6).

Are you known as a servant among those who know you best? Would your spouse, children, friends, and those who work alongside you describe you as humble? Is your life characterized by making sacrifices for those who are closest to you? Do you serve your wife or husband, children, and friends? Are your loved ones the first to benefit from edifying words and daily expressions of love, joy, peace, patience, kindness, goodness, faithfulness, gentleness, and self-control (Ephesians 4:29; Galatians 5:22, 23)? If you are a Christian leader who humbly and obediently takes the lead to serve your spouse, children, and friends, the church will observe and follow. Conversely, without the example of servanthood, the finest preaching and teaching runs the risk of becoming academic, shallow, and irrelevant. Listen for the Spirit to speak to your heart about any areas of needed change.

How Will We Sense That the Lord Is Transforming Us Into Humble Servants?

The Spirit's sanctifying work of humility will be seen in our obvious **dependency**, the **vulnerability** of our heart, and the **approachability** of our life. Our dependence upon God will be evident through listening prayer and sensitivity to His Spirit. We will see Him birth the directions and plans for our life, lest we labor without His grace or blessing. Humble dependence will also involve a willingness and eagerness to seek the wisdom and input of others, knowing that God's plans are often revealed and confirmed through the counsel of other saints. Vulnerability will be displayed through a willingness to share our struggles, weaknesses, and needs. This evidence of humility will allow us to rest on the promise that His power is made perfect in our weakness (2 Corinthians 12:9). Finally, as humble servants, we will be easily approachable, communicating genuine interest in and care for others, without pretense or haughtiness. Others will sense our heart of compassion, knowing that we will not stand at a distance and condemn or judge, but will, with humility of heart, express God's care for others.

Pause to consider what deepened work of humility the Spirit may want for your life. Quietly listen for His voice as He speaks into your life: "It's not about you, it's about Me!"

Devoted Followers of Jesus Are Humble Servants With an Expectant Faith.

"Without faith it is impossible to please God" (Hebrews 11:6).

Believers are consistently challenged to focus "not on what is seen, but on what is unseen" (2 Corinthians 4:18). Pause to consider any anxieties of your life, those distractions, uncertainties, and fears that steal the wonder of life, hindering your freedom to practice the presence of the Savior. Your anxieties might relate to people or decisions, present provision or future security. Whatever they may be, recall Christ's lesson concerning the lilies of the field and birds of the air: "Do not be worried about your life . . . for your heavenly Father knows that you need all these things" (Matthew 6:25, 32 NASB). Expectant faith in the disciple's heart embraces the glorious truth that "since the Father knows, we do not need to be anxious." Jehovah Jireh will provide, just as surely as He does for the lilies and birds. First John 4:18 reminds us that God's perfect love casts out fear. The devoted follower of Jesus has come to enjoy such a sweet, loving relationship with the Lord that he or she is freed from anxiety because of His care. Fear is removed through the experienced security of His love.

How Will We Sense That the Lord Is at Work in This Transformation of Expectant Faith?

"With humility of mind regard one another as more important than yourselves" (Philippians 2:3).

Our fearful "taking," or demanding of attention and care from God and others, will be replaced by secure trust in Him. Selfishness will give way to the greater blessing of giving, since "It is more blessed to give than to receive" (Acts 20:35 NASB). Expectant faith holds to things unseen, having grown confident in the faithfulness of His presence. Would those closest to you characterize you as one who prioritizes giving rather than expecting to receive? Would your spouse, children, or friends describe you as one who puts others first? Are you confident in God's provision, able to rest secure in His care? Could your heart and life benefit from such freedom? Do you need to be liberated from the anxieties that so easily distract from the practice of God's presence? Could you benefit from more freedom to hold steadfast to things that remain unseen?

Pause to consider what deepened work of faith the Spirit might want for your life. Quietly listen for His voice as He speaks into your life: "I love you, and I know what you need. You can count on Me to provide! Is anything too difficult for the Lord" (see Genesis 18:14)?

Devoted Followers of Jesus Are Humble Servants With an Expectant Faith Empowered by Gratitude.

"The love of Christ constraineth us " (2 Corinthians 5:14 KJV).

It was Christ's love that empowered believers in the early church, motivating them to endure significant hardships with joy and even to embrace death. Profound gratitude to a loving God equipped Paul and the early church for a lifetime of wholehearted devotion and service. As Christian leaders, we must purposefully cultivate hearts of gratitude toward God, and guard ourselves against ineffective and unscriptural motivations. The Spirit's ever-present work will reveal our subtle and not-so-subtle ulterior motives. For example, we might be living to gain approval, or to avoid failure or rejection. These motivations must be exposed, and brokenness must be experienced. A life based on dutiful compliance and diligent striving must be exposed as a life of self-effort. The Spirit's gracious work begins as we recognize that "God demonstrates his own love for us in this: While we were still sinners, Christ died for us" (Romans 5:8). Mature disciples never get over the wonder of such love!

How Will We Sense That the Lord Is at Work in This Transformation of Gratitude?

God's Spirit cultivates grateful hearts in His people as we experience and embrace our identity in Christ. The apostle John referred to himself as the disciple Jesus loved. He was not boasting or exalting himself above others. Rather, John was in awe of this wondrous truth. Believers who accurately perceive themselves as the "disciple Jesus loves" are ready to serve God and others out of humility and deep gratitude. We will know that the Lord has begun to deepen our heart of gratitude as we are able to more fully embrace our identity as the beloved of God (John 13:34).

Second, God's Spirit cultivates grateful hearts as we experience deepened love for the giver of all good gifts (James 1:17). King David admonished himself, "Praise the Lord, O my soul, and forget not all his benefits" (Psalm 103:2). In the next verse, he itemized God's goodness to him: forgiveness, healing, deliverance, abiding love and compassion, fulfilled desires, and renewed youthfulness. Our hearts can be enlarged with gratitude toward God when we consistently come before Him to reflect on all the ways that He has intervened, protected, and provided. God is able to free His disciples from the pain of self-condemnation and to help us embrace our identity as the beloved of God as we consistently recall His blessings and move into deepened intimacy with the One who gives the gifts. The wonder of His grace and love stirs the response of divine gratitude. "Forgetting none of His benefits" becomes intimate and personal, stirring the overwhelming feeling that "I cannot get over the wonder that I get to share today with Him, to serve Him, and to love Him."

Pause to consider what deepened work of gratitude the Spirit might want for your life. Has your heart lost the grateful wonder of being a child of God? Quietly listen for His voice as He speaks into your life: "You are My beloved! I can't wait to share the day with you!"

An Experience With God's Word

"If you believe, you will receive whatever you ask for in prayer" (Matthew 21:22).

Quietly listen before the Lord as His Spirit speaks of needed Christlike character in your life and ministry: ask the Lord to give you discernment and direction as you respond to the following:

"Lord, I sense a needed fresh work of *servanthood* in me, particularly toward _____" (which person/persons in your life?)

"Holy Spirit, I long for the *humility* of Christ to be more real in my life through my dependence upon You, my vulnerability before You and others, and my approachability." (Who might benefit from your dependence on the Lord? Your vulnerability? Your approachability?)

_____

"Lord Jesus, I need a strengthening of Your *faith* in me, particularly concerning _____. Help me to believe You for great things. Free me, Holy Spirit, from all of life's anxieties so that my heart might rest secure in You. Help me to cease any attempts to fearfully and selfishly take that which You've promised to supply."

"Lord, forgive me, as there have been times that I have taken Your grace for granted. I want your Spirit to stir within me a sensitive and *grateful* heart. Overwhelm me with a deep awareness of my identity as the beloved of God. Help me to consistently express my gratitude, particularly for _____."

Now share with your partner or small group at least one of the ways that His Spirit might want to make changes in you. Pray together, with each of you asking God to change you in these ways. Ask Him to deepen your servant's heart and to humble your walk before Him and others. Implore Him to strengthen your faith, casting out all of your anxiety. Ask His Spirit to fill you with the gratitude for His wondrous love.

As each of you pray, believe together that you will receive this deepened work from the Spirit and that your life's transformation will be miraculously evident!

THE CALLING TO MINISTER

"Equipping of the saints for the work of service . . ." (Ephesians 4:12 NASB).

Christ's saints are called to minister. Just as surely as the Spirit is encouraging us to become humble, faith-filled, grateful servants, He also wants to empower us to fulfill His divine calling on our lives. The Word calls us to fulfill the ministry God has given us by employing the gifts we have received through His Spirit (2 Timothy 4:5; 1 Peter 4:10). The Greek word *diakonia,* or *minister,* literally means "to serve." We see this portrayed in the Book of Acts as the deacons served food to the widows who were being overlooked (Acts 6:1–4). It is this same calling to serve that we see clearly illustrated in the Upper Room as Christ washed the feet of each disciple (John 13:5–17). Pause again to reflect on the fact that Jesus was only hours away from His own betrayal and torment, yet He chose to spend a significant portion of the night before His death washing feet! Carefully consider how much time it must have required to wash 12 disciples' feet. For those of us who live in the Western world, with its frantic pace, Christ's act of service might seem like a supreme waste of time. But John 13:1 explains the motive behind the act: "Having loved his own who were in the world, he now showed them the full extent of his love." Some might view His gesture as an error in efficiency or as evidence of poor judgment, but in reality, it was a natural expression of Christ's calling. Jesus was called to love and to serve, and up until the very moment of His death, He did just that.

As we trace the principle of ministry through the New Testament, we identify at least four significant dimensions of serving to which the followers of Jesus have been called: ministering to the Lord, ministering His Word, ministering His love to others, and becoming ministers of reconciliation (Acts 13:2 NASB; 6:4; Galatians 5:13; 2 Corinthians 5:18). As we begin to restore the relational foundations to our homes and churches, we must focus upon these callings and assess our cooperation with the Spirit's work.

Ministers to the Lord

Both our personal lives and our ministries will see significant change as we come to prioritize the One who gave, served, and ministered grace.

One of the significant descriptions of the first-century disciples was that they could be found "ministering to the Lord" (Acts 13:2 NASB). As we make ministering to the Lord a priority in our own life, we will experience a much-needed restoration of intimacy in our relationship with Jesus. Both our personal lives and our ministries will see significant change as we prioritize the One who gave, served, and ministered grace. This restoration of intimacy with the Lord will restore our awareness of the wondrous truth that our faith is primarily and ultimately about a person—the God-Man, Jesus! Imagine the wonder of both personally and corporately loving Jesus and yielding our hearts as we serve the One who loves us so! Key elements in such a "ministry to Jesus" are illustrated by the one returning leper of Luke's Gospel, by Mary, the friend of Jesus who listened at His feet, and by the man born blind in the Gospel of John. Join us now as we learn from these New Testament examples.

Ministry to the Lord Means Giving Him Praise.

As we look toward restoring relational foundations to life and ministry, we must first give priority to our ministry to Jesus. We must come to identify with the returning leper of Luke 17:11–19, who, after he found that he was healed, could not wait another minute or take another step without returning to honor Christ. Christ received the leper's praise and declared that the man had given God glory (v. 18 NASB). Our present-day ministry to Jesus will involve looking expectantly for opportunities to bring honor and glory to Him. As we consistently stop to reflect upon the marvelous grace that the Lord has provided on our behalf and voice our gratitude to Him, we minister to the Savior. As the created ones give praise and honor to the Creator, we fulfill His desires and He receives the glory.

As we seek to minister to the Lord, we will have to shift our primary focus away from human-focused questions such as, "What do I need to do?" or "How might we be more effective in our ministry?" Rather, our focus must be upon how our lives and our ministries might bring glory to Him. We must begin to ask the questions, "What is Christ receiving from my life? What is He longing to see in my marriage, my family, and my friendships? What is the Lord receiving from our ministry? How is He being lifted up?" The apostle Paul reminds us of this truth in his second letter to the church at Corinth: "For the ministry of this service is not only fully supplying the needs of the saints, but is also overflowing through many thanksgivings to God" (2 Corinthians 9:12). In our personal devotion and corporate worship, we want our spirits to whisper, "It is all about You, Lord. It is all about You."

Finally, while this focus on ministry to the Lord certainly acknowledges the essential elements of faith and obedience, the believer who seeks to minister to Jesus does not stop there. Unlike the nine lepers, faithful followers of Jesus conclude that there is much more to life in Christ than merely believing the right things and behaving in the right way—and that "much more" is an intimate relationship with Him! As we enter into minister to Him, we will discover that our commitment to trust and obey is important, but not sufficient. In fact, our trust in Jesus and our obedience to Him are meant to lead us back to the One in whom we trust, the One whom we have been called to obey.

My Personal Journey

When the busyness of ministry seems to have me focused on every imaginable issue except the Person whom it is all about, I often pause to consider the sadness in Christ's words: "Were there not ten?" As His Spirit moves within me, I am filled with compassion for the Savior, and there arises in my heart a prompting, a longing, and a passion not to leave Jesus alone. I imagine Christ looking around at those who are before Him, giving Him praise. I never want Him to have to ask in sadness, "Where's David?" Christ's Spirit leads me back from the busyness of activity, and I find my place at His feet, giving Him glory.

Ministry to the Lord Means Listening to the Spirit.

Relevance in life and ministry will only come as we learn to remain still and listen to the Savior's promptings, allowing Him to reveal more of Himself, His heart, and His hope for our lives. As we seek to fulfill our calling to minister to the Lord, we will emulate Mary of Bethany. The Gospel of Luke records one of Christ's many visits to this small village (Luke 10:38–42). Jesus undoubtedly saw the town of Bethany as a refuge, a safe haven from the harsh realities that awaited Him in Jerusalem. Only a short time before His betrayal and arrest, Christ returned to this place of welcome, to friends that loved Him dearly.

On this particular occasion, we learn of an important difference between Mary and her sister Martha, a difference that faithful followers of Christ will not want to miss. Martha was capable, eager to serve, energetic, and enthusiastic about ministry and service. Yet in her efforts to serve and demonstrate acts of kindness, Martha, in some important way, missed the eternal. Instead of affirming Martha's efforts, Christ brought attention to Mary. And what did Mary do? All Mary did was to pause, slow down, and sit! Yet it is where she sat that made the difference. Mary was not distracted by the things of this world, the relentless needs that come with ministry, or the external pressure to "have things just right." Instead, she was focused upon listening to Jesus, and as she sat at His feet, Mary blessed the Savior. As Christ affirmed His friend, He said something quite extraordinary about what Mary did: "Mary has chosen what is better, and it will not be taken away from her" (v. 42). Mary's choice to fellowship with the Lord would count for all of eternity! Those who seek to minister to the Lord long to become a friend like Mary, attentively listening to the Savior's heart.

Take a moment and consider your own passion for simply sitting and listening to the Lord. How often do you pause to pray and sit at the feet of Jesus, simply listening to the Spirit's voice, hearing the heart of your Friend? Has your journey with Him moved you beyond a pursuit of His provision to a longing for His presence? Have you been so busy, worried, or preoccupied with the challenges of life and ministry that you have forgotten to listen for the Savior's voice?

Relevance in life and ministry flows through people who become like Mary—those who choose to listen to Jesus, sit humbly at His feet, and prioritize their relationship with the One who gave His life that we might become His friends (John 15:13–15).

Ministry to the Lord Means Yielding to Him.
One of the most powerful testimonies of listening to the Lord comes when we submit ourselves to the wonder of His ways, even though we may not fully know or understand them. Recall the blind man from the Gospel of John. He was simply lying beside the road when his life was miraculously interrupted by the gracious touch of the Master. John tells us that controversy arose after the man's sight was restored, and that the religious leaders threw him out of the temple. Now pause and reflect on the initiative and care of Jesus: "When Jesus heard what had happened, he went and found the man" (9:35 CEV). Christ then issued this challenging question: "Do you believe in the Son of Man?" The blind man responded, "Who is He, sir? Tell me so that I may believe in Him" (vv. 35, 36). This man who had only recently received his sight, been deemed an outcast by the religious leaders, and been shunned by his family had already yielded himself to believe in the Lord, even before he could be certain about the Savior's identity! How was this possible? How could this blind man be so open to believing in the Son of Man? The answer is simple: in his previous experience with Jesus, he had received amazing grace, undeserved mercy, astounding blessing, and immeasurable abundance. From this foundation of trust, the blind man yielded in faith. It was as if he said, "I am committed to yield to the Son of Man. Just reveal Him to me!"

As we seek to fulfill our calling to minister to the Lord, we will be called upon to yield to Jesus. If we truly want to bless His heart, we will faithfully trust in Him even before we fully know His plans. Our yielding, our willingness to hear from Jesus, and our faith in His care will minister to the Lord.

Is such yielding taking place in your life today? Are you yielding in faith to Him or yielding to the pleadings of men? Is your fellowship so intimate and supportive that your faith can be declared even before the realities of provision come forth?

Pause and Reflect

What might be hindering you from more intimate ministry to the Lord? What keeps you from experiencing more of a close relationship with Him? What hinders you from praising Him? Listening to Him? Yielding to Him? Trusting Him?

Could it be . . .

- a matter of wrong priorities?
- a struggle with materialism?
- fearful anxiety?
- concerns about receiving others' approval?
- over-attention to activity or achievement?
- pre-occupation with your own plans and goals?
- other factors?

My "ministry to the Lord" might at times be hindered by . . .

Share your response with your partner or small group. Take time to pray together about these issues, asking God to remove these entanglements that so easily beset us, that we might run the race with endurance (Hebrews 12:1).

Relational Ministry Places Priority on Ministering to Jesus.

Churches seeking this restoration of relevance may be challenged to redefine the focus of ministry and corporate worship. If we indeed are called to minister to the Lord, then both our lives and our worship must reflect this calling. Therefore, churches and ministries will want to ask themselves:

- Do our ministry methods equip saints to minister to Jesus?

- Do we consistently experience Jesus and give honor to Him? How is this preeminent purpose reflected in each worship service? What changes might be necessary?

- How might Christ become "the audience"—the One to whom our thanksgiving and praise is focused?

- How might performing for the approval of man be replaced by giving Him glory?

- How might the exercise of spiritual gifts call attention to the Giver of those gifts?

- Could the exposition of Scripture involve the Spirit leading individual hearts to experience a deeper love for the One who wrote it?

- Could individuals come to not only know the truth, but to have that truth set them free to more deeply love the One who gave it?

- Could our times of personal response, altar calls, and invitations somehow become more about how individuals encounter God and less about tradition, man's expectations, or the approval of people?

Relational Ministry Is in Contrast to Event Ministry.

Relational ministry can be contrasted with "event ministry." An event-driven approach to ministry tends to attract participants through strategic planning, promotion, and personality. An event-focused ministry can become overly preoccupied with measuring numbers, filling calendars, and designing promotional pieces. If true ministry involves genuinely serving those within the body and those outside of Christ, then events in and of themselves have limited relevance for our culture. Events can serve the purpose of bringing people together around God's Word and God's Son, but they must also present opportunities for deepened relationships. In Chapters 4 and 5, we explored the crisis of aloneness and argued that only deep, intimate relationships can remove aloneness. Event ministry may produce an increase in numbers, and those in attendance may gain more knowledge, but numbers and knowledge do not make disciples. In many cases, people often leave events feeling just as alone as when they came. As noted above, an essential element of relational ministry is the consistent creation of opportunities to experience deepened intimacy with Jesus because intimate relationships are God's provision for aloneness. Aloneness has both a spiritual, or "vertical" component, and an intra-personal, or "horizontal" component. In a relational ministry, there will be opportunities for praise, meditation, listening to the Holy Spirit, and fellowshipping with Jesus. These are some of the components that address the vertical, spiritual dimension of aloneness.

Regrettably, much of the ministry in our Western world has devolved into a quest for competitive advantage. Churches and ministries may find themselves making ministry decisions based more on what others are doing than on what they have heard from the Lord. Ministry leaders of the Western world may even work to outdo their peers in ministry, hoping to have bigger numbers, more grandiose productions, or more cutting-edge events. Relevance will return, and Christ will be blessed when His saints turn aside to minister to the Lord rather than filling the calendars of men.

An Experience With God's Son

Reflect on the needed priorities of . . .

- sharing praise with Jesus, as the returning leper did.
- listening to Jesus, as Mary did.
- yielding to Jesus, as the blind man did.

Consider which of these might need renewed emphasis in your life. Then spend time meditating on one of these Scripture passages.

Sharing praise with Jesus: "Where are the other nine" (Luke 17:17)?

Pause and allow the Holy Spirit to remind you of Jesus. He longs to receive praise from one of the many He has blessed.

In your heart and mind, picture Christ uttering these words: "Where are the other nine?" Reflect again on the probable emotions of His heart. Was this yet another time that He was acquainted with sorrow (Isaiah 53:3)?

Allow the Spirit to move your heart to respond to Him. Can you sense sorrow for Him? Can you fellowship with His sufferings? Can you sense a "godly sorrow that produces repentance" (see 2 Corinthians 7:10)? Allow His Spirit to renew in you a longing to give Christ praise.

Imagine now that you are bowing before Christ, giving Him praise. Tell Him of your renewed desire to praise Him often. Praise Him for who He is and for all He has done.

Listening to Jesus: "Mary . . . sat at the Lord's feet listening to what He said" (Luke 10:39).

Pause and allow the Holy Spirit to bring an image of Jesus to your mind and heart. Picture Him as He withdrew from the rejection of Jerusalem, finding refuge in Bethany at the home of His friends. Possibly sensing the Savior's troubled heart, Mary sits before Him, listening quietly. You are shocked by Martha's self-focused interruption, but also startled by Christ's clear words of affirmation for Mary: "Mary has chosen what is better" (v. 42).

Now imagine that you have an opportunity to be with Jesus. You might want to move to your knees and sit quietly with a reverent heart. Do not speak; just listen. The Savior longs to share His heart. Wait before Him. Listen for His words of pleasure: "You have chosen well."

Pray a quiet prayer similar to young Samuel's prayer. "Speak, for your servant is listening" (1 Samuel 3:10). Allow the Spirit within you to commune with the Savior.

Yielding to Jesus: "Tell me so that I may believe in him" (John 9:36).

Jesus has loved you well, just as He loved the man born blind. He has given you spiritual sight, a new identity, and the promise of eternal life in heaven.

"He who did not spare his own Son, but gave him up for us all—how will he not also, along with him, graciously give us all things" (Romans 8:32)?

If you had a stingy God, He would have never given you Jesus! Since He has blessed you with "everything we need for life and godliness" (2 Peter 1:3), can you now trust Him for certain, smaller things in life?

What discernment do you need concerning decisions or direction? What answers are needed concerning people or provision?

Pause now, and thank God for past blessings. Then imagine yourself bowed before Him, yielding to Him. Declare your intentions to Him:

I yield my choice, my will, my future to You. As You reveal, my heart is yielded to follow in the power of Your Spirit.

Share your responses with your partner or small group, and close with a prayer confirming what God has revealed to you.

Lord Jesus, I sense in my heart the need to be more like _____ *(the leper, Mary,* or *the blind man) by giving priority to* _____ *(sharing praise with You, listening to You,* or *yielding to You).*

Ministers of the Word

"But we will devote ourselves to prayer and to the ministry of the word" (Acts 6:4 NASB).

The disciples of the New Testament were known for their commitment to minister the Word, and this must become a priority for us as maturing disciples. If we want to see relevance restored to the 21st century church, we must see the number of true "servants of the Word" multiplied among God's people. Truly ministering the Word requires going beyond a devotion to right doctrine or persuasive speech. It must include a commitment to humbly take the Word of God and share its relevant message by first vulnerably proclaiming how it has been relevant in your own life, marriage, family, and ministry.

Ministers of the Word Demonstrate Humility.

> **Truly ministering the Word requires going beyond a devotion to right doctrine or persuasive speech. It must include a commitment to humbly take the Word of God and share its relevant message by first vulnerably proclaiming how it has been relevant in your own life.**

A minister of the Word must have a humble heart, allowing (not forcing) the Word of God to do its work in human lives. It is the testimony of the Word, not the teacher of the Word, that condemns sin. It is the Spirit of the Word, not the teacher of the Word, that convicts the sinner. It is the power of the Word, not the teacher of the Word, that brings healing to the human heart and life. An authoritarian teacher may open a few minds, but the Holy Spirit ministers through a humble teacher to open hearts.

Ministers of the Word Share From Their Own Experience With the Word.
"Let the word of Christ dwell in you richly as you teach and admonish one another"
(Colossians 3:16).

It is a common misconception that the disciple's primary task is to bring people to Christ and
help them grow in Him. We assume that our own spiritual growth will occur as a by-product
of ministering to others. We study God's Word in order to preach, teach, and share it with
others. But we rarely slow down long enough to contemplate what God wants to do in our
own lives, apart from what He does through us for others.

Teaching and admonishing without first allowing the Word to dwell in us propagates irrelevance.
Instead of studying Scripture primarily to prepare us to preach sermons, teach classes, or
lead small-group Bible studies, we must approach the Word with the intention of knowing and
loving God more intimately. This approach seems consistent with Paul's testimony, "I consider
everything a loss compared to the surpassing greatness of knowing Christ Jesus my Lord"
(Philippians 3:8). The humble leader or teacher who wants to restore relevance to his or her
own life and ministry will first begin to prioritize personal time in the Word. This time will be
dedicated to truly knowing the Lord and strengthening an intimate relationship with Him. A
separate time will be set aside to study and prepare lessons for others.

A Demonstration of How to Minister the Word
Join us now as we recount a worship service in which one of God's leaders made a serious
commitment to begin truly ministering the Word, thus serving others with its life-changing truth.

Pastor Ben Anderson normally preaches from behind a large, oak pulpit on a raised platform.
But today, instead of stepping to the pulpit, Ben descends the platform steps and stands in
front of his congregation on ground level.

He begins in a conversational tone. "Our text today is Ephesians 4:31, which admonishes us to
'get rid of all bitterness, rage and anger.' Before I talk about the Greek words and their meanings,
I want to share with you how God has been dealing with me through this text."

Several members of the congregation look puzzled. They are not accustomed to their pastor
speaking about his life with such transparency.

Ben pauses, drops his head, and wanders a few steps to his right. He speaks haltingly. "It may surprise you to learn . . . that I have a problem . . . with anger." He lifts his head to resume eye contact, but he does so with difficulty. "I am a driven, task-oriented person, and when something or someone blocks my path to a goal, I can get pretty upset. If you don't believe me, ask Martha and Janet." Pastor Ben nods in the direction of his wife and college-age daughter, who are sitting in the second pew on the side aisle. They smile at him encouragingly.

Ben ambles across the front of the sanctuary as he speaks. Every eye is riveted on him. "For years, I have excused my angry outbursts as an expression of my Type-A personality. But this week, God arrested me with the first three words of Ephesians 4:31: 'Get rid of.' I sensed Him saying to me, 'Ben, I never tell people to get rid of something they cannot get rid of. You are not so hard-wired to respond to problems with anger and rage that you have no control. You are hurting the very people you love the most by excusing your anger. I want to heal the pain that is fueling your anger and to give you victory through my Spirit so you can get rid of it.'"

Pastor Ben drops his head again and stands silent and motionless for a full minute. When he lifts his head, his eyes glisten with tears. He continues: "So before I could share Ephesians 4:31 with you today, I had to experience it myself. Some healing had to take place so that I could find additional freedom in this area of my life."

His voice breaking, Ben proceeds. "I grew up in a home that was characterized by anger, abuse, and fear. I will never forget the day my dad came into the barn and told me, 'Your mother and I are getting a divorce. She's moving to Michigan, and you're staying here with me to work the farm.' At that moment, my heart seemed to turn to ice. I didn't feel mad. I didn't feel anything but numbness."

Ben wipes a tear from the corner of his eye. "For 40 years, I buried my pain. That unresolved hurt has been with me all these years. Too often, it has come out in angry outbursts aimed at my wife and daughter and at many of you here in this church."

Tears now trickle down Ben's cheeks. Scattered sniffles can be heard in the sanctuary, and a number of people reach for handkerchiefs and tissues.

The pastor continues. "This week, for the first time in my life, I allowed my deep, inner pain to be comforted by my loving wife, Martha, and my sweet daughter, Janet. I was deeply grieved over the anger that has gripped my heart for decades. But I was also overwhelmed with gratefulness for God's forgiveness, and I was able to find freedom from my bitterness. I then sought Martha's and Janet's forgiveness for my hurtful anger, and they forgave me as well. Now I need to seek forgiveness from some of you."

Ben focuses his attention on a man sitting in the sixth row on the center aisle. The pastor says, "Allen, during the trustees meeting last week. . . ."

"Just a moment, Pastor," interrupts Allen Dixon, chairman of the trustees, rising to his feet. "I need to say something before you go on."

Allen steps into the aisle and makes his way toward the pastor. "I certainly forgive you," he says warmly. "But I also want to tell you how sorry I am for the loss you suffered and the pain you have carried all these years."

The trustee embraces his pastor and tearfully shares words of comfort. Other church leaders quickly step forward and join the caring, comforting huddle. Parishioners weep openly in their pews at the sight of such compassion.

By the time Ben Anderson steps behind the pulpit to preach, the congregation is leaning forward in anticipation. Ben's message from Ephesians 4:31 rings with relevance because of his personal testimony. The Word has dwelt deeply in him, and his teaching and admonition are now shared with genuineness and sincerity. People eagerly welcome the Word, which has already been experienced by their transparent shepherd.

Ministers of the Word Focus Upon Relationships.

Relevant ministry of God's Word not only challenges hearers to obey, but brings them to the point of experiencing deeper relationships with God and others. We must never exalt experience above God's truth, but scriptural truth is to be experienced and lived out through the power of the Holy Spirit, thus having a positive impact on relationships. The task of Christian leaders is to challenge, inspire, and motivate others to experience truth in relationship with God and one another. Faithful disciples will not be satisfied with simply "knowing" Scripture, which tends to promote arrogance, but will approach the Word with a passion to experience deepened love with the One who wrote it, and with those He loves (1 Corinthians 8:1).

Relevant Christian ministry, from weekly sermons to summer youth camps to the Bible stories that parents' tell their toddlers, is designed to lead students to experience God's Word in relationship. We call this *experiential Bible teaching*, by which we mean challenging students to apply a scriptural passage by living it out in relationship with God and others.

To accomplish this goal, Christian education may need to be redefined and restructured in some of our ministries so that it becomes a means by which the Word is truly ministered. Experiential Bible teaching should be added to the "life application" method already practiced in many circles of Christian education. Life application teaching helps students identify right beliefs and apply those beliefs to right behavior. While this application of Scripture is important, we must go further.

Ministers of the Word Lead Others to Experience Scripture.
A critical element in moving beyond biblical application to actually experiencing Scripture can be found in the words of the apostle Peter on the birthday of the church, the Day of Pentecost. Referring to the dramatic outpouring of the Holy Spirit upon the believers of that day, he announced, "This is that which was spoken by the prophet Joel" (Acts 2:16 KJV). Three little words, "this is that," give us insight into one of the secrets of 1st century church relevance. Imagine Peter using his index finger. As he says "this," he points to the believers upon whom the Holy Spirit has been poured out. When he says "that," he taps his finger on God's promise that was penned in a scroll by the prophet Joel: "I will pour out my Spirit on all people" (v. 17). "This" that they were experiencing was simply "that" about which the prophet wrote!

The dynamic of the Day of Pentecost, and a secret to the early church's ongoing relevance, was that God's Word was being experienced! That is why they were able to turn their world upside down (17:6 KJV). Restoring relevance to the 21st century church is possible when we return to this forgotten purpose of God's truth. God's Word is not only to be believed and obeyed; it must also be experienced within the context of our relationships. Relevant relational ministry will challenge churches to ask, "Where in our ministry are people experiencing God's Word?" Ministry leaders may find that their Christian education structures must be altered in order to effectively address this need.

Ministers of the Word Serve the Truth That Sets Us Free to Love.
Christ's Great Commandment love flows through the channel of experienced truth. In an age of rising rationalism, we may be tempted to substitute simply knowing and obeying truth for

allowing the Word to become spirit and life (John 6:63). Mere knowledge "puffs up," and edifying love is thus quenched (1 Corinthians 8:1). When biblical truth is not experienced, love grows cold.

The 21st century church must place a priority on experiencing biblical truth. Even as we rightly defend the priorities of believing and behaving correctly, we must move beyond them to emphasize loving relationships with God and others. Biblical truth was intended to be lived out experientially in relationship as the Father's love is shared in our hearts. Our culture needs to encounter a relational theology that brings the relevance of God's Word to their lives and relationships. Experiencing the truth of God's Word is a fulfilling and attractive journey!

Pause and Reflect

What might hinder you from being consistently nourished by the Word as you encounter God through the Scriptures? Has your ministry to others been preceded by genuine experiences of the Word in your own life? What has hindered you from moving beyond merely learning and applying God's Word to truly experiencing it?

Could it be . . .

- following the cares of this life?
- pride about what you already know?
- fear of being real and vulnerable with others?
- unresolved pain, similar to that of Pastor Ben?
- feelings of inadequacy?
- a lack of role models of such ministry?
- anxiety to please others?
- other factors?

My faithfulness in ministering the Word to others might, at times, be hindered by . . .

Share your responses with your partner or small group. Pray together as time allows. Ask the Holy Spirit to deepen your desire to minister the Word and to equip you to truly experience God's Word and then share it with others.

Relational Ministry Is in Contrast to Propositional Ministry.
Relational ministry differs significantly from propositional ministry, which presents rational arguments for the Christian faith through an emphasis on education, exposition, and knowledge. As noted in Chapter 3, an over-emphasis on the rational purpose of truth can subtly promote prideful knowledge as a substitute for actually living out what we are encountering in the Word. Rather than centering on what the hearer of the Word will learn, understand, or know, relational ministry begins with a focus on what the hearer of the Word will experience. What Scripture will be experienced? What sort of intimacy with the Son will be experienced? What dimension of fellowship will be experienced among the saints?

At this point, we feel that a cautionary note is needed: as relational ministry presents the challenge to go further with biblical propositions by actually experiencing God's Word at church, misunderstandings are almost inevitable. It will be important to convey that this fresh emphasis on experiencing Scripture does not diminish the importance of biblical truth, though some may fear this is the case. Effective leaders will provide reassurance that it is essential to embrace and convey truthful propositions, but will then go on to help others experience those same biblical truths. The needed transition is from an atmosphere of knowledge, which can promote arrogance, to a culture of love, which edifies (1 Corinthians 8:1). It is critical for the Christian leader to demonstrate his or her own vulnerability concerning the Word in order for this transition to successfully take place.

Ministers of His Love
"Through love serve one another" (Galatians 5:13 NASB).

A third important dimension of both individual and corporate calling is the ministry of God's love to others. Out of our ministry to the Lord and our life-changing experiences with His Word flows the empowering grace to share His life and love with others.

The Ministry of Love Begins at Home.
The Christian disciple's nearest "neighbors" are God's ordained starting places for exercising a ministry of love. Whether it is our spouse, our children, or dear friends, a ministry of love begins with those closest to us.

Husbands are to follow Christ's example by taking the initiative to serve the needs of their wives and children (Ephesians 5:25; Psalm 127:3). Wives are to demonstrate a ministry of love by serving their husbands and families in countless ways (Proverbs 31:10–31). Single adults are to live out the loving testimony of Christ's care, just as He did for His "singles group" from Bethany—Mary, Martha, and Lazarus.

> **The Christian disciple's nearest "neighbors" are God's ordained starting places for exercising a ministry of love.**

In the home of a faithful disciple, the anger-dissolving gentle answer of Proverbs 15:1 is continually practiced and perfected. The disciple's nearest ones benefit from edifying words that build them up according to their needs (Ephesians 4:29). The disciple's home is the proving ground for the daily expression of love, joy, peace, patience, kindness, goodness, faithfulness, gentleness and self-control (Galatians 5:22, 23). Rejoicing together is commonplace, God's blessings are routinely celebrated, wrongs are quickly confessed and forgiven, and emotional pain is lovingly comforted and healed (Romans 12:15; Psalm 103:2; James 5:16; Ephesians 4:31, 32; 2 Corinthians 1:2–4).

As Christ's faithful followers boldly and obediently take the lead in living out relational intimacy with their spouses, children, and friends, others in the church will observe and follow, and the world will take note that we, like the 1st century disciples, have been with Jesus (Acts 4:13). If needed, you may want to review our explanation of this critical priority in Chapters 4 and 5. Without this example of a ministry of love in the disciple's inner circle, the finest preaching and teaching about love will be only a noisy gong or a clanging cymbal (1 Corinthians 13:1).

Pause and Reflect

What might hinder you from serving others with God's love, beginning with those nearest you? What keeps you from living out the truth with your spouse, children, family members, or friends?

Could it be . . .

- misplaced priorities?
- insecurity or uncertainty about how to minister love in these relationships?
- unresolved, emotional pain in these relationships?
- other factors?

I may be hindered at times from serving others with His love because of . . .

Share your responses with your partner or small group. Consider spending a few moments in prayer together. Ask the Holy Spirit to empower you to serve others in love, beginning with those nearest you.

Relational Ministry Is Family-Centered.
In addition to encouraging an intimate relationship with God, relational ministry exists to encourage God-ordained relationships among people. When the relational needs of spouses and children are being met in the family, the church's overall health and relevance in the community are greatly improved. When friendships are made vibrant and vulnerable through the ministry of mutual care, we become living epistles that clearly declare God's love to those around us.

A key goal for marriage, family, and singles ministry should be to equip individuals to meet relational needs and foster growing intimacy, thus removing aloneness. Ongoing ministry by trained lay leaders and mentors should be the rule, with one-time events regarded as supplementary. For example, the annual couples retreat should not be a substitute for week-by-week ministry to couples in classes or small groups. The summer youth camp should not be the primary vehicle through which the church ministers to children and young people. A local single adult conference should not be viewed as an acceptable substitute for ongoing ministry to singles through classes, small groups, or weekly fellowship gatherings.

Periodically, the church might offer a family Bible study where parents, children, and perhaps extended family members experience Scripture passages together. The object of such family-focused Bible studies is to deepen relationships through vulnerable self-disclosure and to learn how to identify and meet specific relational needs. These encounters allow adults, children, and youth to deepen their intimacy with God and capture his heart of care and compassion for one another. Additionally, married couples, singles, students, and children should, at times, minister and receive ministry together, across generational and marital status lines. These experiences will reveal the mystery of fellowshipping as God's family.

If Great Commandment love is needed anywhere in 21st century culture, it is needed in the realm of parenting our children. A key philosophy of ministry concerning parenting is that parents are to be the primary "disciplers" of their own children. The church, with effective youth and children's ministries, plays a supportive role, but it is the parents who must be reached and trained in how to impart a living legacy of love. However, we must go beyond simply instructing, exhorting, and encouraging parents in church and expecting them to go home and parent effectively. Many of today's young parents lack adequate parenting models. We need the "new wineskin" of an intergenerational focus, which brings families together to provide on-the-job training.

Relevant, relational ministry will make special provisions to include single adults, teens without church families, widows and widowers, and single parents in this intergenerational focus. Those without families are folded into nuclear families as "adopted" parents or extended family members so that no one in the church feels alone.

Relational Ministry Is in Contrast to Segmented Ministry.

Much ministry today is segmented to the point that God-ordained relationships like marriage and family are made secondary to individual ministry. While specific ministries for specified age groups are important, and ministries that encourage individual spiritual growth are certainly needed, the culture of our day is groping for help with the God-ordained relationships of marriage, family, and friendships. Relevant, relational ministry must provide a blueprint for these relationships that really works. This will require ongoing ministry opportunities for married couples, single parents, blended families, and single adults. It will also require that ministries designed specifically for women and men give priority to developing and enriching the friendships within these ministries. Biblical study and acts of service are important, but ministry leaders will also need to assess how members are being encouraged to deepen their relationships with God and one another. Regularly offered relational classes with a high level of visibility within the church send an important message: "Marriage, family, and friendships are a top priority for us because they are important to God!"

Ministers of Reconciliation

Ultimately, our culture's gravest problems cannot be remedied by political, social, or economic means. We throw more laws, programs, and money at these problems every year, yet they continue to increase. The solution to the alienation and aloneness of the human heart can be found only in God's offer of reconciliation through His Son, Jesus Christ. As individuals establish and maintain intimate relationships with their Creator through the Spirit's power, abundant life and meaningful relationships with others are possible.

Christ has entrusted this ministry of reconciliation to us, His church. God is at work in us, calling a hurting world to Himself. He is the solution to the heartache of our world, and because He is in us and we are in Him, we have the awesome ministry privilege of co-laboring with Him to see people reconciled to God and to one another.

Paul's inspired message to the Corinthian church is as pertinent today as it was then. "Working together with Him, we also urge you not to receive the grace of God in vain . . . so that the ministry will not be discredited, but in everything commending ourselves as servants of God" (2 Corinthians 6:1–4 NASB). This call from God is being restored to the 21st century church. The call is to relevance in ministry, applying the Great Commandment principle of love in His church and beyond. Only as we hear and heed His call will we give evidence that we are His disciples.

Pause and Reflect

What might be hindering you from living as God's ambassador of reconciliation to those around you?

Could it be . . .

- feeling unequipped or unprepared?
- misplaced priorities?
- being distracted by the challenges of life or by other activities?
- lack of a burden for others?
- fear of rejection, or of being misunderstood?
- other factors?

I am hindered, at times, from living as God's ambassador of reconciliation by . . .

Share your responses with your partner or small group, and pray together that God would empower each of you to be a minister of reconciliation.

When we truly experience Great Commandment love in our lives, it will startle the world around us. Consider the startling nature of Jesus' ministry. People were often startled by the things that He said: "Stretch out your hand"; "Pick up your mat and walk", and "I and the Father are one" (Mark 3:5; John 5:8; 10:30). They were also startled by the things that He did, such as turning water into wine, walking on water, and eating with tax collectors. But most importantly, the world was startled by His love. His love startled the woman at the well, Zacchaeus, and the woman caught in adultery. But the most startling expression of His love was the giving of Himself as a sacrificial atonement for a skeptical and rebellious world.

Pause now and consider how startling it is that He demonstrated a love that was so undeserved! He loved us when we were unlovable. He was moved with compassion when, from His eternal perspective, He saw us suffering in our alienation and aloneness. His love led Him to a painful death upon a cross in order to make abundant

> **When we truly experience Great Commandment love in our lives, it will startle the world around us.**

provision for you and for me. Hear His startling cry of love for those who betrayed, tormented, and rejected Him: "Father, forgive them, for they do not know what they are doing" (Luke 23:34). Listen again as He speaks accepting words to the thief by His side: "Today you will be with Me in paradise" (v. 43). Then, "He said to his mother, 'Dear woman, here is your son,' and to the disciple, 'Here is your mother.' From that time on, this disciple took her into his home" (John 19:26, 27).

We, too, are the beneficiaries of His forgiveness and compassionate care. Humbled by such matchless grace, we have been made partakers of His love. But our world needs to be startled by this same love. They need to see a living model of Great Commandment love in action. Let us go forth with gratitude and compassion and begin to startle our world with God's love.

An Experience With God's People

"We are therefore Christ's ambassadors, as though God were making his appeal through us. We implore you on Christ's behalf: Be reconciled to God" (2 Corinthians 5:20).

Consider again Christ's startling love at Calvary . . .

- forgiving those who had wounded Him.
- accepting a thief before he changed.
- supporting His own mother, even while suffering excruciating pain and sacrificing Himself.

Think of His loving initiative. Remember His forgiveness, acceptance, and support. Then pause to review the traffic patterns of your life. You have been placed there as His ambassador. He longs to share His love through you. He hopes to demonstrate His forgiveness and acceptance through you. He wants to communicate His support through you to others.

Who among your family, friends, co-workers, and acquaintances could benefit from . . .

- His forgiveness through you (no matter what their sin)? _____
- His acceptance through you (even before they change)? _____
- His support through you (even if they have not asked)? _____

Share these responses and specific people with your partner or small group. Pray together, asking the Spirit to remove hindrances to your witness and to empower the sharing of God's startling love through you.

For Further Study

CHANGING CHURCH CULTURE

As we conclude our exploration of the relational foundations that gave the 1st Century Church relevance and enabled it to impact the entire world for Christ, we must note that God's Spirit seems to be at work in our day. He has begun "the removing of what can be shaken . . . so that what cannot be shaken may remain" (Hebrews 12:27). We have been challenged with the "fresh wine" of relational theology as we have explored the following:

- A Relational Christology—"seeing Christ as He really is"
- A Relational Hermeneutic—"experiencing Scripture with the One who wrote it and with those He loves."
- A Relational Anthropology—"seeing people as God sees them."
- A Relational Ecclesiology— "experiencing fellowship with those God loves."
- A Relational Apologetic—"imparting not only the Gospel, but also our very lives."

The Challenge of Fresh Wine

We have proposed that a return to these 1st century relational foundations will restore relevance, bringing impact, meaning, and purpose to our lives and ministries. Such a shaking of our message brings challenging considerations for each of us. In my own life, I have been challenged with these questions: "Have I not been seeing Christ as He really is? Have I not been representing to others who Christ really is?" Similar shaking may have occurred as you have been challenged to ask yourself, "Have I truly been experiencing Scripture? Do I see people—particularly those nearest me—as God sees them? Do I impart life by ministering to the aloneness of others, or do I focus too readily on sin?" Such questions can be not only challenging, but possibly convicting.

The Challenge of Fresh Wineskins

Not only does our theology need shaking in order to remove those man-made things that can be shaken, but our wineskins, or ministry methods, must be shaken as well. **Relational theology**

can only be contained in and expressed through relational ministry. This shaking of wineskins may require significant changes in the way we approach both our personal life journey and our ministry. We will be challenged with questions such as the following:

- Where, in my personal life and in corporate ministry, am I experiencing consistently deepened intimacy with Jesus?

- Is priority being given in my personal devotions and times of corporate fellowship to periods of "waiting"—listening before the Lord for His affirmation, calling, and direction?

- Has a spirit of yielding to Jesus in my personal walk and corporate ministry replaced a reliance solely upon knowledge, which can lead to arrogance?

- Have times in the Scripture become more about truly encountering God rather than simply learning about Him?

- Before seeking to share, teach, or preach the Word, do I first allow His Word to dwell deeply in me?

- Where, in corporate ministry, am I routinely experiencing the closeness and blessing of meaningful, vulnerable fellowship?

The Challenge of Changing Church Culture

To better understand the challenge of restoring relevance, consider that a church's message (whether relevant or irrelevant) has, over the course of time, been expressed through certain wineskins—methods, approaches, and priorities—that have combined to create a church culture. As we will see, it is primarily a church's culture that interacts with and influences (positively or negatively) the unbelieving world.

A simple portrayal of church culture might be represented by the following:

Message + Method = Church Culture $\longrightarrow$ interacts with an unbelieving world

or

Wine + Wineskins = Church Culture $\longrightarrow$ has a relevant or irrelevant impact on an unbelieving world

Simply stated, the unbelieving world is not primarily attracted or repelled by the validity or truthfulness of our message, but by the way in which our message is being lived out and expressed. Particularly, in our 21st century, postmodern world, unbelievers do not seem to be asking, "Is the Bible true?" but rather, "If the Bible is true, so what?" A relevant church culture provides the answers to these "so what" questions. Unbelievers may attend our events or benefit from our services, but their ultimate response to us and to the Gospel will largely be shaped by the church culture they encounter.

Understanding Church Culture

Every church tends to be culturally characterized by such things as their . . .

Identity—How we come to view and describe who we are.

Values—The crucial priorities that have become an outgrowth of who we are.

Language—The distinguishing aspects of our communication.

Norms—The common anticipations or expectations we share.

Traditions—The rituals, events, programs, and processes that tend to provide security and hope for the future.

For example: The Westminister Community Tabernacle might describe their culture as follows:

Identity—We are Christian believers committed to the proclamation of God's Word concerning Jesus Christ as the only answer for a sinful world.

Values—We give priority to preaching and teaching the infallible Word of God, in order that we might see lives changed and the lost saved.

Language—"That was a powerful, 'right-on' message that our community needs more of."

"God taught me from my early days as a believer about the importance of tithing, witnessing, and having a devotional time."

"Our part is to share the Gospel and leave the results to Him."

Norms—"What did you get from your study of the passage?"

"Let's pray and ask God to be all you need in the midst of this crisis."

"I'll see you at Monday night outreach, won't I?"

Traditions—Typical events: annual Bible conferences, summer mission trips, Easter pageant.

Acknowledging celebrations: recognition of high attendance, children's Scripture memory, building dedications, budget receipts, baptisms.

Dealing with losses: "God can be trusted; we'll praise Him anyway!"

The Process of Changing Church Culture

- **Experience** elements of a fresh, relational theology.

Pastor Andy introduces several topics from John 13–14 in order to focus worship and preaching on the need to experience Jesus as He really is. Those present are led to personally respond to Jesus as they encounter Him in worship and the Word.

- **Incorporate** this fresh message into ongoing aspects of relational ministry.

Pastor Andy's emphasis on experiencing the truth that Christ is "excited to share in our love" has had a great impact on the congregation. The elders and worship team begin to plan worship services that will allow Westminister Community to truly experience Jesus more consistently. Through drama, music, sermons, and meditations, worship services will be tailored to help those in attendance to experience Christ, to leave less alone than when they came, and to be motivated and empowered by gratitude to share His life and love in their daily walk.

- **Celebrate** relevant refinements in church culture.

A New Year's communion service kicks off a January emphasis on "Experiencing His Love," as Westminister's new identity statement is presented and lived out in each worship service.

- **Engage** the community and world around you with the testimony of this new church culture.

During the Easter season, Westminister focuses on "Experiencing His Love From the Cross." During the service, attendees are given the opportunity to forgive one another just as Christ forgave His tormentors. Outreach events are organized in order to demonstrate acceptance to those beyond the church's walls. Community service activities are undertaken in order to give support to widows, single parents, the unemployed, and the homeless.

The Sequence of Changing Church Culture

"You are going to have the light just a little while longer. Walk while you have the light, before darkness overtakes you" (John 12:35).

Address these three questions, in this order: Who is He? Who are we? Why are we here?

- Begin with Christology, which redefines your church's identity. The goal is to move from a methods-based identity or a rational/behavioral identity to a secure identity as the beloved of God.
- Reframe your church's values in relational ways that are consistent with a Relational Hermeneutic, Anthropology, Ecclesiology, and Apologetic. Begin with ongoing, relational ministry to married couples, families, and single adults, in order to strengthen and empower God's planned purposes for these relationships.
- Revamp mission statements, doctrinal statements, ministries, budgets, and staffing to make them consistent with an emphasis on "loving as we have been loved."

For example: The Westminister Community Tabernacle has worked toward changing their church culture in the following ways:

Identity—We are followers of Jesus who are seeking to live out a lifestyle of loving God and others, even as we have been loved.

Values—We want to experience Jesus in our worship, experience His Word in our Bible teaching, experience genuine fellowship with His people in our families and small groups, and be empowered to share His life and love with those who do not know Him.

Language—"I am coming more and more to see how hindered my view of Jesus has been."

"It is amazing how safe and transparent God is making our small group."

"I am so sorry for all that you are going through."

Norms—"God is here for you during this tragedy, and so am I."

"I know that I need to apologize to my co-worker for my judgmental attitude. Would you pray for me now that God's gracious acceptance will be very real through me?"

"We are excited to share a little of His loving support with you! You are worth it!"

Additional Resources

David S. Dockery, *The Challenge of Postmodernism: An Evangelical Engagement,* second edition (Grand Rapids, MI: Baker Books, 2001).

Hubert L. Seals, *Spiritual Renewal in Your Family* (Cleveland, TN: Pathway Press, 1999).

John Kie Vining and Hubert L. Seals, *Family Ministry Frameworks* (Cleveland, TN: Pathway Press, 2003).

Appendices:

- **Ten Key Relational Needs**

- **Relational Needs Questionnaire**

- **The Potential and Pain of Relational Needs**

- **Emotional Responding Chart**

Ten Key Relational Needs

ACCEPTANCE: Being received willingly and unconditionally, especially when one's behavior has been less than perfect (Romans 15:7).

AFFECTION: Expressing care and closeness through appropriate physical touch, saying, "I love you" or "I care about you" (Romans 16:16).

APPRECIATION: Expressing thanks, praise, or commendation to one another (Colossians 3:15; 1 Corinthians 11:2).

APPROVAL: Building up and affirming one another; affirming both the fact of and importance of a relationship (Ephesians 4:29).

ATTENTION: Conveying appropriate interest, concern, and care; taking thought of one another; entering another's world (1 Corinthians 12:25).

COMFORT: Responding to a hurting person with words, feelings, and touch; hurting with and for others in the midst of grief or pain (Romans 12:15; 2 Corinthians 1:3, 4).

ENCOURAGEMENT: Urging another to persist and persevere toward a goal; stimulating toward love and good deeds (1 Thessalonians 5:1).

RESPECT: Valuing and regarding one another highly; treating one another as important; honoring one another (Romans 12:10).

SECURITY: Harmony in relationships; freedom from fear or threat of harm (Romans 12:16–18).

SUPPORT: Coming alongside and gently helping with a problem or struggle; providing appropriate assistance (Galatians 6:2).

Name:_____

Relational Needs Questionnaire

While we all have the same relational needs, the *priority* of those needs is different for each person. Your greatest need may be for *affection*, while your partner's greatest need may be *security*. One child may have an acute need for *comfort*, but another sibling's greatest need may be *encouragement*. *Appreciation* may be at the top of the list for your next-door neighbor, while your tennis buddy needs *approval* more than anything else.

An important aspect of learning to love others is taking the time to know them and to discover what their priority needs are. This questionnaire will help you assess your most important relational needs. Answer the questions, then score the questionnaire to identify which needs you perceived as most important. Have family members, friends, and ministry team members complete the questionnaire and then discuss the results.

Instructions: Respond to these questions by placing the appropriate number beside each item:

Strongly Disagree	Disagree	Neutral	Agree	Strongly Agree
-2	-1	0	+1	+2

_____ 1. It's important that people receive me for who I am, even if I'm a little "different."

_____ 2. It's important to me that my financial world be in order.

_____ 3. I sometimes become "weary in well doing."

_____ 4. It's vital to me that others ask me my opinion.

_____ 5. It's important that I receive physical hugs, warm embraces, etc.

_____ 6. I feel good when someone "enters into my world."

_____ 7. It's important for me to know "where I stand" with those who are in authority over me.

_____ 8. It is meaningful when someone notices that I need help and then they offer to get involved.

_____ 9. If I feel overwhelmed, I want someone to come alongside me and help.

_____ 10. I feel blessed when someone recognizes and shows concern for how I'm feeling.

_____ 11. I like to know if "who I am" is of value and is meaningful to others.

_____ 12. It is important to me to express myself—what I think, feel, etc.—to those around me.

_____ 13. It means a lot to me for loved ones to initiate saying to me, "I love you."

_____ 14. I resist being seen only as a part of a large group—my individuality is important.

_____ 15. I am blessed when a friend calls to listen and encourage me.

_____ 16. It's important to me that people acknowledge me not just for what I do but for who I am.

_____ 17. I feel best when my world is orderly and somewhat predictable.

_____ 18. When I've worked hard on something, I am pleased when others express gratitude.

_____ 19. When I "blow it," it's important to me to be reassured that I'm still loved.

_____ 20. It's encouraging to me that others notice my effort or accomplishments.

_____ 21. I sometimes feel overwhelmed with all I have to do.

_____ 22. I want to be treated with kindness and equality by all regardless of my race, gender, looks, or status.

_____ 23. I like to be greeted with a handshake or other appropriate friendly touch.

_____ 24. I like it when someone wants to spend time with me.

_____ 25. I am blessed when a "superior" says, "Good job."

_____ 26. It's important to me for someone to express care for me after I've had a hard day.

_____ 27. When facing something difficult, I usually sense that I need other people's input and help.

_____ 28. Written notes and calls expressing sympathy after a serious loss or difficulty are (or would be) meaningful to me.

_____ 29. I feel good when someone close to me shows satisfaction with the way I am.

_____ 30. I enjoy being spoken of or mentioned in front of other people.

_____ 31. I would be described as a person who likes hugs and/or other caring touch.

_____ 32. When a decision is going to affect me, it's important to me that I am involved in the decision.

_____ 33. I am blessed when someone shows interest in what I'm working on.

_____ 34. I appreciate trophies, plaques, or special gifts as permanent reminders of something significant I have done.

_____ 35. I sometimes worry about the future.

_____ 36. When I'm introduced into a new environment, I typically search for a group to connect with.

_____ 37. The thought of change (moving, new job, etc.) produces anxiety for me.

_____ 38. It bothers me when people are prejudiced against someone just because they dress or act differently.

_____ 39. I want to be close to friends and loved ones who will be there "through thick and thin."

_____ 40. I am blessed by written notes and other specific expressions of gratitude.

_____ 41. To know that someone is praying for me is meaningful to me.

_____ 42. I am bothered by "controlling" people.

_____ 43. I am blessed when I receive unmerited and spontaneous expressions of love.

_____ 44. I am pleased when someone carefully listens to me.

_____ 45. I am blessed when people commend me for a godly characteristic I exhibit.

_____ 46. I typically don't want to be alone when experiencing hurt and trouble.

_____ 47. I don't enjoy working on a project by myself; I prefer to have a partner.

_____ 48. It's important for me to feel a "part of the group."

_____ 49. I respond to someone who tries to understand me and who shows me loving concern.

_____ 50. I would rather work with a team of people than by myself.

Relational Needs Questionnaire: Scoring

1. Add up your responses (-2, -1, 0, +1, +2) to items:

     1 _____

   19 _____

   36 _____

   38 _____

   48 _____

Total   _____

These responses relate to the need for ACCEPTANCE.

2. Add up your responses to items:

    2 _____

   17 _____

   35 _____

   37 _____

   39 _____

Total   _____

These responses relate to the need for SECURITY.

3. Add up your responses to items:

        18 _____
        20 _____
        25 _____
        34 _____
        40 _____

Total _____

These responses relate to the need for APPRECIATION.

4. Add up your responses to items:

        3 _____
        15 _____
        21 _____
        33 _____
        41 _____

Total _____

These responses relate to the need for ENCOURAGEMENT.

5. Add up your responses to items:

        4 _____
        14 _____
        22 _____
        32 _____
        42 _____

Total _____

These responses relate to the need for RESPECT.

6. Add up your responses to items:

        5 _____
        13 _____
        23 _____
        31 _____
        43 _____

Total _____

These responses relate to the need for AFFECTION.

7. Add up your responses to items:

6	_____
12	_____
24	_____
30	_____
44	_____

Total _____

These responses relate to the need for ATTENTION.

8. Add up your responses to items:

7	_____
11	_____
16	_____
29	_____
45	_____

Total _____

These responses relate to the need for APPROVAL.

9. Add up your responses to items:

10	_____
26	_____
28	_____
46	_____
49	_____

Total _____

These responses relate to the need for COMFORT.

10. Add up your responses to items:

8	_____
9	_____
27	_____
47	_____
50	_____

Total _____

These responses relate to the need for SUPPORT.

For Reflection or Discussion:

1. What were your three highest totals? Which needs do they represent?

   - _____
   - _____
   - _____

2. What were your three lowest totals? Which needs do they represent?

   - _____
   - _____
   - _____

3. If others are completing this questionnaire with you (friend, spouse, fiancé, other family members, ministry team members, etc.), what were their highest and lowest totals?

   Highest:
   - _____
   - _____
   - _____

   Lowest:
   - _____
   - _____
   - _____

4. What might be the implications of your scores compared to their scores?

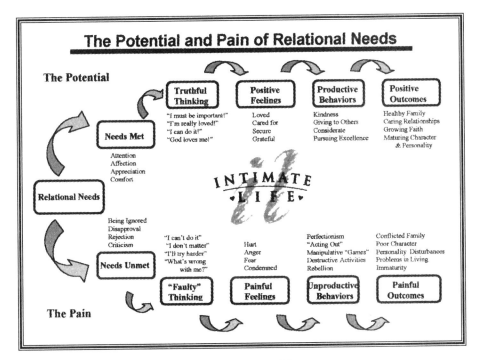

The Potential and Pain of Relational Needs

The Potential

Truthful Thinking
"I must be important!"
"I'm really loved!"
"I can do it!"
"God loves me!"

Positive Feelings
Loved
Cared for
Secure
Grateful

Productive Behaviors
Kindness
Giving to Others
Considerate
Pursuing Excellence

Positive Outcomes
Healthy Family
Caring Relationships
Growing Faith
Maturing Character
& Personality

Needs Met
Attention
Affection
Appreciation
Comfort

Relational Needs

INTIMATE LIFE

Needs Unmet
Being Ignored
Disapproval
Rejection
Criticism

"Faulty" Thinking
"I can't do it"
"I don't matter"
"I'll try harder"
"What's wrong with me?"

Painful Feelings
Hurt
Anger
Fear
Condemned

Unproductive Behaviors
Perfectionism
"Acting Out"
Manipulative "Games"
Destructive Activities
Rebellion

Painful Outcomes
Conflicted Family
Poor Character
Personality Disturbances
Problems in Living
Immaturity

The Pain

Implications for Childhood

Personality development is intense during the first six years of life as a child experiences the complex maze of physical, social, emotional, intellectual, and spiritual needs that are normal for human beings created in the image of God.

Unmet needs are inevitable as imperfect children grow up in imperfect families in an imperfect world. We have all been "under-nourished" in some areas of need. **Healthy** families address the hurt of unmet needs as they inevitably occur; **dysfunctional** families deny the hurts, ignore the needs, and/or shame the child for being needy!

Children don't comprehend their needs, so it is essential for parents to understand these needs, validate their importance, and focus on giving to meet each child's needs.

Implications for Adult Relationships

Unmet childhood needs "follow" us into adulthood. Without realizing it, we often enter adult relationships expecting to receive the acceptance we missed, the affection we longed for, or the attention we desired but did not get in childhood.

Great hurt is experienced when needs that went unmet in childhood remain unmet in our adult relationships. Sadly, many receive the opposite of what is needed--rejection when they longed for acceptance, coldness rather than affection, or neglect instead of attention.

Great love is felt when needs that went unmet in childhood are fulfilled in our adult relationships. Spiritually healthy adults work to understand the relational needs of others and consistently give to meet such needs.

Implications for Parenting

Unmet needs underlie a great deal of a child's acting-out behavior. For example, lack of attention might evoke anger, and missing out on approval and acceptance might prompt withdrawal. Successful parents address inappropriate behaviors as well as explore unmet needs. In the parent, this requires awareness of one's own needs, openness about feelings, and a healthy self-image.

Need frustration is seen as a factor that contributes to living difficulties (labeled "pathology" by many). Unmet needs contribute to lack of identity, low self-worth, insecurity, discouragement, self-defeating attitudes and behaviors, loneliness, and abusive or addictive patterns harmful to oneself and others.

Developing Intimacy Skills—Emotional Responding

Unproductive Responses

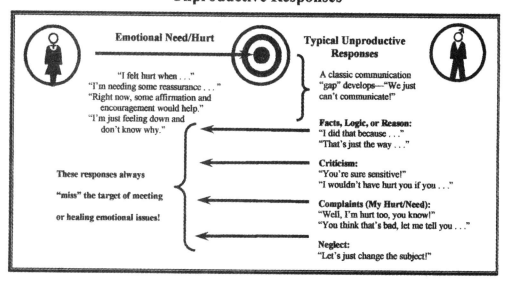

Emotional Need/Hurt

"I felt hurt when . . ."
"I'm needing some reassurance . . ."
"Right now, some affirmation and
encouragement would help."
"I'm just feeling down and
don't know why."

These responses always

"miss" the target of meeting

or healing emotional issues!

**Typical Unproductive
Responses**

A classic communication
"gap" develops—"We just
can't communicate!"

Facts, Logic, or Reason:
"I did that because . . ."
"That's just the way . . ."

Criticism:
"You're sure sensitive!"
"I wouldn't have hurt you if you . . ."

Complaints (My Hurt/Need):
"Well, I'm hurt too, you know!"
"You think that's bad, let me tell you . . ."

Neglect:
"Let's just change the subject!"

Emotional Responding

Emotional Need/Hurt   **Emotional Response**

Brings:
- healing
- understanding
- fulfillment
- closeness

Always includes:
- understanding
- empathy
- gentleness
- reassurance
. . . and often must include confession!

Examples of Productive Emotional Responses

Comfort	**Confession**
"I can really see that you're hurting (or_____)."	"I genuinely regret my part in hurting you."
"I'm sorry to see you hurting."	"Can you share with me how I've hurt you and
"It saddens me to see you so fearful (or_____)."	how it made you feel? I want to fully
"I deeply care about you and love you."	understand and make it right."
"I'm committed to go through this with you."	"I now see that I hurt you by my and that was wrong of
	me. Will you forgive me?"

About the Author

David Ferguson, along with his wife, Teresa, has shared a biblical message of health and relevance for more than 25 years. Their passion for seeing the Great Commandment of loving God and loving others lived out among God's people has enabled them to impact thousands of ministers and their laity. As co-directors of Intimate Life Ministries, they direct a multi-disciplinary team that serves more than 35,000 churches in the United States and abroad with training and resources through the strategic partners involved in the Great Commandment Network of denominations, movements, and ministries. David serves as co-director of the Center for Relational Leadership, which provides training and resources in church, business, and community settings

About The Great Commandment Network

The **Great Commandment Network** is a team of denominational partners, churches, para-church ministries, and strategic ministry leaders that is committed to the development of on-going Great Commandment ministries worldwide. Great Commandment ministries help us love God and our neighbors through deepening our intimacy with God and with others in marriage, family, church, and community relationships.

The **Great Commandment Network** is served by *Intimate Life Ministries* through the following:

- **The Center for Relational Leadership (CRL)**—Their mission is to teach, train, and mentor both corporate and ministry leaders in Great Commandment principles, seeking to equip leaders with relational skills so they might lead as Jesus led. The CRL then challenges leaders to train their co-workers in these relevant, relational principles because great relational skills can and will impact customer/member satisfaction, morale, productivity, and, ultimately, an organization's measurable success.

- **The Center for Relational Care (CRC)**—Their mission is to equip churches to minister effectively to hurting people. The CRC provides therapy and support to relationships in crisis through an accelerated process of growth and healing, including Relational Care Intensives for couples, families, and singles. The CRC also offers training for counselors and caregivers through More Than Counseling seminars.

- **The Center for Relational Training (CRT)**—Through a team of accredited community trainers, the CRT helps churches establish ongoing Great Commandment ministries. They offer an online supported, structured process for guiding church leaders through relational ministry training. Training is available in a variety of relational areas: Marriage, Parenting, Single Adult Relationships, Leadership, Emotional Fitness, Care-giving, and Spiritual Formation.

- **The Galatians 6:6 Retreat Ministry**—This ministry offers a unique, two-day retreat for ministers and their spouses for personal renewal and for reestablishing and affirming ministry and family priorities. Co-sponsoring partners provide all meals and retreat accommodations as a gift to ministry leaders.

- **Great Commandment Radio**—Christian broadcasters, publishers, media, and other affiliates build cooperative relationships in order to see Great Commandment ministries multiplied.

- **Relationship Press**—This team collaborates, supports, and joins together with churches, denominational partners, and professional associates to develop, print, and produce resources that facilitate ongoing Great Commandment ministry. Experiential, user-friendly curriculum materials allow individuals, churches, and entire denominations to deepen Great Commandment love. Great Commandment Ministry Online provides tools for relationships and the workplace including helpful downloads such as family night tips, marriage staff meeting ideas, daily couple devotionals, and ways singles can reach out to other single adults by meeting relational needs. Tools for the workplace include goal setting, time management, and life balance assessment.

For more information on how you, your church, ministry, denomination, or movement can become part of the Great Commandment Network and take advantage of the services and resources offered by Intimate Life Ministries, write or call:

Intimate Life Ministries
P.O. Box 201808
Austin, TX 78720-1808
1-800-881-8008

Or visit our website:
www.GreatCommandment.net

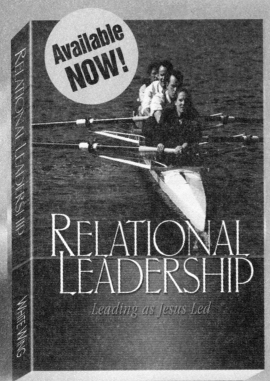